ECONOMIC SOVEREIGNTY AND
REGIONAL POLICY

Economic Sovereignty
and
Regional Policy

A symposium on regional problems
in Britain and Ireland

EDITED BY JOHN VAIZEY

Gill and Macmillan

First published in 1975
Gill and Macmillan Ltd
Dublin 1
and internationally through
association with the
Macmillan Publishers Group

7171 0743 4

Printed in Great Britain by
Bristol Typesetting Co. Ltd
Barton Manor, St Philips
Bristol

GLOSSARY OF ABBREVIATIONS USED

AIFTA Anglo-Irish Free Trade Area Agreement
CAP   Common Agricultural Policy
CET   Common External Tariff
CTT   Coras Trachtala Teo. (The Irish Export Board)
DTI   Department of Trade and Industry
EAGGF European Agricultural Guidance and Guarantee Fund
ECSC   European Coal and Steel Community
EEC   European Economic Community
EFTA   European Free Trade Area
FAO   Food and Agricultural Organisation
GATT   General Agreement on Tariffs and Trade
GDP   Gross Domestic Product
GNP   Gross National Product
IDA   Industrial Development Authority
IDC   Industrial Development Corporation
ILA   Intermediate Level Authorities
IMI   Irish Management Institute
LDC   Less Developed Country
NIEC   National Industrial and Economic Council
OECD   Organisation for Economic Co-operation and Development
REP   Regional Employment Premium
SET   Selective Employment Tax
SITC   Standard International Tariff Classification
u.a.   units of account
VAT   Value Added Tax

Contents

SECTION FOUR

SECTION FIVE

List of Contributors

Norman Cuthbert, Professor of Economics, Queen's University, Belfast

Norman Gibson, Professor of Economics, New University of Ulster, Coleraine

David Law, Department of Economics, University College of Wales, Aberystwyth

Dermot McAleese, Department of Economics, Trinity College, Dublin

Gavin McCrone, Scottish Economic Planning Department, Edinburgh

P. S. McMenamin, Industrial Development Authority, Dublin

Barry Moore, Department of Applied Economics, University of Cambridge

John Rhodes, Department of Applied Economics, University of Cambridge

Paul Romus, Directorate General for Regional Policy, E E C Commission

Christopher Smallwood, Department of Economics, University of Edinburgh

John Vaizey, Professor of Economics, Brunel University

John Williamson, International Monetary Fund, Washington, and Professor of Economics, Warwick University

Tom Wilson, Professor of Political Economy, University of Glasgow

List of Contributors

Introduction

JOHN VAIZEY

THIS collection of essays is really concerned with the political economy of regionalism. That somewhat cryptic expression needs elaboration.

In economic theory there has for long been a dichotomy between regional economics on the one hand and international economics on the other. But classical political economy developed in a world where there were large empires. During the nineteenth century the emergence of nationalism led to the break-up of some of the larger empires, and with the Treaty of Versailles Europe was effectively Balkanised. This process has continued since the Second World War, and there are now nearly 140 independent nation states. Some of these, like the United States and the USSR, are very large, but the great majority are very small, both in terms of population and of their economic resources. It follows, therefore, that much of the analysis of international trade, which was based upon the inhibitions to free factor movements, is not applicable to some of the new nation states which are part of wider economies. And, furthermore, it may be that economic analysis as applied to regions, which allows for a free movement of factors, may well be more applicable to their circumstances. But this view, of course, immediately runs into the difficulty that in fact the nation states are states in the full sense of the word, and have independent jurisdiction over their economies. The countries in the British Isles represent a fascinating example of this series of problems.

One country, the Republic of Ireland, is completely independent, whereas the four other territories are mutually interdependent within one overall political jurisdiction, but with separate constitutional arrangements, namely England, Scotland, Wales and Northern Ireland. The Royal Economic Society and the

British-Irish Association thought that it would contribute to theoretical and political understanding of these issues if a conference were arranged at which these technical and political problems were directly approached, and this was done. These papers were presented at Durham in September 1973.

In the first place, it will be seen that this collection of essays constitutes an original and important break-through in the field of regional economics. The work which Moore and Rhodes have done on the problem of a regional economy tends to argue (from a post-Keynesian position) that the true economic cost of supporting a region which has substantial unemployed resources, especially labour, is negative—that is to say, that there is a net gain not only to the region but to the community as a whole from such a policy. This important and valuable conclusion was rigorously tested at the meeting, and much discussion and controversy arose. It was supported also on the monetary side by an important and fruitful analysis by Professor J. H. Williamson of the economic effects of monetary integration. This is something which, of course, applies to all regional economies, and increasingly, in the modern world, with the development of such international organisations as the European Economic Community, it will apply to formerly independent nation states. It is on this basis, therefore, that these two papers represent complementary statements on an issue which has become increasingly complex.

There follow a series of important papers on the economic consequences of different forms of political autonomy within one large nation state. Dr McCrone of the Scottish Office makes a particularly penetrating analysis of the Scottish situation, and there are also special considerations of the problems of Wales, and also of the English regions following the result of the important Royal Commission under the chairmanship of Lord Kilbrandon, which considered these questions. Mr Smallwood's work was particularly devoted to the vexed question of financial support of quasi-autonomous regional governments, and this problem clearly is of great significance in the support of regional territories within such growing communities as the E E C. The Northern Irish problem is elucidated in two extremely important papers, one of which, by Professor Gibson, tends to show that the consequences of a greater degree of devolution to the

Northern Ireland government from the United Kingdom, even
to such a point as independence, would not be so grave as they
have often been thought to be. This assertion might rest upon
two separate considerations. One is whether or not the facts
about the existing degree of support are correct, and Professor
Gibson suggests that they are not; and the other concerns the
development of a body of theory which would enable the facts
to be explained in a comprehensive and comprehensible form.
It is at this target that my own paper, and the important paper
by Professor Tom Wilson, is particularly directed. The proof of
this pudding is, in a sense, in the eating. There is one part of
the integrated economy of the British Isles which has for over
50 years been independent, namely, the Republic of Ireland,
formerly the Free State. The problems and benefits of independence are discussed in an important series of papers originating
in the Republic. In this context, several points may well be
made. The first is that we are dealing here not so much with
a distinction between regional economics on the one hand and
international economics on the other, but with a continuum, a
sort of rainbow where one colour shades into another, and
this continuum is perhaps one of the most important contributions that economics has to make to these important questions of
political and nationalist independence.

Secondly, it is shown that all the economies within these
islands are to a greater or lesser extent mutually interdependent,
and that variations in the relative strengths of different parts of
the whole economy immediately affect all the other parts. As
the world becomes a more interdependent place, this is likely to
be increasingly true of nation after nation and region after
region.

Thirdly, it is shown how extremely complex is the relationship between different political and constitutional structures, and
different rates and patterns of economic development and
change. This complexity has been far too little understood in
the past.

Fourthly, and this is perhaps not the least important contribution that these essays make, the relationship between Ireland
on the one hand and the other nations which make up the
British Isles on the other is shown to be a particularly complex
and close one. It may well be that approaching the problem of

these relationships from economics may tend to defuse the atmosphere, for certainly the experience of the conference in this respect was particularly positive and valuable.

It remains for me, on behalf of the British-Irish Association which organised the conference, to thank the Royal Economic Society, and particularly its Secretary, Professor Charles Carter, for its help in arranging the conference and in helping to finance it, and secondly, to thank Nick Stadlen, the Secretary of the British-Irish Association, for all the work that he has devoted to organising it. Above all, we must thank the authors of the papers, not only for writing and presenting them, and for re-writing them in the light of the discussion which took place at the University of Durham, but also thank them for allowing us to publish this volume. We hope that the volume will contribute not only to the development of economic reasoning but also to friendship and harmony between the peoples of these islands and the rest of Europe.

SECTION ONE

Economic Sovereignty

TOM WILSON

'Shake a sieve, and the rubbish remains.'

Ecclesiasticus

Introduction

WHAT economic advantages can be obtained when an area has a government which can exercise sovereign authority? The question is far from being merely academic at a time when the governments of a number of countries have surrendered the right to independent action over various important matters and may continue to do so. Moreover while sovereign power is being abridged in some places and in some respects, there is a continuing demand for more independent power elsewhere. Admittedly the number of separate national groups that have not yet achieved independence is fairly small, at least in the Western World, but in many countries there continue to be demands for greater regional autonomy, if not for independence. In Britain this has been the problem with which the Commission on the Constitution has been concerned.

Is economic sovereignty on balance something so desirable that it ought to be sought or preserved? The question is important but it is also somewhat vague. If progress is to be made and the possible benefits and the possible drawbacks assessed, it seems necessary to distinguish between different functions and between different areas. This, at least, is what common sense would suggest; but we must first satisfy ourselves that the term 'sovereignty' is being used in a permissible manner. If a sovereign authority is one than which, in law, there can be none higher, is it possible to adopt a functional approach which would seem to imply that the sovereign authority might be limited in certain directions? Again the question is not simply academic, for those who oppose any form of economic union appear at times to feel that sovereignty must in some ultimate sense be destroyed if it is in any respect abridged. Perhaps this fear is more natural in a unitary state than it would be in a federation. For the sovereignty of the state governments in a federation is real enough, though limited in scope, and the same is true of the federal governments themselves within their respective spheres. At all events a functional approach to sovereignty seems to be the natural and useful one from an economist's point of view.[1] It will be helpful, moreover, to bring within our scope the autonomous powers exercised by subordinate governments which cannot be described as 'sovereign' at all without an improper use of language. The local authorities in Britain are an example. So was the former Parliament of Northern Ireland and so is its new Assembly.

Although a government may have the legal right to act as it pleases in certain respects, this is 'negative freedom' and the scope for practical action may naturally be circumscribed in a variety of ways. If this is so with regard to a particular function of government, then the sacrifice of *de iure* authority over that particular function may cost little in practice and may well be worth making if there is a good prospect of advantage in other respects. This possibility is one of the questions with which we shall be concerned. Other questions concern the relationship between governments which are members of a federation or members of an economic union and also the relationship within a unitary state between the central government and the local authorities or the regional authorities (if any). For the manner in which these relationships are conducted, in particular in the financial field, can have an important bearing on the degree of independence that is exercised in practice. Thus such concepts as 'fiscal harmonisation' and 'equalisation' and 'parity' will obviously need to be examined.

There is another word in our opening sentence which clearly calls for preliminary comment and warning. This is the word 'advantages'. From which point of view are the advantages to be assessed? It is easy to slip unconsciously into the habit of speaking as though (i) the advantages were simply those likely to accrue to the area in question and (ii) the assessment of these advantages were to be made only by the government of this area. Both a wider view and a narrower view are needed. The benefits conferred or the losses imposed on an area wider than one particular nation or region cannot be left out of account without adopting a highly nationalistic or even highly parochial set of values. To use economic jargon, 'externalities' must not be disregarded when we are dealing with governments any more than when we are dealing with consumers or firms. This is why a wider view of government is needed. A narrower view of the role of government is also required because we must not suppose that government, even when democratically elected, can fully ascertain and adequately respect the preferences of large numbers of individuals over the vast and complex range of economic activity. Thus we come to the metaphorical use of the term 'sovereignty' which, as it happens, is its most common use in economic literature : that is to say, 'consumers' sovereignty'. There is a corresponding need to set some limits to the scope of official action.[2]

It goes without saying that this range of topics extends far beyond the scope of a single paper. These include such familiar and much debated topics as neo-colonialism and the role of the multi-national corporation. The differences between planning on a national and planning on a regional basis are also relevant. We shall, however, confine our remarks to two issues : first, the control of exchange rates, and secondly, fiscal policy. Even with this limitation, the range is far too great for more than summary comment; but these two topics have been chosen because, as we shall see, they hang naturally together.

Exchange Rates and Currency Areas

The old debate about exchange rates, far from subsiding, has been renewed with intensified vigour. To some economists the sovereign power to determine exchange-rate policy is one which should, on no account, be surrendered to any international authority or economic union. This is 'the price of economic freedom',[3] and it is a freedom which should be used, whether in order to adjust the pegs or in order to allow currencies to float. For there are bound to be structural changes in both demand and supply and there may also be differences in national propensities to inflate which it might be difficult to contain adequately without imposing monetary discipline so severe as to be unacceptable. It is held that such disturbances can be dealt with more effectively and less painfully if rates can vary. To other economists, this *de jure* power is of little significance *de facto*. In particular, a fall in the exchange rate will soon be offset by rises in domestic costs and the advantages to be derived in other respects from stable rates will thus have been sacrificed to no avail. This argument appears to rest mainly upon a theory of cost inflation[4] and one imagines that its force and relevance will depend upon circumstances in particular cases. A similar comment may be made about the plea for variations in exchange rates or for freely fluctuating rates. Is it inferred that if the United Kingdom can benefit from such policies, Scotland would also do so if she had the appropriate sovereign power? Has the Republic of Ireland, for its part, been wrong to keep its pound pegged to the British pound?

The discussion of optimum currency areas, which has been the subject of a number of articles in recent years, is of obvious relevance in attempting to deal with questions of this kind. As McKinnon has observed,[5] this has added an important and previously somewhat neglected dimension to the debate.

A currency area may be defined as an area with a common currency or, if there are several currencies, these currencies must—in the language of the Werner Report—be fully convertible and have their relative values fixed irrevocably. The value of the common currency, or of the group of linked currencies, may vary relatively to those of other currencies. Indeed such external variations *should* take place if we continue to accept Mundell's observation that: 'The optimum currency area is not the world'.[6] But the boundaries of the 'optimum' currency areas need not, of course, coincide with the boundaries of areas that have governments that are sovereign in this sense.[7] Nor is it to be expected that the latter will in general be re-drawn with this objective in mind! If, however, the characteristics of an optimum currency area can be identified and assessed, this should, in principle, be helpful in several contexts. It should allow an area which is not independent to decide whether to place much or little weight on the legal right to follow a separate currency policy which independence would convey. It should also help a country that is already independent in this respect to decide whether to use this power in practice in such a way as to follow a fully independent line, or whether to peg is currency to that of some other standard. Still more topical, of course, is the question whether a group of countries, such as the members of the European Economic Community, are right in aiming at monetary union. The main issues, as presented in the growing literature on the subject, may be briefly summarised.

Consider two economies of equal size one of which is more open than another. The difference may reflect one or both of two factors : first, differences in preferences between domestic and foreign goods; secondly, differences in the costs of obtaining these two classes of goods whether as a consequence of differences in transport costs or of differences in domestic production possibilities. Suppose now that both countries seek to eliminate deficits by restricting domestic expenditure. It has been pointed out by Corden that : 'The higher the marginal propensity to import, the less the expenditure reduction required to eliminate any *given* initial deficit.'[8] It would seem to follow that a fixed parity will be more costly for the more closed economy. We must, however, note the crucial nature of the assumption that the deficit is 'given'. For the adverse developments which produced the deficits would have to be more severe in the case of the more closed economy in order to yield the same deficit. The comparison does not, therefore, seem to be altogether fair. There is the further point that, even if the excess cost of adjustment were greater in the more closed economy, it might suffer less in its export industries. Clearly the possibilities need to be teased out more fully and the verdict will depend upon the precise assumptions made as, indeed, Corden subsequently concedes. Thus the effect of a reduction in the exchange rate is more likely to be offset by changes in domestic costs when imports are high relatively to gross domestic product, both because the import content of output will be higher and also because wages and other incomes are then more likely to be forced up in response to dearer imports. If, then, the economy is very open, it may be harder to achieve a devaluation that is effective.

Consider now a different situation where the two economies are in surplus but in danger of importing inflation from the rest of the world. In each case a rise in the value of the currency would seem appropriate but the case for it would naturally be greater in the more open economy. The latter would have to deflate more with greater excess costs in order to offset the rise in import prices—and this, of course, throws us into the Phillips curve controversy.[9] The foreign surplus would also be increased still more and this might not be an appropriate outcome, either nationally or internationally.

If, indeed, we lay heavy stress on the difficuty of dealing with a deficit by means of a fall in the exchange rate because money illusion may not prevail, we find ourselves with an awkward ratchet mechanism in the machinery of international adjustment. A lower rate of exchange may not do much good in such circumstances but, in the opposite circumstances with a surplus and the danger of imported inflation, a higher rate of exchange may be helpful. From a national point of view, appreciation may sometimes be appropriate, depreciation never!

We cannot explore this difficult area further in the present context. There are, however, some other considerations which may help in reaching a conclusion.

If the movement of labour between two or more areas is easy, then two consequences follow. First the linking of their currencies will present fewer problems. The free movement of labour can ease the social hardship of unemployment that may be caused by a balance-of-payments deficit when parities are fixed. Migration may also provide some solution in that imports to the deficit area will be reduced when the migrants depart and will be correspondingly increased in the surplus area. Ease of migration is thus one of the tests for identifying a currency area.[10] To look at the matter from a different angle, an area which is not at present part of a sovereign state could expect to gain less from independence if, as a consequence, the movement of labour became much more difficult. There is a second point which may not have received enough attention. This is that ease of migration will make people more conscious of differences in real wages and will therefore make it more difficult to reduce relative real wages by means of a lower exchange rate.

What has been said relates only to the movement of labour. We shall discuss the movement of capital at a later stage. Meanwhile, it will be seen that the factors mentioned above have an important bearing on the consequences of different propensities to inflate. If wages rise faster relatively to changes in productivity in some countries than in others, then difficulties will be encountered when priorities are fixed. This is also true with regard to other factors, although the labour market is likely to be the most important. As a result some members of a monetary union will have balance of payments deficits. The severity of the consequential deflation and unemployment will depend partly upon the importance attached to inflation by the central authority. (The same is true in a single country where there are regional differences in unemployment.) But, as we have seen, the outcome will also depend partly upon the openness of the particular members' economies and upon ease of migration.

Enough has now been said to indicate that the expression 'optimum currency areas' is misleading. Relevant and important though the various issues may be, these are usually questions of degree. This is clearly so with regard to migration and openness. Such reasoning does not lead to the definition of an 'optimum'. On the contrary there are a variety of opposing considerations to be placed in the balance on either side. As far as I am aware, little attempt has been made to specify the problem of assessment in precise terms, and statistical solutions for particular countries lie still further ahead. Indeed it is hard to see how some of the relevant factors could be quantified, in particular the advantage in terms of convenience and less uncertainty that may be expected to follow from the irrevocable fixing of parities. In short we still lack models which are sufficiently operational and the inferences that can be drawn from the theory are therefore limited. Some suggestions can, however, be made as the following examples may show.

With these various considerations in mind, we can now return to some of the questions posed at an earlier stage. Should the Republic of Ireland have followed an independent exchange rate policy in the past? I do not think so. But it is very important to recall that the Republic used other measures to influence the flow of international payments: tariffs and also export bounties in the form of a tax holiday for certain profits earned on exports. Plausible assumptions about elasticities would suggest that such measures would probably be more effective than an independent exchange-rate policy would have been.[11] The future will be different in two respects. First, the Anglo-Irish Trade Agreement is bringing down, if it does not completely eliminate, the barriers to imports from the United Kingdom.[12] Secondly, membership of the E E C may not only mean a customs union but may set limits to indirect protection through regional devices although Eire may escape from interference for a long time as a 'peripheral' area. Agricultural exports will also do well, and this will lessen any hardship imposed by monetary union.

Let us next ask whether an independent currency policy would have been more appropriate if the island of Ireland had been united under a single independent government.[13] The answer is almost certainly in the negative. The North has a substantially more open economy than the South, and a united Ireland would be more open than the existing Republic of twenty-six counties. This is the first point. The second concerns migration. Over the years the net outflow of people to England has been much larger from the South than from the North—although such migration from the South was international and from the North only interregional. One could reasonably expect unification to be followed by substantially larger migration because the North would then be cut off from the relatively high British social security benefits which have fostered immobility.

Let us now turn to a different area. If Scotland were politically independent, with sovereign power to determine its own exchange rate policy, would it be sensible to let the Scottish pound depreciate relatively to the English pound in order to reduce unemployment? Again the answer must almost certainly be in the negative. As it happens, this particular question has been posed by Corden and he goes on to say: 'If Scotland had never been joined to England, one could well conceive of Scotsmen accepting wage settlements fixed in their own currency irrespective of prospective exchange-rate changes. But this is less likely if Scotland, after more than two hundred years of union, were newly turned into a separate country.' More generally he concludes that: 'A very small open economy is not really a feasible area, since there would be no significance in its having its own exchange rates. Its own currency would have no liquidity value, and the population would choose to strike wage bargains and accumulate wealth in terms of foreign currency.'[14]

European monetary union is a very different matter. There are two aspects to be kept in mind. First, there is the tying of the British currency to those of her E E C partners, or the substitution of a new currency, Europa, for all these national currencies. Some common exchange rate in terms of other world economies which might be more appropriate for Western Germany might be less so for the United Kingdom or Italy. The common rate is likely to be a compromise reflecting the outcome of different pressures. Again we must be careful to recall that the advantages may be assessed from different viewpoints and it will not do to assume implicitly that some national viewpoint is the only one that matters. If we can bring ourselves to think as Europeans, a common external rate may have advantages and this is important, even apart from the possibility that the individual countries may themselves benefit in the long run. In short, the political assumptions should not be submerged. But the quantities are also important. The tying of the Irish pound to the British pound has not only affected the flow of trade, payments and factors between Ireland and Britain; it has also affected Irish relations with the rest of the world. The relevant facts here are that trade with Britain has accounted for a proportion of total Irish trade that has been much higher than British trade with the EEC countries as a fraction of total British trade. A common Anglo-Irish parity was therefore more appropriate than a common European currency. The second question is the effect of European monetary union on British relations with Europe. The situation is, of course, changing but would have to change a great deal before about half of British trade is with the EEC. Not only is the British economy far less open relatively to Europe than is Scotland, or Northern Ireland, or even the Republic of Ireland, relatively to England; migration is bound to be far more difficult, even if there are no legal obstacles. Moreover, there is no traditional link between the British wage-level and the average European wage-level as there is between wage-levels in the different regions of the United Kingdom. Perhaps there will ultimately be some effective move towards wage-bargaining on the European level; but this is still a nightmare rather than a reality.

It may be held that Britain might just as well accept fixed parities with her European partners because the trade unions in Britain are not so subject to money illusion as to allow real wages to be lowered by devaluation.[15] In reply it can be pointed out that, if this is so, what is required is fixed exchange rates with the rest of the world, or much the greater part of it, not just with Europe. But it has not, in my view, been shown conclusively that exchange-rate adjustments will always be so fully offset by rising domestic costs as this reasoning seems to imply.

As we have observed, this remains a highly controversial matter but some of the recent arguments advanced on the pessimistic side seem to me to be as unconvincing as some of the earlier rival claims that it is easy 'to float' along to prosperity. Indeed I am not sure that I understand what Johnson has in mind when he argues that, if elasticities of substitution between domestic and foreign goods are high, a successful devaluation requires that 'workers will be content to accept wages below the international value of their marginal product, and that employers will not be driven by competition for labour in the face of this disequilibrium to bid wages up to their marginal productivity levels'.[16] For this reasoning seems to imply that there was equilibrium before the devaluation occurred. In fact the starting point would rather be one where labour and, perhaps, some other factors were receiving *more* than their marginal products valued at international prices, or would have been doing so with exports at the volume needed in order to achieve solvency. The excess would be at the expense of profits which might be negative, so that the required flow of exports could not be sustained. Devaluation would be designed to correct this position.

More generally devaluation, or a downward drifting rate, need not imply an absolute cut in real wages if growth is taking place or if the composition of domestic expenditure can be altered in favour of consumption. It must certainly be conceded that domestic cost-inflation may nevertheless offset any competitive gain that has been achieved; but it is surely not necessary to make a desperate choice between optimism and pessimism.

Moreover if the extremely pessimistic verdict on exchange rates is accepted, we have to ask how the balance of payments can ever be adjusted. For deflation and rising unemployment must also be regarded as unacceptable—unless one postulates some kind of political fairyland—a rather unpleasant fairyland at that! The true verdict would then appear to be that, if changes in the exchange rate are useless, a free economy has been made unworkable and certain strategic freedoms must be abandoned—in particular collective bargaining and free trade unions. It is, one hopes, a little premature to accept this conclusion but it is important to see where totally fixed parities might lead in a world where deflation and heavy unemployment are also politically unacceptable.

To say this is not to ignore the difficulties involved in a falling exchange rate or to overlook the positive advantages which some stability in rates may confer.

Fixed parities reduce the administrative costs and the uncertainties of trade, travel and the movement of capital. It is true that uncertainty can also be reduced by futures markets but only at some cost. The complexity and cost of such dealings and the difficulty in establishing and operating such markets effectively would be great if there were a very large number of freely fluctuating currencies. These considerations can be accepted but it does not necessarily follow that any one of the main trading nations should abandon its independence by joining a currency area. Thus there is a balance of considerations to be taken into account. What we can say is that the balance may tilt more towards fixity if an economy is very 'open' *vis-à-vis* the economies of the other members of some actual or prospective union, and if the economy is relatively small.

There is a further point which may have received too little attention. This is that fixity, at least for a reasonable period, is necessary for the transmission of competitive pressures. It is an odd feature of the discussion of optimum currency areas that attention is so much concentrated on monetary expenditure as it affects, and is affected by, the balance of payments. Much less is said about changes in efficiency. Even migration is discussed largely from the point of view of the effect on expenditure. The fact that migration is nevertheless one of the central features of the analysis of optimum currency areas undermines any attempt to defend the comparative neglect of changing efficiency on the ground that the analysis is concerned only with the short term. Although it would be going too far to say that the production-possibility functions are taken as given, it is the case that changes in efficiency receive less attention than might have been expected in view of the arguments originally deployed in favour of common markets. For it was held that efficiency would be better stimulated if barriers to trade were lowered and economies were thus made more open. The gain would flow not merely from a better allocation of resources and some further realisation of comparative advantage, but also from the stimulus to X-efficiency that might come from foreign competition. Precisely how this stimulus was to be transmitted was not very adequately explained but it is surely important to observe that competitive pressures will be weakened if exchange rates can be changed too easily and too often.[17] This does not amount to a plea for parities that are fixed indefinitely, for countries may get into positions where profits are so squeezed as to leave too little finance for investment in response to these competitive pressures. The fact remains that the desirability of transmitting competitive pressure provides support for some stability in exchange rates, even if this implies a peg that is adjustable rather than one that is immovable.[18]

An inflow of capital from other areas may also help to bring about 'desirable' adjustments. But what adjustments are to be deemed 'desirable', and by whom? If a wide viewpoint is adopted, it may be held that some areas should be net exporters of both capital and labour. If, on the contrary, the less prosperous areas are to be net importers of capital, then this may be justified (*a*) on political grounds (common citizenship, solidarity within a community, etc.) or (*b*) on what may be broadly described as infant-industry grounds. Even if a case can thus be established for a net inflow, it does not follow that such an inflow will take place in the absence of special encouragement. This encouragement may come through fiscal policy. But fiscal policy entails many wider issues.

Fiscal Policy

Let us first begin on a negative note by recalling that the surrender of sovereign power over exchange rates in itself entails some further restriction of the exercise of sovereignty. Thus monetary policy may be determined by a central bank set up to serve a new economic community or, if there are still central banks in the member countries, by a supra-national currency board of some kind. There are then further implications for public finance. Obviously a Government will not be able to finance a net borrowing requirement by the creation of money on whatever scale it thinks fit, without regard to the degree of inflation thought to be acceptable for the community as a whole. Apart from any such implications for net borrowing requirements monetary union clearly implies that taxes which raise prices can be changed only with a careful eye on the balance of payments. This is directly so in the case of taxes based on the origin principle (such as payroll taxes) as compared with taxes based on the destination principle (such as Value Added Tax). When exchange rates can be varied it is possible to argue that differences in payroll taxes need not distort trade. Even with monetary union, payroll taxes levied at different rates in different member countries in the past will not necessarily have to be made uniform, for these differences should also have been reflected in exchange rates in the past and will therefore be reflected in the rates to be frozen when a monetary union is established. But subsequent changes in such taxes will have to be made with caution. Thus both the choice of tax and, in some cases, its level will be affected by monetary union with implications that are likely to be particularly important for social services by payroll taxes.[19]

Some limits to the exercise of autonomy in national fiscal and monetary policies[20] are thus required, but this is only one aspect of the matter. For account must also be taken of fiscal and monetary policies at the level of the economic community itself which may provide some compensation for the loss of sovereignty at the national level. This is a theme that has not been neglected by E E C spokesmen, but the scale on which such policies are operated is still quite modest. More is to be learned by looking at developments *within* various national economies than by looking at the E E C—which is scarcely surprising at this stage. Moreover, apart from any lesson which may thus be learned for subsequent application within a relatively new economic community, these national developments are of interest and importance in their own right. As we shall see, these matters are highly relevant to any study of economic sovereignty.

Fiscal transfers between different areas within a nation[21] are made with the objective of achieving greater equality in the provision of public services than that which exists in output a head. These transfers may take place as a consequence of the normal activities of central government, possibly without any explicit expression of intent, and probably without any statistical calculation. This in large measure is what happens within

Britain and, in varying degree, within most countries. But the relationship between different types of government may also be involved: the relationship between a central government and the local authorities, or between a central government and a subordinate regional authority; or between a federal government and the state or provincial governments. A question which then arises is whether greater equality can be achieved only at the cost of imposing some restraints on the freedom of action of the local or the provincial governments. Or the point could be put in this way: fiscal transfers may be regarded as compensation for having no control over exchange rates, but these transfers may themselves be made in such a way as to impose further restrictions on regional autonomy. Is this a real issue or only a hypothetical one?

There are two methods of achieving greater regional equality:

(i) by aiming at parity through the detailed control and adjustment of expenditure;

(ii) by the equalisation of revenue in order to permit parity in expenditure.

In principle the two could yield the same *total* figure for transference, but their respective effects on regional autonomy may well be different.[22]

In the United Kingdom, the evolution of financial relations between Westminster and the Government of Northern Ireland has been a particularly illuminating example of the effects of controlling expenditure. The former Parliament was responsible for a far wider range of public services than are the state or provincial governments in the great federations, and the same is true of the new Assembly. But Stormont was given a very limited power to raise taxes and, under the legislation establishing the new Assembly, Westminster not only retained its old taxing power but took over responsibility for 'existing Northern Ireland taxes and taxes substantially of the same character as any of those taxes'. A new regional rate (property tax) will be levied as a consequence of the reorganisation of local government. The Assembly would also be able to levy taxes other than those retained by Westminster but some ingenuity would be required in order to devise new taxes of much quantitative significance. The new Executive has suggested that it may wish to discuss with Westminster the possibility of revising the constitution with regard to taxing powers but there the matter rests at the time of writing.

Westminster has therefore been obliged to make available revenue raised in the province by reserved taxes. The original formula of the nineteen-twenties was that, in addition to the modest proceeds of its own taxes, Stormont would receive the proceeds of this reserved taxation *less* a prescribed deduction for defence, interest on the national debt, etc.—the so-called 'Imperial Contribution'. This arrangement, which put Northern Ireland implicitly in a worse position than the other less prosperous regions of the United Kingdom, was modified gradually and the criterion of 'parity' was ultimately accepted.[23] This meant that, with taxes imposed at the same *rates,* expenditure on the services transferred to Stormont could be on the same scale as in Great Britain. It was the contribution towards 'imperial' costs which then became the residue. The latter was positive in the boom years of the Second World War but has been negative for extended periods. This negative contribution[24] has often been described as a 'subsidy' but it should be clearly understood that other parts of the United Kingdom with relatively low output a head and relatively heavy expenditure are also making negative 'imperial contributions'. Over the whole field of public expenditure there is no reason to suppose that Ulster was more 'subsidised' than any similarly situated region.[25] To take one specific example, no one has ever suggested that South Wales or Clydeside should balance their national insurance accounts!

This assistance would naturally be lost if Ulster became independent—and it would be hard to believe that the new power to devalue a new Ulster currency would afford much compensation! If Ulster joined the Republic, the North would then not only lose this assistance from Westminster but might have to provide assistance to the South where, on average, output a head is a sixth below the level in the North and the tax base is therefore smaller. (Given time, the latter problem might be resolved by faster growth in the South.)

Parity in expenditure need not mean that the public services must be identical.[26] In principle, more expenditure on some services could be offset against less expenditure on others, but the administrative difficulties become formidable. It is true, of course, that in certain fields differences in policy may not have important financial implications. It is also true that even with regard to the most costly services, Stormont's policies diverged in some interesting respects from Westminster policies. But, on the whole, the public services have developed along lines very similar to those of the rest of the United Kingdom—a fact which one would never suspect if one relied upon impressions received from the mass media! The administrative difficulties in arranging a trade-off between one service and another would be far more formidable if all the main regions of the United Kingdom had their own assemblies and obtained finance on the basis of parity. It would not make much difference to this particular issue if they were able to raise 10 or 20 or 40 per cent of the revenue from their own resources. The application of the criterion of 'parity in expenditure' implies surveillance over the whole field and the administrative pressure towards uniformity would still be strong.

As we have noted above, an alternative method of achieving parity, or of moving towards it, is to make tax-equalisation payments. In this case, Canada must serve as the example.[27] The move towards parity was made later in Canada than in the United Kingdom, as was perhaps to be expected in view both of the size of the country and its tradition of provincial autonomy; but large changes have occurred over the last decade or so.[28] The arrangements for equalisation are associated with the arrangements for sharing the proceeds of certain taxes between the federal government and the provincial governments : personal income tax, corporation tax and succession and estate taxes. The share of these taxes going to the provinces is calculated on the basis of average yield for the country as a whole. Since 1967, the other provincial sources of revenue have also been adjusted according to the same principle—though with greater administrative and statistical difficulty, as might be expected. Thus sixteen sources of revenue are now adjusted up to the Canadian average. This does not, of course, imply complete equality in the proceeds because those provinces with yields above the average are not deprived of their surplus (Ontario, Alberta and British Columbia, in 1972–73). The deficiency payments made to the other provinces comes from federal revenue. The cost will, of course, ultimately fall more heavily on the richer provinces.[29] The position has been further complicated by recent windfall revenues accruing to certain provinces through oil and gas. The Federal Government has made a ruling to exclude these windfalls from the equalisation formula. This implies some qualification of the equalisation scheme.

Equality of revenue *per capita* is not to be identified with equity. Suppose the revenue available to each of the provinces were, in fact, exactly the same *per capita*. Such an arrangement would not take account of differences in needs arising from a whole variety of different circumstances. The arrangements for tax equalisation would have to be based on some more refined formula, or would need to be supplemented in one way or another. Large sums are in fact provided in Canada—as in the U S A—often on a cost-sharing basis : in particular, in Canada, for health, education and roads.[30] A quite different approach is for the federal government to extend its activities and raise its own direct expenditure in fields where differences in 'needs' are most likely to occur. The outstanding example in all the federations has been the great expansion in federal expenditure on social security. (Let us recall, by way of contrast, that the old government of Northern Ireland was responsible for the whole range of welfare services as well as for education at all levels. The new Assembly will also have these responsibilities.) Another important example is assistance to the less prosperous areas whether in the form of inducements for industrial development or in the form of assistance with infrastructure in addition to the shared-cost programmes mentioned above. Canada has had a large number of agencies designed to achieve this objective, such as the Atlantic Provinces Development Board; most of these have now been brought together within the Department for Regional Economic Expansion.

As one reflects on these developments, a dilemma of policy becomes increasingly apparent. It is this attempt to cope with differences in *needs* that is likely to have two results. First, the central government will assume more and more direct responsibility for certain services. Secondly, the payments made to provincial governments will involve supervision in varying degree by the central government over the uses to which these moneys are put. Thus greater 'equity' can be achieved, but at the cost of some loss in provincial autonomy. This leads on to the next

B

question. How far is it possible to devise more refined formulae for the equalisation of revenue which will make some allowance for differences in needs? This, after all is what Westminster has attempted to do with regard to the equalisation grants paid to local authorities—as distinct from its method of dealing with the one regional government in Britain.[31] These precise formulae used are, of course, open to criticism and can perhaps be improved. It is probably the case that no formulae can be as sensitive and flexible as direct bureaucratic control can be, at its best. The question then is how much equity should be sacrificed for the sake of preserving or strengthening local (or provincial) autonomy.

It would be too much to hope that all such difficulties can be completely resolved and all hard choices avoided. But an important conclusion remains. This is that devices for equalising revenue, even if imperfect from the point of view of equity, make it possible to go a very much further way towards reconciling territorial redistribution with territorial autonomy than is possible by applying a parity formula directly to expenditure.

Assumptions Uncovered and Conclusions Suggested

It is easy for an economist to become so absorbed in the technicalities of policies such as those described above as to neglect certain underlying factual assumptions about political behaviour and social attitudes and to leave unrevealed and unexamined the value judgements on which any recommendations must partly rest.

Underlying much of the discussion in the preceding section has been the assumption that there should be a substantial degree of genuine autonomy at the local or provincial level. If the fundamental basis of the argument is a belief in local or provincial democracy, then we need to be able to assume that representative government is working reasonably well at these levels. This raises questions about efficiency, integrity and apathy; and about the danger that government at these levels may be dominated for long periods by a single party which is less likely to be the case at the national level.[32]

Then there is the further assumption that freedom of choice at these levels of government, if permitted *de iure* and made possible *de facto* by the financial arrangements, will be exercised on a significant scale in practice. The validity of this assumption depends very much upon the extent to which the nation under consideration is a tightly knit community. The differences that would emerge in Great Britain, if regional governments were to be established, might be far less than is sometimes supposed. No doubt there would be strong demands in some regions for increases in some services above the national average; but the crucial question is then to decide which services would be accepted at levels *below* the national average. The administration of the parity arrangements for Ulster no doubt encouraged uniformity—the policy of 'step-by-step' as it came to be known. Equalisation operated on the revenue side would have been less inhibiting. But we need to assess the grounds for supposing that large departures from step-by-step would take place—at least when large financial outlays were involved. In short, the considerations similar to those raised with regard to real wages in earlier discussions of currency areas are relevant in the present context as well. The degree of social cohesion, or the strength of the 'demonstration effect', will be crucially important.

Next we must note the assumption that there should be equality in the provision of public services, qualified only by some allowance for differences in needs. It is an assumption that will be more enthusiastically supported in the poorer than in the richer areas,[33] but even an 'impartial spectator'—to use the language of Adam Smith—would no doubt wish to note that there are other considerations to be taken into account. Growth in the nation as a whole *may* be adversely affected—though this is not certain—and what is also likely to follow is a higher level of regional unemployment because mobility will be discouraged. Neither of these points should be regarded as decisive objections; but both are points which should not be ignored.

Parity, however reached, will result in higher public expenditure as a percentage of local output a head in the poorer areas than in the richer. May it not be more sensible to suggest that, with any *given* scale of transfers, those in the poorer areas should be able to choose lower taxes with correspondingly lower public expenditure if they should prefer this alternative? If the answer is in the negative does this imply a paternalistic approach and a lack of faith in the local democracy mentioned above? Equalisation of the *tax base* should permit such a choice to be made. The resources element in Westminster's aid to local authorities can be operated flexibly in either direction although its quantitative significance is limited. Tax-sharing after the Canadian model does, of course, ease the administrative difficulties involved in imposing taxes at different rates in different provinces, but equalisation is conditional upon taxes being levied at certain minimum rates. This arrangement does not prevent surcharges and it is interesting to note that several provinces have in fact chosen to have such surcharges added to direct taxes in excess of the federal abatement. This indicates a preference for higher taxes in order to support higher expenditure even in the poorer provinces. The old Parliament of Northern Ireland was also empowered under the Government of Ireland Act, 1920, to ask for lower rates of personal income tax but the cost, in terms of lower expenditure, was never thought to be acceptable. These are interesting pieces of evidence but do not, of course, destroy the case for allowing a choice to be made.

Next let us turn to 'externalities' which received a passing mention above. Local or regional governments may not pay sufficient regard to these wider considerations and this fact is sometimes used as a defence for shared-cost programmes (e.g. roads). This is an exceedingly crude way of dealing with the matter and may well produce distortions in other respects. A national plan for public investment, designed to co-ordinate the different provincial plans, would be more appropriate and is obviously possible in Britain. We must recognise, however, that in a federation the sovereign rights of states or provinces may prevent the kind of action, supported if necessary by powers of veto, that is possible in a unitary state where all lower levels of government are subordinate.[34] Joint planning and negotiation may help but it may be that there is a reason here for expanding federal expenditures under direct federal control, where possible, with correspondingly smaller federal transfers to the provinces through shared-cost programmes.

Conflict may arise on a different and still more important plane. If large powers are exercised by provincial governments and if these governments are helped to finance these programmes on a generous scale by unconditional grants of one kind or another from the central government, *counter-cyclical* policy may become rather more difficult to implement with the speed and sensitivity required. It is hard enough to do so in a unitary, highly centralised state, as we all have occasion to know!

If we now turn back to a consideration of the E E C, what general conclusions have been drawn? It is frequently emphasised that, if there is to be monetary union, there must be corresponding adjustments in fiscal policy. Let us note at once that the harmonisation of some of the main taxes, though obviously desirable in an economic community, may create difficulties for stabilisation policy. The harmonisation of V A T and ultimately of excise duties and of corporation tax will curtail severely the fiscal measures at the disposal of each of the member countries for controlling the rate of growth of expenditure. Correspondingly greater reliance will have to be placed upon changes in personal income taxes on the revenue side and upon changes in public expenditure. We know from experience that the difficulties may then be enhanced partly because of the time-lags involved in carrying out effective adjustment on an adequate scale. It is true that the harmonisation of V A T, the excise taxes and corporation tax need not mean that the rates at which these taxes are levied must be frozen. Variations could still be made on a European scale. These variations might not be what the individual nations acting on their own would choose but might be more appropriate from the point of view of the whole Community. Again one's assessment of the desirability of the outcome will depend upon one's point of view—whether national or European. If we assume that a European standpoint is adopted it still remains important to distinguish between harmonisation of rates on the one hand and the indefinite freezing of rates on the other. It is also important to appreciate that the adjustment of harmonised rates in whatever manner seems appropriate from the Community's point of view will present Brussels with a new and difficult task which has not I think been much discussed so far.

If this problem is set aside, then fiscal harmonisation can be viewed under two headings:

(i) Measures that should help to correct fundamental disequilibria in balances of payment on the assumption that exchange rates were fixed. (Short-term measures would also, of course, be needed in the form of drawing rights, adjustments in short-term interest rates, etc.)

(ii) Fiscal benefits might provide a form of compensation substantially broader than what would be regarded as an alternative corrective mechanism for the balance of payments. That is to say there might be some approach towards equalisation in public expenditure and this could be regarded as a compensation for the sacrifice of sovereign authority over exchange rates. Naturally such transfers would affect the balances of payments of the member countries and affect their development and employment. But the poorer areas are not necessarily those with balance-of-payment difficulties or even those with more unemployment. Even if they were, the criterion would be differences in the tax base, as in Canada, and the quantitative adjustment would then be different. Moreover some fiscal transfers of this kind may increase local unemployment by reducing mobility.

Under the first heading, regional policy is usually mentioned, but the term 'region' acquires a bewildering ambiguity at this stage. For the detailed discussion of regional policy has been concerned with (*a*) establishing some rules of the game with regard to regional policies as practised by the member nations and (*b*) with the prospect of some financial assistance from the E E C. But the balance of-payments problem will affect *nations. That is to say, the 'regions' in this context are the former currency areas.* This requires a different approach and a clear recognition that the scale of assistance might have to be on a quite massive scale. (The idea of having a European Regional Employment Premium is surely the final folly.) There is, of course, no reason to suppose that transfers on such a scale would be forthcoming in practice, which is another reason for viewing monetary union with scepticism. If E E C assistance is to be as effective as possible, it must be directed at raising efficiency and changing industrial structures; and this means primarily assistance with investment. Labour subsidies, if any, should be related to training programmes.[35] This assistance with investment would be designed in part to cope with the problem that, in the case of capital, greater mobility might result in an outflow that would make the process of adjustment in a monetary union more painful, not less, as is assumed in the case of labour.[36] But it really will not do to speak of regional policy as a substitute for exchange-rate adjustment as though regional policies had been so successful in the member nations that we had now simply to apply the lessons of this experience on a European scale!

We must also take account of the length of time required before efficiency can be raised and structural change effected even if the most generous policies are adopted and vigorously applied. It will not do to rely upon short-term measures on the one hand (borrowing arrangements, interest-rate differentials) and, on the other, on quite long-term measures for development. When proper regard is paid to the question of time, it becomes clear that a vast gap is left in the middle which a flexible exchange-rate policy might help to fill.

Harmonisation of fiscal policies under the second heading is much more mysterious. Is it really contemplated that there should be some approach to parity as attempted, for example, in a federation such as Canada? There is an immense and obvious difference between the federations and the E E C. This is the great importance of federal sources of revenue which are not only large but usually more important than the sources of revenue of the individual states. Over the years federal revenue has proved to be more buoyant and has been further strengthened in some federations (Canada, Australia) by what were originally wartime leasing arrangements. The E E C has no such sources of independent finance and, in order to obtain it, political integration on some kind of federal model would be required in order, *inter alia*, to provide the representation that goes with taxation.

We have already argued that for Britain at least the sacrifice of sovereign control over the rate of exchange would imply a real change and not merely the abandonment *de iure* of a power that was in any case demonstrably useless *de facto*. We have now seen that, at least as far as fiscal transfers are concerned, the offsetting advantage would have to be on a far greater scale than appears to have been contemplated. It does not follow, of course, that there is no scope for co-operation in exchange-rate policy if more flexibility is permitted than would be implied by a commitment to parities that were irrevocably fixed. Nor does it follow that there is no case for moving towards greater harmonisation in various economic policies, including fiscal policies.

In criticising the proposal to fix European rates of exchange relatively to each other, one is in danger of being labelled 'anti-European'. But that is not the point. The point is rather that the E E C might be damaged or even destroyed by an over-rapid attempt to achieve monetary union in the sense of parities irrevocably fixed before the implications of such a commitment had been adequately understood and the necessary implications accepted by the members of the Community.

APPENDIX

1. The effect of a rise in import prices on domestic prices may be illustrated by the following expression based on simple adaptive assumptions.

$$\dot{p} = \dot{m} \left(\frac{M}{Y} \right) \left[1 + \left[\frac{W + P}{Y} \right] + \left[\frac{W + P}{Y} \right]^2 + \dots \right]$$

$$= \dot{m}$$

where $\dot{p}$ is the percentage rise in domestic costs;
$\dot{m}$ is the percentage rise in import prices;
M is total imports;
Y is the value of national output;
W is wages;
P is profits.

Thus the final percentage rise in domestic costs will be the same as the percentage rise in import costs.

The limiting assumptions are, of course, crucial. The adjustment lags, which may be important, have been ignored in this simple expression. Moreover M/Y may not remain constant. Wages may not be pushed up by just the amount required to offset rising prices. (The danger here is that the rise may be greater than p.) The profit margin may not be fixed.

The possibility of a less rigidly deterministic reaction will, however, depend partly on the size of M/Y, and this is one of the respects in which differences in the openness of different economies is important.

For trade between Eire and the United Kingdom, the ratio is about 25 per cent.

For trade between Northern Ireland and Great Britain, it is believed to be something like 80 per cent.

For trade between the United Kingdom and the E E C, it is about 5 per cent.

Where the percentage is small, the possibility of offsetting action is obviously enhanced.

2.   Suppose the rise in wages can be represented as follows :

$$\dot{W} \ = \ f(u, \ \hat{p}, \ \dot{e})$$

where u stands for unemployment, and $\hat{p}$ for expected increases in prices. The final item, $\dot{e}$, stands for rising efficiency on the assumption that there is a positive correlation between the latter and wage demands.

If government expenditure can be reduced and indirect taxes correspondingly lowered, then the effect of x on p may be offset and thus $\hat{p}$ may also be reduced.

I do not think we have much precise information about the link between $\dot{w}$ and $\dot{e}$, but we may assume that it is not a constant. It may also be possible, perhaps by means of an incomes policy, to reduce this relationship $\dot{w}$ and $\dot{e}$, subject no doubt to the constraint that

$$\left(\begin{array}{c} w \\ / \\ p \end{array}\right)_n \ \gtreqless \ \left(\begin{array}{c} w \\ / \\ p \end{array}\right)_{n-1}$$

These offsetting adjustments will obviously be more practicable if

$$\dot{m} \left(\frac{M}{Y}\right) \ \text{is small.}$$

First Choose Your Theory

JOHN VAIZEY

'IRISH history is a subject for Irishmen to forget and Englishmen to learn'. (Ancient saying.)

It may seem perhaps appropriate for an official of the British-Irish Association to begin with ancient history, and in this case literally so. A recent book on Arthur's Britain has pointed out that the distinction between the island of Great Britain and the island of Ireland, which has had the most lasting effect on the relationships between the peoples of these islands, was the Roman dominance of the greater part of Great Britain and the absence of the Caesars' empire of Rome in Ireland.[1] Great Britain was a Roman unity for nearly four centuries (AD 50–450) and the consequent and subsequent development in Great Britain of a Romano-British empire during the period of the Dark Ages (which subsequently acquired the legendary glamour of Arthur's Britain) led the peoples of Great Britain throughout the last fifteen hundred years usually to acquiesce in the notion of a common allegiance to the Crown. This acquiescence has not been extended to the people who form the greater part of the inhabitants of the island of Ireland. The author's argument is that these long traditions manifest themselves not only in political forms, particularly in the case of Ireland the long nationalist struggles which culminated in the achievement of the Free State and then the Republic and which still continue, but they also affect the economic and social philosophies which embody the ideals and aspirations and experience of the peoples.[2] I would agree with him that these long historical trends are not without significance, and I shall present the case for that view. In particular they have led to the view of the economic relationships between Great Britain on the one hand and Ireland on the other being widely held, that they partake far more of the nature of a 'colonial' relationship than do the relationships between England on the one hand and either Scotland or Wales on the other. Other speakers in this Symposium will be drawing lessons from these basic social and political facts, but they certainly affect the nature of the argument that I wish to present, which is that the different styles of economic analysis adopted by different participants in the debate owe a great deal to certain deep historical elements in the mutual economic relationships.

It is also important to recall that classical political economy, which developed in Scotland and later in England in the last quarter of the eighteenth century and the first quarter of the nineteenth century, coincided with a period of great difficulty in British and Irish relationships which centred around the Rising of 1798 and the subsequent Union of the Parliaments.[3] It is less often recalled that the full growth of *laisser-faire* and neo-classical economics in the period from John Stuart Mill to the publication of Marshall's *Principles* and the widespread assumption of the Jevons-Austrian doctrines as being in some sense scientifically true coincided with a lengthy period of Anglo-Irish political struggle—a struggle which culminated in the Rising of 1916, and Anglo-Irish War and the Treaty of 1922. The Treaty of course was followed by the Civil War, a period culminating in the Anglo-Irish Trade War and the subsequent partial divorce of the Southern Irish economy from that of the United Kingdom in the Second World War.

My own reading of the history of economic thought suggests that while there were those in the United Kingdom who dissented from the prevailing trend of economic doctrines, regarding particularly *laisser-faire* as a Weltanschauung whose *raison d'être* was to justify the exploitation of the working class, it was only in Ireland that the economic doctrines which formed the basis of the Zollverein and other autarkic mechanisms in Europe, namely the German historical doctrines, played any significant part in economic training.[4] If you read the work of Professor Tom Kettle, the leading Irish nationalist, who was Professor of National Economics at the National University of Ireland, or the work of Arthur Griffith, who was the first Prime Minister of the Free State, you will find constant parallels drawn between the case of Ireland and the case of Hungary. The view was strongly put that the major function of the Union

of the Parliaments had been to enable English manufacturers
and to some lesser extent Scottish businessmen to deprive Ireland
of its own industries and to use Ireland as a market for British
goods and keep it purely as an agricultural dependency.[5] Professor Lynch and I have argued elsewhere that this view of the
relationship between the two economies is both factually false
and analytically weak,[6] but nevertheless it would be unwise to
assume that this version of the economic relationships between
these economies has not dominated some aspects of economic
teaching and policy up to the present time. Indeed it forms the
basis of the current analysis of the relationships between Great
Britain and Ireland adopted by the Provisional I R A, whereas
the Official I R A has adopted a Marxist-Leninist interpretation.[7]

I wish to put the problem of the relationships of all our
economies in a more general context. It is necessary to apologise
to my colleagues who specialise in regional studies for having
broken into their own specific domain. The traditional difference
between regional economics on the one hand and international
trade theory on the other is that regional economics is concerned
with the relationships between separate geographical areas within
one political jurisdiction, whereas international trade is concerned with relationships between the economies of sovereign
states.[8] There is, further, a difference in the freedom with which
goods may be transferred from one area to another, and in particular a break in the factor markets which makes the migration
of labour and of capital (whether in the form of financial claims
or of capital goods), more difficult in the case of international
trade than it is in the case of inter-regional transactions. Having
stated this, it will at once be clear that the difference between
the various sub-economies of these islands and the main
economy which has its axis on the north-west/south-east corridor
between Manchester and London is in this sense a somewhat
blurred one. The Republic of Ireland has a separate political
jurisdiction. It is a fully sovereign state. But nevertheless there
has been from the earliest times a substantial movement of
labour and of goods and of financial claims, as I shall subsequently draw your attention to, between Ireland and Scotland,
Wales and England. (St Patrick seems to have been English and
St David was Irish. St George, of course, was a Lebanese while
St Andrew was a Jew.) In part, this relationship is due to the

historic fact that for seven centuries there was (to a greater or less extent) a common political jurisdiction between England and Ireland. Particularly from 1801 until 1922, from an economic point of view, the countries of the then United Kingdom were administered as one unit, with certain minor caveats to that general statement. In a sense, had the two countries been politically separate during the nineteenth century, when modern economic structures were established, the common economic relationships might have not persisted in quite the form that they have after the achievement of independence in 1922. Nevertheless, such was the fact—there was a political and economic union—and it is true to say that at the moment there is a considerable degree of interpenetration between the economies. More to the point, there is little reason to suppose that this mutual interpenetration will diminish in the future.

The meaning of this from the point of view of contemporary economic policy analysis is that it makes little sense to analyse Irish economic conditions by themselves. Irish economic conditions only make sense in the broader context of the movements of the economies of these islands as a whole, for reasons which I shall subsequently spell out. But, at this point, all I want to say is that this fact does raise substantial and interesting questions about the nature of the economic consequences of different forms of political sovereignty in conditions where there is (to put it mildly) considerable contiguity. We are at the position where, by joining the E E C, the United Kingdom and the Republic of Ireland have thrown in their economic lot not only with each other but with seven other sovereign states, and increasingly the question will be asked as to what the relationship is between theories of international trade concerned with political jurisdiction at the national level on the one hand and economic relationships at the international level which are subject to formal co-ordination through such mechanisms as the Brussels economic policy-making intruments. These distinctions between regional and international analysis have received increasingly detailed and analytical attention.[9]

Perhaps before I turn to this matter it might be as well if I briefly draw your attention to the distinctions between the politico-economic status of the different economies which make up these islands at the present time. In the first place there is

England itself, which has no Parliament of its own and is subject entirely to United Kingdom legislation in which Members of Parliament from Scotland, Wales and Northern Ireland habitually vote on English questions. The English regions, which get regional assistance, have themselves no independent political institutions at the regional level, except the newly formed Metropolitan Councils which are considerably smaller than the regional economic areas. Wales has some all-Wales institutions of an advisory character, together with the Welsh Office, an administrative department which operates largely in the social field and has a Member of the Cabinet as its spokesman. Wales has however no elected representative body. Scotland has gone considerably further along the road of autonomy. Scotland has a separate body of law; its Members of Parliament habitually meet in the Scottish Grand Committee to deal with specifically Scottish legislation; it has had for ninety years a separate Member of the Cabinet representing its interests, and it has a government department, the Scottish Office, which deals not only with social affairs but to an increasing extent with economic policy. It also has to some degree an autonomous banking system which is, however, closely linked with the English banking system and is subject to the Bank of England which, despite its title, is the United Kingdom's central bank. Northern Ireland, on the other hand, has had a parliamentary system of its own, together with separate legislation from that of the rest of the Kingdom, largely derived from the Irish legislation which was on the Statute Book before 1922, and the laws subsequently passed at Stormont. Northern Ireland is an area with, to all intents and purposes, a separate jurisdiction in economic affairs except in the case of foreign trade. Finally, the Republic of Ireland is a completely autonomous independent nation state.

The questions that I wish to raise concern the difference which these political institutional differences between the jurisdiction actually make to economic activity and to economic policy. In so doing I wish to put forward certain simple-minded facts and statements which will form, I hope, the basis of subsequent fruitful discussion.

In the first place, the central point to make about the relationship of these countries is that we have here a series of small regional economies which are organised around a central axis of larger size, and theoretically the problem arises of the form of the relationship between this centre and the other smaller economies. The questions could be posed at a very general level —viz: is the relationship 'exploitative', as Bob Sutcliffe suggests the relationships between the third world and the Western industrial world are;[10] or (as classical free trade theory would support) are not all better off because we can specialise, and resources can flow to points of least cost and greatest surplus? Or the questions could be posed at a detailed level—what are the facts about flows? In the first instance we must take these circumstances which prevail which may tend to reinforce the situation in which resources flow to the centre. One such is that there is free movement of labour, and that the labour to a large extent has characteristics (language, upbringing, skin colour etc.) which make it, broadly speaking (on any given skill level) acceptable throughout the whole area. Professor Brinley Thomas, who has exhaustively studied the relationships of labour migration between different parts of the Atlantic economy in response to differing stages of the economic cycle, is fairly clear that at times of economic upsurge the flows towards the centre tend to be strongly positive, at times of economic depression the flows tend to slow down and occasionally even to become negative.[11] In those circumstances in which there is an upsurge in one particular part of the smaller regions, as in the case of Scottish oil, there is a possibility of an inflow of resources to that region, but the circumstances in which this has occurred have not been frequent.

At the same time as a common labour market there is a common framework of law, and an identity of business custom in many of the ordinary affairs of economic life. This common ground particularly applies to the business community, in which many of the firms are operating across the whole area as though it were all one country; and in this respect many firms, big and small, tend to operate in the way in which multinational corporations are said to operate in the Atlantic economy as a whole. It is especially within this context that it might be said with some deep meaning that there is a common capital market which affects investment in an immediate sense. Most investment is done by firms themselves and these firms are operating across the area as a whole (or in several parts of the area), and are using their own investible funds as they see fit, without much regard for 'political' considerations. The common capital market also takes the form of raising money on the London Stock Exchange and of using the London-based financial institutions, particularly the merchant banks, in close alliance with the financial institutions in the other major cities which tend to be closely linked to London institutions. This applies even in the Republic of Ireland, and most particularly to the Irish commercial banks. Thus there is a substantial flow of finance from the area as a whole into and out of London. There are within the individual jurisdictions of the islands particular local owners of finance, particularly the state savings banks and institutions, which are separate, but these are more conveniently considered under the terms of fiscal policy. The major exception to this generalisation is housing finance. There is also, as a result probably of the interlocking of financial institutions, a common currency between the Irish Republic and the United Kingdom. The Irish Republic formally has currency independence, both in its membership of international institutions, and because it has its own Central Bank. But in fact the two pounds are pegged to each other and there is virtually complete identity of operation between the two central banks and the institutions which they affect. British currency is acceptable in the Republic of Ireland (and Irish coins may be used for parking meters in London). My conclusion, therefore, is that political independence has not seriously affected labour, capital or the money market. How far political intervention can affect any or all of them seems to me to be a matter for serious discussion. It was certainly assumed by the original Sinn Fein supporters that political independence included 'freedom from the English bankers' (as Madame Maud Gonne MacBride said on a famous occasion to the Banking Commission) and the common pool of labour has always been a serious affront to the strongly held feelings of nationalists.

We may next turn to fiscal policy, which might seem the practical object of political separation. It is obvious that fiscal policy throughout the islands is necessarily determined with reference chiefly to the most powerful economic forces which are those that originate within the jurisdiction of Great Britain, and relates chiefly to the macro-economic balance of forces within the central corridor of Great Britain. In this respect, because of size, the other economies are 'peripheral'. When father turns we all turn. In the case of Northern Ireland, although formally the budgetary process has been separated from that of Westminster, in practice the operation of taxes and of public expenditure has been closely related to the legislation which has been adopted at Westminster, and the differences which exist, though perceptible, are marginal. In the case of Scotland there is no serious fiscal independence, though there are differences in expenditure which may best be discussed under the heading of regional policy. In the Republic of Ireland the problems of fiscal autonomy arise in the following forms; viz. that the pressures for public expenditure are in part based on expectations aroused in the United Kingdom, from the freedom of travel, the common labour market etc., and from the close links of prices and demand pressure because of the foreign trade multipliers, and in part from domestic pressures which may run counter to those of the United Kingdom. These pressures may be political: in particular, for example, there was the opposition in the 1950s to the copying of the British National Health Service, and there are substantial differences in the finance of education as a result of domestic Irish considerations; or they may be structural, as when agricultural interests differ from industrial interests, as in the case of the Common Agricultural Policy. On the revenue side fiscal policy has to be affected by the extent to which differences in tax rates are likely to lead either to migration of members of the labour force or to flights of savings to or from Dublin to the United Kingdom. The degree to which there is genuine fiscal autonomy available to the Irish government is therefore total in theory but limited in fact by the contiguity of the major United Kingdom jurisdiction, resembling in this respect the relationship of Canada and the United States.

The independence of fiscal policy over a period of fifty years has cumulatively led to differences between the Republic of Ireland and the rest of the islands, largely because changes introduced in the United Kingdom have not necessarily been introduced into the Irish legislation, while at the same time there are close similarities because they both started from a common basis of legislation which applied throughout the islands. In many respects, therefore, an examination of Irish fiscal legislation is an examination of fiscal legislation as it used to prevail in the

United Kingdom, though there have been certain innovations in Irish fiscal policy, particularly on the taxation side, which preceded United Kingdom changes and which formed interesting and important examples of the consequences of such changes. In addition, the differences in jurisdiction have cumulatively also led to differences in the legal structure within which the economy operates, which, though small, are sufficiently significant to merit attention in particular cases. But the consequences of autonomy, it is important to note, are complexity and barriers to movement of people and goods, otherwise what is the point of autonomy?

The rest of the paper comes more properly under the heading of regional policy. Regional policy may now be interpreted in the E E C context as policies adopted at national and international level, affecting different parts of the E E C. In the case of the Republic of Ireland these are policies affecting the whole of the jurisdiction and in the United Kingdom they are affecting substantial parts of it. Let us recollect that if you look at the international trade figures for the Irish Republic and the United Kingdom, the United Kingdom forms the largest single market for Irish exports and the largest single source of imports, while for the United Kingdom the Irish Republic forms a large market for exports and a large source of imports, despite its relative absolute smallness. This is surely another way of saying that the Irish Republic was once part of a total economy which included the rest of the United Kingdom and the Irish Republic. Similar figures produced for Scotland and its trade with the rest of the world indicate the importance of the rest of the United Kingdom in this total picture,[12] and so, too, for Northern Ireland.

If we look at regional policy, then, in this context we see certain problems. What we are concerned with in regional policy is an attempt to stimulate economic activity in the relatively low income areas. These areas happen to include the politically distinct jurisdictions of Ireland, North and South, Scotland and Wales. Regional policy, in this particular context, operates with constraints. Changes in monetary policy affecting any one part appear to be ruled out *de facto*, and in particular changes in the parity of the currency are ruled out *de iure* in the case of the nations within the United Kingdom and apparently *de facto* in the relationship between the Irish Republic and the United

Kingdom. It follows, then, that the bulk of the activity for regional development must take place at the fiscal level. This has taken the form in the United Kingdom of tax remissions, adopted autonomously in the case of the Northern Ireland jurisdiction and by the United Kingdom Parliament on behalf of Northern England, Scotland and Wales; of fiscal subsidies, again adopted autonomously in Northern Ireland and by the United Kingdom Parliament for the other regions and nations; fiscal subsidies given both for investment and for manpower utilisation, together with differences in the level of public expenditure, particularly on the infra-structure, and positive discrimination in the form of the relocation of government activities, as in the dispersal of offices from London to other regions. The Republic has adopted its own forms of fiscal policy designed to encourage investment from overseas, particularly from England, by substantial grants to capital investment.

It is my submission that it is in this area that debate and discussion must be concentrated. It raises all the familiar problems of harmonisation. But it also—negatively—indicates the limitations of political independence.

The Economic Case for Constitutional Reform

CHRISTOPHER SMALLWOOD

T H E Royal Commission on the Constitution is shortly to publish its long-awaited Report—to be known, no doubt, as the Kilbrandon Report. Exactly what the proposals of the Report will be it is impossible to say at this moment, but a number of things are already clear. In the first place, it has already been reported that the Commission may be in favour of the establishment of elected assemblies with legislative powers for Scotland and Wales, and whether this will indeed prove to be the case, or whether more conservative recommendations will be made—for instance, for a system of elected authorities for Scotland, Wales and the regions of England without legislative powers but with significant administrative discretion—it is clear that the Commission will advocate the creation of a number of authorities with extensive administrative and perhaps legislative responsibilities at this intermediate level. Secondly, if the creation of an additional level of government in this country is to be proposed, it is clear that the Commission must have considered a number of basic economic and financial questions in this connection. For instance, if there is to be a number of Intermediate Level Authorities (referred to hereafter as IL As) and they are to be given significant freedom of action, is this to say that they should be permitted autonomously to vary the amount and the pattern of their expenditures? Further, where should their revenue come from? Should they be given the power to levy their own taxes? If so, what types of taxes would be appropriate, and at what rates should they be levied? Moreover, what should be the nature of the relationship between each I L A and the central government? How can the inescapable need of certain intermediate areas for financial help from the centre be accommodated without undue restriction of the independence of the intermediate authorities concerned? And how can the degree of financial and economic independence which is undoubtedly required at the intermediate level, if the purpose of constitutional reform is to be realised, be reconciled with the requirement that the central government should continue to be responsible for the management of the national economy and should continue to have the means to fulfil this responsibility? These are formidable problems, and in considering them many have concluded that although devolution might be desirable on political grounds, there would be an economic price to pay, and that price would probably be too high. At first sight it does seem that the creation of a number of I L As with significant fiscal powers and the ability to control the use of economic resources in their areas, would make the main economic aims of the nation much more difficult to fulfil. It could be argued that the loss of central control would lead to a much less efficient allocation of resources; that the pursuit by authorities at the intermediate level of independent revenue and expenditure policies would make the Treasury's task of stabilising the national economy and maintaining full employment virtually impossible to fulfil; and that the national growth rate would suffer accordingly. The purpose of this paper, on the other hand, in reconsidering the economic implications of the creation of an additional intermediate level of government in this country, is to indicate the opportunities which would thereby arise for improving the management of the economy, and to demonstrate their importance, to present in effect the economic case for constitutional reform.

The case is presented within the framework of a specified comprehensive scheme of financial and economic arrangements. This procedure has been adopted because it is impossible to discuss any one of the major areas of interest—planning responsibilities, expenditure control, revenue powers, techniques of demand management—without making quite specific assumptions about the others. It must be understood, however, that the purpose of the exercise is not only to present a scheme of financial and economic arrangements capable of exploiting the opportunities offered by a reformed constitution; it is rather to demonstrate in more general terms the nature of those possibilities, of the economic opportunities which will be there to be exploited if the Constitutional Commission's recommendations for a devolved system of government are accepted.

The argument may be summarised in the following way. The central problem is to establish the maximum degree of financial and economic independence at intermediate level consistent with the continued ability of the central government to manage the United Kingdom economy as a whole, and to retain responsibility for the general level of employment, the national economy's rate of growth, and the state of the balance of payments. It is demonstrated in the paper that a system of financial and economic arrangements may be devised capable of providing the I L As with a considerable degree of independence. It is shown that they might be permitted subject to minimal supervision from the centre, to determine the pattern of their expenditure. Further, each I L A might be given the responsibility of planning the future development of its area, and could be provided with the means, after negotiation with the central government to see that the provisions of its plan are fulfilled. And, thirdly, each I L A might be given the power to levy its own taxes, and to influence the rates at which these taxes are set. By the judicious use of the powers of expenditure and taxation granted to it, the I L A would be able by its own efforts to alter the rate of growth and the level of unemployment in its area. At the same time, things could be arranged in such a way that the central government's ability to manage the national economy and achieve the major goals of domestic economic policy—full employment, a faster rate of growth, a satisfactory balance of payments would be enhanced more than it would be impaired by a system of regional finance. The economic case for devolution is that the setting up of a number of intermediate authorities, together with a system of regional finance and expenditure, would create new opportunities to improve the efficiency of economic management. In essence, the case consists of two parts. Firstly, it is argued that inroads might be made into the problem of regional unemployment by utilising the techniques of demand management at the intermediate level. It is explained (pages 56-9) that the difficulties which this might be expected to create for the Treasury in its attempts to control the pressure of demand over the economy as a whole could adequately be overcome. And if the difference in unemployment rates in different parts of the country were significantly reduced, the

Treasury's task of overall demand management would become easier, and for the first time there might be something like full employment in all parts of the United Kingdom. Secondly, it is shown that the setting up of a number of I L As responsible for planning the development of the intermediate areas, in consultation with the central government, would make possible the creation of a fully viable system of national planning. Such a system would put the United Kingdom on the road to achieving many of the goals which the old National Plan defined but had not the means to attain. Then the nation's seemingly immutable 'underlying rate of growth', which has been so low for so long, might begin to rise.

I

It is necessary to give a general outline of the proposed financial and economic system before considering its various provisions in detail. This is because the main aspects of the scheme are inter-related, and it is necessary to understand the relationship of each to the whole system before the reasons behind the particular arrangements proposed can be appreciated. What follows, then, is a summary statement of the scheme : a full discussion of it is given in the next section.

The starting point is planning. Each I L A could be required to draw up a set of projections of the likely development of its area over the next five years, assuming the continuation of 'present policies'. Estimates of the demand for each of the public services under the control of the I L A would be made on the basis of projections of likely demographic changes and indus-trial developments. The I L As would then enter into negotia-tions with the Treasury and establish a set of 'reasonable stan-dards' of service for each of the categories of expenditure— education, health, water and so on—for which they were responsible. Estimates of the cost per head of meeting these standards in each area would then be made, whereupon the total amount of expenditure on each category of public expendi-ture administered by each I L A would be fixed. Hence the total expenditure of each I L A on public services in its area would be fixed, and the 'demand effects' of this, or the claim on the area's resources represented by this could be estimated, over the period of the plan. Given the *totals*, each I L A would be permitted to determine the *pattern* of its expenditures as it wished. Decisions about this would be taken in the course of an Intermediate Expenditure Survey procedure, which each I L A would follow, and which would be similar to the Public Expenditure Survey which takes place at national level at present. When the I L A had settled on the allocation it desired, the Treasury would again be consulted with the object of ensuring that the sum of I L A expenditure intentions did not represent too severe a demand on any particularly scarce resources. Totals and allocations then finalised, projections of actual I L A expenditure could be published for the next five years, and the five-year forecasts of expenditure would be rolled forward every year against the background of the regional development plans, the procedure for finalising which is still to be described.

How is the expenditure of each I L A to be financed? The proposal is that it should be financed partly from a mix of supplementary taxes levied in the intermediate area itself, and partly from an equalisation grant from the central government. The particular mix of taxes which is desirable is discussed in the next section. The rates at which the taxes should be levied and the size of the central government grant to each I L A could be fixed in the following way. Attention would first be focused on the area with the lowest level of public expenditure per head, which in the present situation would also be the most prosperous area, the South East. A decision would be reached that perhaps three-quarters of its expenditure, the total of which has already been fixed in the manner described, should be met from its own resources, say by supplementary taxes on income, sales or value-added, and the rates of these taxes would be set in the negotiations to provide a revenue of this amount. The rates of nationally levied income tax and V A T would be adjusted downwards to the extent necessary to leave the level of demand for the goods and services of the South East unaltered, i.e. full employment in the South East would be maintained. As a working hypothesis, these rates of national and supplementary I L A taxation would be applied to all the other areas, which could then require the central government to grant them sufficient money to bridge the gap between the revenue gleaned from these sources and the agreed totals of intermediate expenditure.

At this point, it is possible to take advantage of the opportunities for regional stabilisation created by the establishment of a system of regional finance. Returning to the development plans which had been drawn up initially, on the assumption of the continuation of present policies, modifications to those plans would be made by the I L As in the light of the decisions as to the total and pattern of intermediate expenditures, and estimates of the likely growth of demand in each area over the planning period would be made, in the light of the decisions about tax rates. Undoubtedly, but to varying degrees, areas other than the South East would find that their resources were to be under-utilised and that they were to suffer some degree of unemployment, the regional problem which is so familiar, over the planning period. A decision would then be taken, again in consultation with the Treasury, as to the desirable 'average' or 'trend' rate of unemployment, abstracting from cyclical movements, and a figure such as 2 per cent might be fixed upon for an 'average' year. Each I L A would then be given the choice either of pitching its supplementary tax rates below those of the South East in order to stimulate demand in its area, or of increasing public expenditure, or of opting for a combination of both things according to which course was the most appropriate under the particular circumstances. If there was a general deficiency of demand, for instance, alteration of tax rates would be desirable, whereas if unemployment was highly localised, public expenditure directed to the areas concerned might be the answer. Which course was followed would be a matter for the I L A itself to decide, although it might wish to make use of the expertise available to it in the Treasury, and the budget deficit required to reduce regional unemployment to 2 per cent would be financed by a grant from the central government made specifically for this purpose—a 'supplementary stabilisation grant'.

The effects of these decisions would be incorporated into the I L As' development plans, which would now assume their final form. The whole planning exercise would be repeated every *three* years, although the projections each time would cover a *five* year period : this would ensure that there were always at least three planned years to serve as a background to the Intermediate Expenditure Surveys which would be carried out each year. For each planning exercise, new equalisation formulae

would be produced, standards presumably being revised upwards as the economy grew, and new expenditure totals fixed.
Supplementary tax rates and differentials would be reassessed,
but the object would be to alter these as infrequently as possible
so as to interfere with the Treasury's attempts at national
demand management as little as possible. The principal problem
associated with attempts to manage the pressure of demand at
the intermediate level is the 'spill-over' problem—changes in the
level of demand engineered in its own area by any one ILA
would to some extent spill over into the other intermediate
areas in an unpredictable fashion, thereby making it extremely
difficult for the other ILAs to formulate sensible demand
management policies of their own, and for the Treasury to
manage the economy as a whole. However, as is explained in
detail (pages 56–9), this problem can be substantially overcome.
The central suggestion is that a reasonably stable differential
structure of intermediate level tax rates and expenditure policies
should be established which would adjust the levels of demand
and activity in the different areas, equalising as far as possible
the rates of employment in each. Changes in the structure once
established would be made infrequently, and in a properly
co-ordinated manner. The Treasury would thus remain free to
pursue national policies of demand management, as it does at
present, and regulate the growth of demand for the economy as
a whole, but on the basis of a differential system of intermediate
level payments.[1]

Thus the economic unity of the United Kingdom is not weakened: the Treasury retains the means to manage the national
economy. Yet the ILAs are given the maximum freedom consistent with this: they are given control over the pattern of their
expenditures, the ability to plan the future of their areas and
significant influence over the rates of supplementary taxation
which are levied.

II

Now that the general outline of the scheme has been set out it is
possible to consider each of the main categories of concern in
detail, and to explain the reasoning behind the recommendations.

Planning

The intermediate area plans are omnipresent in the procedure outlined in the previous section. The process begins with a set of estimates of the development of the area 'on present policies'; these estimates are modified as the relevant decisions about expenditure allocation, taxation and stabilisation are taken by the I L As; and at the end of the day there exists a complete and comprehensive intermediate area plan. It is worth enquiring what the nature and aims of a plan of this type should be, and highlighting the advantages of a planning mechanism of the type which is being suggested.

The purpose of the intermediate level plan is to ensure that expenditure at the intermediate level is allocated more rationally, and matches regional needs when projections of the likely development of the private sector of the intermediate economy are taken into account. At present, governmental and more general administrative activity is carried on at the intermediate level by a multiplicity of different bodies—the regional 'outposts' of central government departments, planning councils, and 'ad hoc' bodies both commercial and non-commercial. There is a clear need to co-ordinate their work, and the most rational context in which to do this is within the framework of a comprehensive intermediate area plan. In addition to co-ordinating the work of these bodies, it is also necessary to rationalise the plethora of measures designed to counter the 'regional problem'. A more effective way of dealing with this has of course been put forward in the previous section but it might still be very helpful to retain the various inducements to investment and employment in the regions for use in conjunction with the I L A economic plans. Financial inducements might be selectively employed, although grants and allowances would have to be available on the same terms and at the same rates in the different areas; and the physical inducements which have been used—the provision of 'advance factory units', the siting of new towns, the establishment of training centres and so on, are the essence of planning, and would no doubt comprise the section of the plan financed from the 'supplementary stabilisation grant' from the central government referred to earlier.

An I L As' economic plan is a method of co-ordinating and rationalising the various types of expenditure made at the intermediate level. More than this, however, it sets out the likely economic development of the whole area, and sets spending plans in the context of this. What should the nature of such a plan be? It is clear that it should not be a highly detailed document, providing targets for industries and sectors as did the old National Plan. It should be concerned more broadly with strategies of area development, attempting to foresee what types of action would be necessary at the intermediate level to cover a series of possible eventualities. Forecasts should be built up on a variety of different assumptions and the plan should be as flexible as possible to enable action to be adjusted to circumstances as they unfold. The approach of the latest Public Expenditure White Paper[2] is instructive. There, although quite precise estimates of Public Expenditure are set out for the next five years, the figures are set in the context of different assumptions about the rate of creation of resources over the medium term, and no attempt is made to provide precise forecasts of movements in the main economic aggregates. An intermediate economic plan, then, would take close account of the likely economic developments in the area concerned, but would not stand or fall on the basis of precise forecasts or targets; it would be concerned with strategies and retain sufficient flexibility to accommodate the contingencies arising in an uncertain future.

The series of intermediate area plans would become a system of national planning as soon as an attempt was made to co-ordinate them at the centre, as would necessarily be the case. Individual I L As would not be permitted to make indiscriminate claims on scarce resources without due regard for the needs of other areas. Many important allocative decisions could only be taken at national level where the relative needs of different regions could be judged and where the total demand for resources could be brought into line with the capacity of the nation to produce them. There must necessarily be consultation between intermediate authorities and the central government.

It is suggested here that the procedure would be that the I L As would have the responsibility for drawing up their plans, for identifying problems and proposing solutions to them—the initative would rest with them—but that the central government would have the responsibility for reconciling competing claims on resources and in the last resort could have the power to cancel particular I L A proposals altogether. However, lest this should give rise to concern, it should be remembered that the I L As, as directly elected bodies with a mandate from the electorate to pursue specific policies, would be in a very strong bargaining position in negotiations with the Treasury.

The I L A plans would therefore be drawn up in consultation with the centre, where they would be co-ordinated, and reconciled with the assessment of the progress of the economy as a whole in the medium term, the amount of resources available in total for public expenditure, investment and so on. The concept of national planning which emerges is a novel one. It is planning 'from the ground up', and therefore quite different in kind from the old National Plan, which was imposed on the economy from on high and therefore bore no relation to what was happening therein. The National Plan failed because it lacked the means of implementation. The system of national planning, on the other hand, which emerges from the co-ordination of a number of intermediate plans, themselves drawn up in the face of likely developments in the private sector of the economy, and taking account of the reaction of the public sector to them, is in contrast a fully viable planning mechanism, and provides the means for a more rational allocation of resources than this country has enjoyed before. Considering the wider implications, it provides the means to achieve the goals which the National Plan failed to achieve, not the least of which is a more rapid rate of economic growth.

Expenditure

At present, the Government's expenditure policies are administered and executed at the regional level by departmental regional offices, through regional boards of various types, and in vague and tenuous conjunction with the regional planning councils. If the I L As were empowered to co-ordinate and administer these expenditure policies, they would become responsible for at least half of the central government's present expenditure on supply services.

According to the procedure set out in part I, a set of 'reasonable standards' of service for each of the categories of expenditure for which they were responsible would be established by the I L As in negotiation with the Treasury. These, together with estimates of the cost per head of meeting these standards in each area would fix the totals of expenditure to be undertaken by the various I L As. It may be asked why this procedure in particular should be followed in fixing the totals of I L A expenditure. The general principle behind it is that economic resources should be directed in such a way that all parts of the United Kingdom have the means of enjoying equality of standards in the provision of services. This is not to say that all parts of the United Kingdom should necessarily enjoy equality of standards, but should have the opportunity of establishing such standards if they so desire. Now an alternative procedure would be for the central government to stipulate 'minimum standards' which had to be observed throughout the country. However, there is little doubt that this would lead the central government to scrutinise the intermediate authorities' affairs fairly closely, and would therefore detract from the avowed aim of giving the I L As as much independence from the central government as possible, consistent with the continued ability of the central government to manage the United Kingdom economy as a whole. Under the procedure set out earlier the totals of public expenditure in each intermediate area are defined and fixed, which is highly convenient from the Treasury's point of view for the management of the domestic economy; secondly, the I L As have freedom to allocate the totals of expenditure as they wish between different categories, free from the scrutiny from the centre which the alternative proposal would entail; and thirdly, there is no reason to believe that the procedure as set out in this chapter will lead to unacceptable inequalities in the standards of service provided in different intermediate areas—after all, the I L As are subject to democratic control and therefore will be responsive to any grievances arising on this score.

Having established the desirable method of fixing the totals of I L A expenditure, it is necessary to enter a qualifying note. It is probably the case that the relevant figure for control purposes is not the total of I L A expenditure in 'cost' terms, to use official parlance—i.e. the total amount of money which is actually spent—but in 'demand' terms—i.e. the demand for goods and services to which this expenditure gives rise. These two figures are not identical. In so far, for instance, as transfer payments are saved by people, or flow back to the government in taxes, they do not lead to an increase in the demand for goods and services produced by the economy. Various types of public expenditure give rise to 'leakages' from the flow of spending of this kind, but to different extents, which is to say that different types of public expenditure cause the level of demand for goods and services to rise by different amounts. It is the demand effect of public expenditure which the Treasury is primarily interested in in connection with its stabilisation policy, the object of which is to equate the level of demand in the economy with the capacity of the economy to produce goods and services, thereby producing full employment. Therefore, when total expenditure has been fixed for a particular I L A, it will not in fact be appropriate for that authority to reallocate its expenditure between different categories and maintain the same total of expenditure 'in cost terms', it will have to maintain the total 'in demand terms', which may entail some alteration of the money outlay. No issue of principle is involved here. Each I L A remains free to allocate its expenditure as it wishes, but the total it is required to maintain if it does so is not the most obvious one.

The freedom of the I L As to allocate a significant proportion of the nation's resources as they wish should not be under-emphasised. Within the given totals, the decisions on which the annual Intermediate Expenditure Surveys are based are their decisions, and their expenditure is allocated in accordance with their priorities which may well differ from those of the nation as a whole.

Taxation and Stabilisation

In the general outline of the scheme, it was suggested that the expenditure of each I L A should be financed partly from a mix of supplementary taxes levied in the intermediate area itself, and partly from a grant made by the central government. Each intermediate level Government would : (a) levy a supplementary income tax; (b) levy either a supplementary V A T, or a sales tax; (c) receive the proceeds of the whole of the vehicle excise duty and petrol duty levied in the area; (d) receive a grant from the central government based on an equalisation formula of the type already discussed. It is envisaged that the independent revenue provided by (a), (b) and (c) would amount to more than half of the money required to finance the expenditure of the I L A and that (*d*) would follow quite automatically in what-ever amount was required to bridge the gap between the agreed expenditure total and the sum total of the independent revenues.

The rates at which these taxes would be levied would be decided first in the manner described in part I, the initial objec-tive being, as described in that paragraph, to fix them at rates which would enable the most prosperous region, at present the South East, to derive a fixed proportion, perhaps two-thirds or three-quarters of its required revenue from these sources. The desired proportion would first be stipulated. Exactly what it would be is not important, but it is suggested that it should significantly exceed half of required revenue. This proportion then given, and the revenue from (*c*) being given also, the rates being fixed by the central government, the only remaining task is to choose the rates at which to levy the supplementary taxes, of which there would be two. It is preferable for reasons con-nected with stabilisation policy which are explained below, that these should be income tax and value-added tax, but income tax and an intermediate sales tax would be an alternative combina-tion, though second best. The decision, then, which has to be reached at this point concerns the desired balance of direct and indirect taxation in the area, which affects directly the distribu-tion of income in the community. Now the distribution of income is clearly a matter which should be decided by the central government. Discussion of the distribution of the national product between different sectors of the community is the essence of the political debate. It divides the political parties at the most fundamental level, and the decision as to the desirable distribution of the national income is perhaps the most basic one taken by the central government. It is pro-posed here, therefore, that the central government should con-tinue to retain responsibility in this area, and that the ratio of supplementary income tax revenue to supplementary V A T revenue should be the same as that of national income tax to national V A T. This principle is sufficient to fix the supplemen-tary rates of income tax and V A T. A supplementary rate of income tax at 10 per cent together with a supplementary rate of V A T at 3 per cent levied by the I L A of the South East, to-gether with the revenue from vehicle excise duty and petrol duty

C

in the South East, would provide at least three-quarters of the revenue required by the I L A of the South East. National rates of income tax and V A T would be lowered accordingly. Then, following the procedure set out in part I, as a working hypothesis these rates of taxation would be applied to all other areas. If no adjustments for stabilisation purposes were required, the rates would be finalised, and the central government would be required to grant each area whatever further revenue was needed to finance the agreed total of its expenditure.

It has been suggested that it might be very difficult to levy a supplementary V A T at the intermediate level. If it did indeed prove administratively impossible, then it would be necessary for each I L A to levy a retail sales tax. This would give a high yield at relatively low cost. The procedure for fixing its rate would be identical to that described in the previous paragraph and the national rate of V A T would have to be reduced in the same way to compensate for the imposition of the sales tax. But for more general economic reasons, a supplementary intermediate level V A T is to be preferred, for reasons which emerge from the discussion of stabilisation policy which follows.

According to the procedure set out in part I, when the basic rates of supplementary taxation had been fixed in this way, it would then be possible to take advantage of the new opportunities for the stimulation of growth in the intermediate areas and the elimination of regional unemployment provided by the establishment of a system of regional finance. Many I L As would find that associated with the rates of expenditure and taxation which had been decided was the likelihood of a fairly high 'average' or 'trend' rate of unemployment—i.e. abstracting from cyclical movements of output. It was suggested in the general outline, therefore, that after consultation with the Treasury, each I L A might:

(*a*) set its rates of supplementary taxation below those prevailing in the South East in order to stimulate demand; (*b*) increase its expenditure in ways most likely effectively to reduce the rate of unemployment in its area; (*c*) do a combination of both these things; according to which course of action was most appropriate in the particular circumstances.

The clear objection to allowing I L As to alter the rates of taxation which they levy in their areas, is that it may make the task of the Treasury in its attempts to manage the national economy and in particular the general level of demand more difficult. Intermediate economies would be very open, which is to say that a large part of the incomes earned in any intermediate area is spent on goods produced in other intermediate areas. Hence the demand effects of tax changes in one particular area cannot be contained within that area. For instance, if the Scottish I L A were to lower the supplementary rate of income tax in Scotland with the result that the rate of expenditure of the citizens of Scotland increased, many of the extra goods purchased would be made in the different areas of England with the result that economic activity would be stimulated in England, instead of in Scotland. Since these spill-over effects would clearly be very difficult to trace out through the whole national economy, the general management of demand would become very much more difficult, and it would be difficult also for each I L A to know how to react to try to maintain the right level of demand in its own area in the face of other I L As' efforts to stimulate demand in theirs, and the consequent spill-over effects.

The system proposed here has been designed so as to minimise the various difficulties to which a regionally differentiated policy of demand management and stabilisation would give rise. It does so in the following ways.

Firstly, differential rates of I L A supplementary taxation would be settled in the general planning exercise which has been described. The rates decided on would then be fixed and immutable until the next planning exercise, three years later. There is thus no question of I L As changing the rates of supplementary taxation frequently and at will, which would make it very difficult for the Treasury adequately to control the general level of demand in the economy. It could be decided, indeed, to fix differentials in supplementary tax rates for six-year periods, to minimise the spill-over disturbances produced by changes in tax rates, but a three-year review might be quite practical. Essentially, then, the aim is *not* to create a system which would produce frequent and spontaneous changes in rates of taxation, but to establish one which encompassed differential rates of taxation, subject to change infrequently and in a co-ordinated fashion. It would be hoped in this way to establish a stable differential *structure* of intermediate level rates of taxation, which would *equalise* the pressure of demand on resources throughout the economy, leaving it to the Treasury, through its manipulation of national rates of taxation to decide in general what that pressure should be. The 'spill-over' problem is therefore substantially solved by the general nature of the approach.

Secondly, however, tax changes will periodically have to be made, and it is here that the virtues of a regional system of V A T stand out most clearly. The fiscal changes which reduce the spill-over problem to a minimum are those which stimulate the exports of the area in which they are made. To the extent that area exports are increased to other areas in the country, the effect of increasing imports from those areas is cancelled out. Spill-over is nullified, and the increase in demand is confined to the area where the tax change was made. Now, if an I L A facing the prospect of unemployment in the area for which it was responsible were to reduce its supplementary rate of V A T, thereby reducing costs of production relative to those prevailing in other areas, it would achieve all the beneficial effects of a regional devaluation, and its exports would increase to counterbalance the increase in area imports which would accompany the rise in internal area demand. This would therefore be the ideal type of I L A fiscal adjustment, leading to minimal interference with the business of managing the economy as a whole. It is recommended therefore that each I L A, in addition to levying a supplementary income tax, should also levy a supplementary V A T to which advantages are attached which would not be shared by a retail sales tax.

Thirdly, it is recommended in part I that each I L A should be able to deploy part of its expenditure for stabilisation purposes. There are a number of advantages in this. For instance, where unemployment is localised, directing expenditure to the area concerned is a more appropriate and effective measure than increasing the general level of demand in the area by reducing taxes. Further, in so far as over the years the fiscal system becomes constrained by 'harmonising' regulations emanating from Brussels, public expenditure may have to become the principal instrument of demand management.

Lastly, however, in relation to the particular problem under consideration in this paragraph, public expenditure may be em-

ployed for stabilisation purposes with minimal regional import
effect. It could be used to purchase goods and services provided
from within the area concerned, thereby leading to a much
smaller spill-over to other areas than tax changes which might
be used alternatively to bring about an equivalent increase in
internal area demand.

The procedure would be therefore that a regionally differentiated structure of supplementary V A T rates and of supplementary income tax rates, associated with alterations in the
levels of I L A expenditure for stabilisation purposes, would then
be established in negotiation with the Treasury, which would be
concerned to co-ordinate the demand management policies of the
I L As and produce a rational and effective system of intermediate payments. If it was the case that the ideal tax for these
purposes, the supplementary V A T, was administratively too
difficult to operate then the various I L As would still be free
to fix differential supplementary rates of income tax and the
retail sales tax, again in consultation with the Treasury, and
following the arguments presented in the previous paragraph
demand management at the intermediate level would still be a
perfectly viable and practical proposition, and the resulting
structure of payments would be highly effective in helping to
eliminate the regional problem. With unemployment rates
reasonably equal in the different intermediate areas, the Treasury would continue to be free to manage the pressure of demand
over the economy as a whole.

The money required to finance the deficits incurred by the
I L As in pursuit of stabilisation policies agreed with the Treasury, would be provided by the central government in the form
of 'supplementary stabilisation grants' specifically for this purpose.

III

It has generally been believed that the establishment of intermediate level authorities in this country with a significant
amount of financial and economic independence from the central government would seriously impair the ability of the central
government to achieve the major objectives of national economic
policy—full employment, an efficient allocation of the nation's

resources, a satisfactory rate of economic growth; in short, that it would make the management of the national economy much more difficult.

The financial and economic system set out in this chapter would however provide the Intermediate Level Authorities which are likely to be proposed with a considerable degree of financial and economic independence from the central government, whilst at the same time *improving* the ability of the central government to achieve its aims for the whole economy.

The impact which the constitutional reforms likely to be recommended by Kilbrandon (when complemented by a scheme of financial and economic arrangements of the type set out in this paper) would have on the efficiency of government and the allocation of resources, the level of employment and the regional problem, and the overall rate of economic growth, would be significant. The proposed system of flexible economic planning at the intermediate and, out of this, at the national level might make feasible many of the goals which the old National Plan set itself but had not the means to attain. The effective utilisation for the first time of the techniques of demand management at the intermediate level would help to transform the situation of the less prosperous regions. For the first time, there might be something approaching full employment throughout the United Kingdom, and the seemingly immutable 'underlying rate of growth', might begin to rise. This, as I see it, is the economic case for reforming the Constitution. To what extent it is also the economic case for Kilbrandon remains to be seen.

SECTION TWO

The Determinants of Regional
Growth Rates

GAVIN McCRONE

T H E purpose of this paper is to set out some of the elements
of an economic theory which explains the type of regional problem which exists in Britain. No doubt it may have a wider
application to other countries which suffer from regional growth
and decline and to separate nations if these are dominated by
the economy of a larger neighbour. But the background against
which the ideas have been developed is of the regional problem in the United Kingdom.

British regional policy is usually thought of as highly prag-
matic; it certainly seems to owe little to economic theory.
Economic theorists have not given the regional question much
attention in the United Kingdom, at least until recently; and
though they have been much more active in other countries,
much of their work has been concentrated on theories of location. The problems which face a practitioner of regional policy
in Britain are mainly dynamic: disparities in regional growth
rates which lead to serious imbalance in the demand for and
supply of economic resources, especially of labour; locational
changes in investment behaviour; and the effect of technical
progress on economic structure.

Theories of location can give some insight into these questions
though it was not the main purpose for which they were
developed. Equally the notion of poles of growth offers some
rationalisation of situations which undoubtedly exist in practice.
Some applications of these ideas are developed before exploring
other approaches but the principal idea put forward in this
paper is that the growth rates of individual industries are determined by national, not regional, factors, and that with economic
structure varying from region to region, imbalance between
regional growth and resources is most likely to arise. No auto-

matic mechanism exists to bring the regional economy into equilibrium as it does for the nation as a whole; the law of comparative advantage does not operate. Indeed in the absence of some interventionist policy a cumulative process is likely to be set up, the most rapidly growing regions continuing to outstrip available resources, the slow growing ones falling behind. The advantages or disadvantages of location no doubt play a part in this growth pattern, but it is suggested that it is not the major part.

Location Theory

Theories of location are mainly of two kinds. The first, which stem largely from the work of Weber, seek to explain the location of a firm in relation to its market, its suppliers and its raw material.[1] Such theories depend heavily on transport costs and economies of scale and are of interest for micro-economic analysis, but they do not attempt to explain the regional pattern of economic activity as a whole, let alone the changes in that pattern which are the principal concern of this paper.

The second group do try to explain the geographical pattern of economic activity. They originate mainly from the work of Christaller and Loesch and have been carried to advanced degrees of sophistication in programming models such as those of Bos and Tinbergen.[2] Like the other theories these too derive their locational aspects from their treatment of transport costs or distance as an economic variable. Sometimes there is an interaction between transport costs and economies of agglomeration or urbanisation. These theories mostly depend on assumptions about the geographical spread of resources, particularly as regards agriculture, to explain the spread of economic activity over space. Agriculture requires population to be spread out and hence determines the distribution of population and markets which then affect the pattern of other industries. Without this the economies of agglomeration would lead to population and economic activity being highly concentrated. Most of these theories tend to lead to a pattern of economic activity based on market areas which has a more or less regular distribution through space; the production units of any particular type of activity are then spaced at intervals whose frequency depends upon transport costs and economies of scale and can, therefore, be determined with precision.

Despite some obvious limitations in these theories, it is worth considering how far they could be 'dynamised' to give a plausible explanation of regional change and the disparities which occur in regional growth rates. If changes in relative costs occur over time, whether reflecting technical progress or simply changes in the costs of factor inputs, this will tend to alter the size of market area served by a particular firm and hence affect the geographical spread of productive units. A reduction in transport costs relative to other costs or an increase in the economies of scale available would both have this effect. One would expect these changes to take the form of increasing the size of market areas over time, thereby increasing the overlap between them and thus intensifying competition between units of economic activity. Stronger centres may tend to grow at the expense of weaker ones. Looking over a long period of time it seems that this process does take place. Certain types of activity become increasingly concentrated in large centres as improved forms of transport make distribution easier and the population more mobile. Even those types of manufacturing activity which were once localised because of the protection which was afforded by distance find that this has been substantially eroded. There has, therefore, been a trend towards concentration in larger units, the weaker ones stagnating or being put out of production.

Other factors which could alter the pattern of economic activity are changes in the industrial structure and in the nature of the products produced. As the economy develops the agricultural population declines and that of the cities expands. Thus the balance of the market alters and those activities which are market orientated in their choice of location will tend more and more to be concentrated in sizeable towns. The change in the nature of products produced has tended to reduce the importance of transport costs and of proximity to raw materials. Typically modern industry has a high value added in relation to weight compared with its nineteenth-century predecessor and often uses man-made materials rather than primary products grown or mined in particular locations of the country. It is therefore free to take full advantage of economies of scale and is much more footloose as regards location. When location decisions are taken they appear to be influenced more by access to a major market or availability of labour than by any other factor.

There is no doubt that these processes have influenced the pattern of economic activity in the United Kingdom. During this century the centre of economic gravity has moved in favour of the Midlands and South East of England and more peripheral locations have suffered. However this has not simply been a question of large towns growing at the expense of smaller; even major cities have been adversely affected. In this respect the change in the economic scene in Glasgow is of some interest. In the last century the industrial growth and prosperity of Glasgow was built by Scottish companies not only in manufacturing but in services—banks, insurance companies and even railways. Over the years the increasing economies of scale have led to mergers and amalgamations, and to the setting up of United Kingdom and foreign companies in Scotland. Sometimes rationalisation has meant the closure of the Scottish enterprise; in very many cases it becomes simply a branch of a much larger concern. Top management and policy decisions tend to be concentrated elsewhere and the more enterprising elements in the population know that ambition and promotion will require them to seek their fortunes elsewhere. It is not surprising that this should be so, since the Scottish market is smaller than that of the English Midlands or of other countries abroad. But undoubtedly it has a damaging effect on enterprise and growth in Scotland.

The development of service activity provides a particularly striking example of this process. This has tended to concentrate to an increasing extent in the South East of England where it accounts for an exceptionally large proportion of total employment. Since the growth of employment in this sector is more rapid than in manufacturing, this trend has had adverse effects on the Development Areas.

Thus the transfer of functions following changes in the structure of the economy and in size of market areas is undoubtedly a factor in the regional problem, especially for peripheral regions; but it does not offer a sufficient explanation. There are important problem regions in other countries which are not peripheral —notably the South of Belgium and the North of France and it cannot explain why Aberdeen should have lower unemployment than Dundee, or Edinburgh than Glasgow. Firms in many industries tend not to be spread out over space in a systematic way, such as the theory of market areas might suggest, but are clustered together or located in particular areas more or less at random. This seems to be because transport costs, while not totally insignificant, are a much weaker determinant of location than the theory allows and are dominated by other considerations. The same factors explain the importance of foreign trade and competition which is otherwise hard to reconcile with the theory. It is therefore necessary to consider more closely why particular forms of economic activity are concentrated in given areas and what consequences such differences in economic structure have for regional growth.

Growth Poles

One approach to this problem is the growth pole idea stemming from the work of Perroux and others.[3] This stresses the interrelationships between various types of economic activity in a region. Certain industries once set up in an area, whether as a result of historical accident or availability of natural resources, induce development in other activities to which they are linked. Sometimes there is a need for these various activities to be located reasonably close to each other, in which case they form a coherent growth pole. Examples of this situation are the growth of iron and steel, engineering and shipbuilding on the Clyde and of textiles in North-West England in the last century. Today the discovery of North Sea oil and growth of related activities in the Cromarty and Moray Firths, in Aberdeen and in Shetland appears to be following a similar pattern.

The performance of a growth pole may depend more on the viability of the complex as a whole than on the competitive position of individual parts, but clearly the key industry round which the rest are gathered is of particular importance. The extent to which inter-industry linkages of this type require physical proximity of location must obviously vary from one group of industries to another. Experience suggests that it was a more important characteristic of typical nineteenth-century industries than of lighter modern industry. Possibly the need for physical proximity has been overstressed in some theoretical work, and this may explain why the secondary development following the development of new steelworks, the discovery of natural gas and other similar developments has often been so disappointing.

If North Sea oil is an exception to this it is only because pipes and production platforms offer classic problems of transport. Servicing activities also have to be as near the oilfields as possible, but the processing of the oil once extracted is not limited in this way at all. The motor industry provides a rather different case. The failure of the motor firms which came to Scotland in the early sixties to generate secondary growth is sometimes thought to disprove the growth pole hypothesis. But recent evidence suggests that the firms are indeed severely handicapped by being so far from their suppliers, more so perhaps than they originally expected.[4] One must presume that the failure of secondary growth is not due to the absence of the linkages, but because the primary developments are not on a sufficient scale to warrant it.

But however uncertain the spin-off effects of expansion may be, it is obvious that this type of analysis can have a precise application to industries in decline. In an area where a major industry is stagnant or in decline, and where secondary industries closely linked to it exist, it is clear that there will be a widespread lack of buoyancy throughout the local economy spreading far beyond the major industry which has run into difficulties. If these inter-industry linkages are known, the effect of a decline in the major industry can then be predicted.

Without doubt this type of analysis has a direct application to the problems which have beset a number of British regions. Several of the older manufacturing industries have been in decline since the middle of the 1950s, notably coal, shipbuilding, certain types of textiles, and locomotive manufacture. Of these, the decline of coal has had relatively little in the way of secondary effects with the major exception that the steel industry has as a result found that its traditional sites of operation became a handicap instead of an advantage and major schemes of rationalisation and relocation were made necessary. But although the secondary effects of a decline in coal mining on other industries may be limited, coal so heavily dominated the economy of some regions in the past that its decline affects them very seriously. Indeed, in some cases it undermines the whole basis of their economic existence.

In shipbuilding, however, the secondary effects are very important and the industries affected are usually closely associated geographically with the shipyards. The situation therefore comes close to the type of inter-related complex described in growth pole theory and the fortunes of the main industry have very serious effects on the local economy. There is little doubt that the economy of Clydeside, for example, has suffered and is still suffering very seriously from this situation as are other shipbuilding centres in the United Kingdom. The recent difficulties of the shipbuilding industry on the Upper Clyde, though perhaps the most dramatic illustration of this are only the last in a long series of problems and disasters which have affected the industry in the last fifteen years. Not only has the industry itself lost ground in a calamitous manner in the face of international competition, but in the process the secondary effects have undermined the buoyancy of the areas concerned. To find a solution for the poor performance of such a region, it is therefore not sufficient merely to bring in new activities which will replace the output and employment lost in shipbuilding; ways have to be found of injecting a new buoyancy right through the economy. In most cases this is an extremely difficult operation because the new industries brought in normally do not have spin-off effects which will inject growth into the economic structure of the region on a scale which can off-set the decline induced by shipbuilding.

Most British problem regions have suffered structural problems of the kind outlined above. Indeed the application of shift-share analysis has shown that there is no major industrial region in a Development Area where the loss of impetus in an important industry cannot be held responsible for much of the economic problem.[5] Naturally the extent of this varies from one region to another and West Central Scotland appears to be the only area where structural factors cannot fully account for the poor economic performance. Regional policy appears to have had a substantial effect in boosting growth, industry by industry, and if the Development Areas had had a structure similar to the United Kingdom average, they would have had a growth of output and employment which considerably exceeded the national performance.

Some interesting light is also shed on this by estimates of job gains and losses recently calculated in the Scottish Office (Table 1). In an attempt to measure the importance of industrial decline as a factor in the regional problem the total job losses by industry at minimum list heading level were aggregated for different periods over the last decade and likewise for job gains. This does not show the full gross movements, since there may be some netting out within minimum list headings, but this effect was thought to be small. The results showed that the rate of job loss in Scotland was considerably in excess of the national average over the last decade; rather interestingly it showed that the job gain rate was also above the national average for part of the period but it nowhere near compensated for the rate of job loss. Rather similar results may be obtained for other Development Areas. It may be concluded from this that the difficulties of the Development Area regions stem principally from their structure. New growth, particularly in the last decade when regional policy has been active, has been as good as or better than the national performance, but the job loss from an over-representation of declining industries continues high and brings down their overall performance.

The Adjustment Mechanism

Structural change of the kind described above would undoubtedly be a discomfiting process anywhere. But if it happened on a national scale it should not lead to substantial unemployment of resources; the price mechanism should adjust in such a way as to avoid this situation. Why then does it happen with a region? To answer this one has to consider some of the essential differences between inter-regional and international trade.

According to the theory of comparative advantage, trade will always be possible and indeed beneficial between two countries even if one is greatly superior to the other in the production of all products. This is because the mechanism of exchange rate adjustment can so regulate factor earnings in the two countries as to ensure that they reflect differences in productivity. Trade can then flow, and if each country concentrates its resources in those sectors where its comparative advantage is greatest, full employment should be reached and income maximised in both of the countries concerned.

This model is, of course, far too simple for the real world. But it none the less explains the basis for trade and why trade is possible between countries so different in productive efficiency as the United States and Britain, the former having productivity levels which are more than twice the latter. The theory breaks down where rigidities of various kinds make it impossible to transfer factors to the sectors in which comparative advantage lies; where the imbalance between factors, labour and capital, is so acute that there is a shortage of one before the other can be fully employed; where protection is necessary to foster the growth of infant industries; and where standards of living and productivity are so low that no amount of exchange rate adjustment can bring real wages to a level at which the labour market produces full employment. Many of these conditions apply to under-developed countries and prevent them from securing full employment or from having a pattern of trade which conforms with the simple model of comparative advantage. But they should not apply to advanced countries, who should, therefore, be able to adjust their economies in such a way as to secure full employment.

Suppose a country were to suffer the *decline* of some of its major industries, whether as a result of technical progress or whatever other reason. If the growth of other sectors was not adequate to absorb the resources there would be two effects. First, the increasing labour surplus would lead the Government to encourage the growth of the economy by boosting demand either from investment or consumption. Secondly, if the sectors affected involved exports or import substitutes, the balance of payments would tend to move adversely. It may be that the slack demand for labour would itself damp down inflationary pressure and thereby gradually improve the country's competitive position, but if such a movement were inadequate some exchange rate adjustment would be necessary to enable the country to regain balance of payments equilibrium. Such an adjustment if carried through successfully would tend both to moderate the decline in the contracting sectors and improve prospects in newer expanding industry. In both cases economic activity would be boosted and investment would be stimulated, certainly in the expanding sector and possibly in the form of re-organisational investment in the contracting sectors also. By the proper management of such stimuli the country could find its way back to full employment.

Difficult though this process of structural change may be, it can be a means of providing a country with a rapid rate of economic growth. Often sectors in decline are labour intensive with low productivity and their replacement with modern industry, though requiring a high rate of investment, results in a sharp increase in the average labour productivity in the economy. Several continental countries have gone through this process in the last twenty years, as resources have been switched out of agriculture, which was over-manned and inefficient, and into expanding sectors with much higher labour productivity.

Unfortunately this process of adjustment is much more difficult to bring about when the problem occurs at a regional rather than a national level. If major industries in a region start to decline, or if they simply stagnate to the extent that output grows more slowly than labour productivity, then labour will tend to be released on to the market more rapidly than elsewhere in the country and regional unemployment will rise. Assuming the national growth rate continues unaltered and the national labour market remains in equilibrium, the regional position may continue to deteriorate.

The problem here is that the forces which would tend to bring the nation back to equilibrium, if the problem was on that scale, are absent in the regional case. The process of structural change means that the region requires a higher level of investment, and is probably capable of more rapid growth, than the nation as a whole. But this the region is most unlikely to get. The main influence on investment in the region is the macro-economic climate of the country as a whole, the expected national rate of growth both of output and of markets.

In the absence of special factors there is thus no reason to expect investment in the region to be any higher than in the nation as a whole. Indeed, the reverse is more likely, since declining sectors are over-represented and growing sectors under-represented by national standards. Assuming that declining sectors will invest relatively little, the growing sectors would have to invest more heavily in relation to their output in the region than elsewhere if the region's investment as a proportion of Gross Domestic Product is to be up to the national average.

Thus, if one can accept that the level of investment and hence the rate of growth in industry is determined by the national macro-economic climate rather than by regional factors, this in itself coupled with differences in economic structure is a sufficient explanation of the regional problem. That the problem does indeed have its origin in these national factors is the central thesis of this paper.

However this is not to deny that there are regional factors. Up to a point investment in the region may be determined by the availability of local labour and this appears to have had an influence on the inflow of foreign capital to Scotland. If this happens it will tend to raise the level of investment. Equally there are the advantages and disadvantages of the region's location already discussed above. If the region is centrally placed in relation to the economy as a whole, it will stand a better chance of attracting new investment from incoming industry than if it is peripheral. The range of industry which will then regard it as a suitable location will be wider. But experience tends to suggest that, while a peripheral location may be an almost insurmountable handicap in some far flung agricultural areas, it is much less serious in most of the major industrial problem areas and may well be outweighed by other factors. Furthermore, problem industrial areas which are not peripheral do exist, the Dutch Limburg and the Walloon coalfield being the most obvious examples.

The root problem is therefore not location or other regional factors such as labour availability but simply that there is no means by which a region can adjust its competitive position. Failure on the part of the region's principal industries may impair its trading balance, but this will not give rise to the normal type of balance of payments problem and hence to the adjustments which would follow. Payments from the region's banks to the rest of the country may for a time exceed the flow of receipts coming in, but with a branch banking system this will bring about no special adjustment. Loss of economic momentum will automatically cause some reduction in the region's contribution to national tax revenue; and various forms of assistance such as unemployment pay and regional subsidies may tend to increase its share of public expenditure. The result may well be that the region ends up with an imbalance in trade which is partly or even largely compensated for in balance of payments terms by an off-setting flow in the accounts of the public sector. This will make it appear that the region is being supported by the rest of the economy and give rise to all kinds of arguments about the rights and wrongs of so doing. But such transfers even on quite a substantial scale may not solve the problem without a mechanism to raise the level of investment and improve the region's competitive position, the only process by which the region could be extricated from this begging bowl situation.

Within a country the existence of a common currency makes exchange rate adjustment impossible. Even if this were not so, labour would stoutly resist the alteration in factor earnings which would be implied if it was to be successful. Demands for the restoration of wage parity would frustrate any process of adjustment in the regional economy. As it is, the tendency for wage rates to be nationally determined owing to the system of national collective bargaining, results in only small regional differences in earnings. As shown by the Department of Employment's Earnings Inquiries, Scottish earnings per head in manufacturing have shown a tendency to approach closer to the British average over the last decade, rising from about 90 per cent of the latter in 1960 to around 97 per cent in 1969.[6] It has become clear that wages and earnings in most sectors in Scotland and indeed in several other British regions are affected very little, if at all, by the local conditions of the labour market, but are simply a function of the United Kingdom figure.

This analysis also sheds some light on the regional consequences of the inflationary process. The structural difficulties of the problem regions are undoubtedly aggravated by inflation, the competitive position of the declining industries being further worsened as a result. It may be that the inflation is simply transmitted to them from the regions in which conditions give rise to it by the demand for factor price parity. Were the depressed regions economies on their own, with factor prices determined purely by conditions in the local market, their competitive position would not be so weakened and they could more readily find the investment necessary to re-organise their industry and restructure the economy. Declining industries of the kind from which Scotland has suffered would, therefore, give rise to less difficulty and stand a better chance of being re-organised on a profitable basis if the inflationary pressures transmitted from other parts of the United Kingdom economy could have been avoided.

Several conclusions follow from the analysis presented above. First, there is no hope that regional unemployment of resources will lead to an adjustment of factor prices through the regional market which would be sufficient to improve the region's competitive position and stimulate investment and growth to a point at which full employment can be regained. With approximate parity in factor price earnings the rules of comparative advantage cannot be made to apply to inter-regional trade. Trade will only follow from an absolute advantage which is obtained either from superior efficiency in production or the production of a good which is not available in precisely the same form elsewhere. The only way in which a region's competitive position can be adjusted so as to stimulate investment and growth and bring a return to full employment is by various types of subsidy. Such measures are the concern of regional policy. In Britain a wide selection of such instruments have been applied including financial inducements to investment, subsidies to labour costs and physical controls. If they have not yet succeeded in eliminating the problem, it is at least clear that the position would have been very much worse without them. To consider the adequacy of such measures, perhaps one should be concerned less with their strict financial cost in budgetary terms but rather consider the adjustment which would be necessary in exchange rates and in real factor prices to produce full employment, for which they are a substitute.

There are however some important respects in which the adjustment attempted by regional policy differs from an alteration in exchange rates. In the national situation where exchange rates are altered, the cost of the adjustment is borne by the devaluing country which must absorb in its living standards the adverse terms of trade effect which results. If unemployment exists and rapid growth results from the devaluation, this loss may be made good very quickly. If full employment exists, of course, the cost is much heavier. Then measures have to be taken to cut consumption to make room for the additional exports. Here the regional situation is not analogous. The cost of regional policy itself, and other measures of regional support such as public expenditure levels beyond what could be financed by regional revenue, involve transfer from the rest of the country to the problem regions. Governments and the public at large especially in non-assisted areas are very much aware of the 'cost' of regional policy and there is often much argument as to whether it is worthwhile. In fact the apparent budgetary cost of regional policy undoubtedly exaggerates the true resource cost. Money spent on bringing idle factors into productive use involves no sacrifice unless previously employed resources have to be diverted to other uses as well. But even if the true resource cost of regional policy is much less than the nominal cost, as has been argued for the Regional Employment Premium, there is always likely to be some burden on the rest of the country. This is because any stimulus to regional incomes will produce spill-over effects in the rest of the country. Regional economies are generally very 'open' and any volume of expenditure will result in a substantial leakage into imports from other regions and abroad. There will therefore be an unwanted stimulus in areas of the country where there is full employment and resources are scarce; there will also be increased demand for foreign imports. With most forms of regional support it is unlikely that these effects can be neutralised by increased regional exports on a comparable scale. To accommodate these effects it will therefore be necessary to cut demand in the full employment regions. The size of the cut should, of course, depend on the scale of the spill-over effects after allowing for any boost to regional exports. It should therefore be substantially less than the full budgetary cost of the regional measures; but there will nevertheless be a significant element of subsidy from the rest of the country.

This inter-regional transfer is of great importance politically. It means, as compared with the devaluation situation, that regional measures must be judged not simply with regard to what is necessary to secure full employment in the region, but also to what other regions are prepared to tolerate. Clearly this factor varies from country to country depending on the scale of the regional problem and on the importance which people in the country as a whole attach to solving it. But it seems that in many countries it is inclined to mean that measures fall short of what is necessary to eliminate the problem completely even if they mitigate it substantially.

Another important difference is that it is impossible to remove a region from the national macro-economic climate of which it forms a part whatever measures are applied. Here again the devaluation analogy does not apply. A state, especially one with a substantial internal market of its own and whose trade is well distributed with other countries, may by devaluation substantially alter its economic climate both by improving its export prospects and substituting home produced goods for imports. The smaller the state and the more it is dependent on a dominant trading partner, the less scope it will have to carry out this action successfully. But a region generally has a small internal market and is likely to trade most heavily with the rest of the country of which it forms a part; the dominant influence on its economy and its export prospects is the macro-economic climate of the country as a whole. Whatever regional measures are employed it is extremely difficult to escape from this influence and very substantial stimuli can be given in the regions without bringing growth on the required scale if the national performance is poor.

These factors perhaps account for the persistence of the regional problem despite the application of regional policy. The latter argument may also explain why Britain has apparently had no more success in solving her problem than either France or Germany despite levels of incentive and regional expenditure which greatly exceed what these countries have provided.

Conclusion

This paper has attempted to argue that the main determinant of regional growth rates is economic structure coupled with a tendency for the industries in the regions to be influenced in their performance by the national economic climate rather than by regional factors. No automatic mechanism for adjustment exists in the regional economy. If the growth of output in the nation as a whole is proceeding in line with the growth of economic potential, it is most unlikely to be doing so at the regional level. In some regions it will tend to exceed potential, creating inflationary pressure, in others it will lag behind. Since there is no automatic adjustment this disequilibrium will tend to be persistent; it may even be in some degree cumulative.

This is a sufficient explanation to account for differences in regional growth rates. But there is also some reason to suppose that structural change helps to bring about increases in labour productivity as old labour intensive industries give way to capital intensive modern ones. The Scottish experience seems to provide some evidence of this. If this is so, it means that economic potential may grow more rapidly than in the nation as a whole. The regional problem therefore arises on two counts: first that the region's actual growth rate lags behind that of the nation; and second that the region's equilibrium growth rate, which would secure full employment, is above that for the nation as a whole. The region therefore needs and has the capacity to sustain a faster growth than the nation but it tends to experience slower growth.

The root of the problem therefore lies in the disparities between national and regional actual growth, as determined by structure and between national and regional equilibrium growth and growth potential. It follows that measures which give the region a growth of output similar to the nation's, as Scotland has apparently had over the last ten years, may not be sufficient to solve the problem.[7] It may also be seen that if the so-called problem regions had been part of a large economy with a faster rate of growth, which brought their actual growth nearer to potential, the problem might not have arisen. Thus if measures can be found to improve the growth performance of the rest of the country, so creating a climate in which the regions can more readily achieve their equilibrium growth, this may prove an effective way of securing regional full employment. In this connection one may perhaps argue that the tremendous inflow of some four million foreign workers to the areas of West Germany where labour is particularly short has, by enabling a high level of economic momentum to be maintained, done as much as anything attempted in regional policy to prevent a serious regional problem.

The paper has argued that locational considerations are much less important than these general factors. Where a region is peripherally located, however, this does undoubtedly aggravate the problem. An adverse location will reduce further the rate of growth which a region can expect to achieve and make the task of improving growth performance more difficult. It will narrow the range of industries which can be expected to operate successfully in the region and hence make it much more difficult to raise levels of investment. Equally where a problem region is favourably located, this will tend to mitigate its difficulties. But the persistence of regional problems in some of the most central parts of the European Economic Community suggests that this factor on its own is not normally sufficient to eliminate a regional problem which arises from other causes.

TABLE 1

Gross changes in employees in employment as % of total employees in employment at the beginning of the period

| | Males | | | | | | | | |
| | 1960–64 | | | 1964–69 | | | 1969–71 | | |
	Loss	Gain	Net	Loss	Gain	Net	Loss	Gain	Net
GB	−3.7	+6.4	+2.7	−7.5	+3.6	−3.9	−5.3	+1.9	−3.4
Scotland	−7.0	+6.8	−0.2	−9.8	+5.0	−4.8	−7.2	+2.1	−5.1
Scotland less GB	−3.3	+0.4	−2.9	−2.2	+1.3	−0.9	−1.9	−0.2	−1.7

Note. Figures are calculated at Minimum List Headings Level.

The Economic and Exchequer Implications of British Regional Economic Policy [1]

BARRY MOORE and JOHN RHODES

Introduction

F o r a long time after the Special Areas Act was introduced in 1934 it was commonly supposed that the justification for regional policy was political and social and that it had a cost in terms of a loss of real income and output arising from reduced efficiency and/or a higher burden of taxation.[2] More recently economists have pointed to some of the possible economic benefits and costs arising from Government regional policy but a satisfactory conceptual and empirical framework for evaluating the *net* economic effects of regional policy has not yet emerged. In this paper we attempt to develop such a framework and make some preliminary estimates of the economic effects of regional policy. It is argued that, in combination with national policy of demand management which aims at maintaining full employment and a satisfactory balance of payments, British regional policy in the 1960s has led to increased output, employment and real income. We shall show, moreover, that the benefits in terms of real disposable income have been shared by *all* regions. This is because, regional policy measures, unlike most types of Government expenditure, bring more new resources into use than they pre-empt through a reduction in general tax rates. These economic benefits are additional to the non-economic local advantages in the form of the preservation of local amenities and the avoidance of the social and psychological costs of migration and unemployment.

Regional and National Economic Policy

It is broadly true that the pressure of demand in the United

Kingdom economy is managed subject to two constraints. Firstly, the Government, by the use of fiscal and monetary policy, aims to manage the level of demand so that it obtains the highest level of employment consistent with there not being labour shortages and bottlenecks in the supply of goods and services which have inflationary consequences. Secondly, the Government will aim to secure a satisfactory balance of payments position : its pursuit of full employment is therefore conditioned by the economy being able to generate sufficient exports to pay for 'full employment' imports. In the absence of a specific regional policy the fulfilment of these two objectives is inconsistent with full employment in all regions. This is because the pressure of demand that would be required to secure full employment in the Development Areas would imply serious production bottlenecks and delivery problems in the full employment areas which would lead to inflationary and balance of payments problems. It is reasonable to assume that the upper limit to the permissible total demand can be thought of as that which secures the desired pressure of demand in the fully employed areas.

It is legitimate to raise the question as to why there should be persistent regional variations in the rate of unemployment. There are two main reasons for this, both of which arise from imperfections in the labour market. Regional wage differentials are never adequate to ensure sufficient incoming firms to eliminate unemployment in the less prosperous areas and given the wage differentials the rate of net outward migration from Development Areas has not been sufficient to reduce unemployment in these areas to acceptable levels.

It is the purpose of regional policy to compensate for these imperfections in the labour market. Regional policy in the United Kingdom attempts to do this in three ways—first, through differential investment incentives designed to divert investment into Development Areas; second, through physical controls in the form of the Industrial Development Certificate policy, designed to divert new factories into areas of high unemployment; finally, the Regional Employment Premiums designed to raise the demand for labour by reducing labour costs in the Development Areas relatively to other areas.

These measures, if effective, will have repercussions on other areas and not just in the regions to which they are applied. They will affect the pressure of demand in the fully employed areas and also, for reasons explained below, the balance of payments position. There will be a dual effect on the pressure of demand in fully employed areas—firstly a diversion (substitution) effect which *reduces* the pressure of demand on account of a diversion of demand to Development Areas; and secondly an income effect on account of the payment of financial incentives which, by increasing incomes and expenditure, *increases* demand in fully employed areas and the Development Areas.[3] When considering the overall net effect of any particular instrument of regional policy it is necessary therefore to take into account these indirect effects on the fully employed areas. If the diversion effect is larger than the income effect general taxation would have to be lower or public expenditure higher (than in the absence of regional policy) if the pressure of demand in the fully employed areas is to be maintained unchanged. The opposite is true if the income effect exceeds the diversion effect. In either case it is necessary to have a counterpart measure in the field of general demand management side by side with the regional policy measures. Hence if we are to identify the net effects of regional policy[4] it is necessary that both the pressure of demand in fully employed areas and the balance of payments position are maintained by macro-economic policy instruments which are brought into operation simultaneously.

The Net Effects of Regional Policy

Ignoring for the moment the complications introduced by inter-regional migration and the balance of payments it can be said unambiguously that whenever regional policy increases employment and output in Development Areas there must be a net increase in employment and output in the country as a whole because, ex hypothesi, employment (or unemployment) is maintained unchanged in the fully employed areas through appropriate counterpart demand management measures. Hence there is a net increase in employment, output and real income which is a clear national economic benefit arising from an effective regional policy.

It should, however, be recognised that even when allowing for successful counterpart measures that would maintain employment in the fully employed areas unchanged, there may be some loss of productivity in these areas due to the fact that the productivity of labour in these areas could have been higher before the initial diversion of demand caused by regional policy. This could happen if there was some redistribution of demand inside fully employed areas towards activities with below average productivity.[5]

It is possible that the productivity of the additional policy-induced employment in Development Areas may be less than the productivity of labour in the same industries and occupations in the fully employed areas.[6] But the important point is that *any* output produced by this additional employment is a net addition to output and real income for the economy as a whole and although the productivity of this extra employment may be below the national average for the same industries, particularly in the short run, the overall output gain could only be eliminated for this reason if the productivity of this employment were near to *zero*.

There is therefore no reason to suppose that, after taking account of these two qualifications, there could be anything but a net benefit accruing from regional policy in the form of a higher total of employment. This is also likely to be true for Gross Domestic Product although in the case of the latter there may be adverse consequences tending to partly offset the beneficial effects.[7]

The net benefits of regional policy will be further reduced by a slowing down in the rate of net outward migration from Development Areas, which reduces the rate of growth of employment and G D P in the fully employed areas. Recent empirical research[8] suggests that new jobs created by regional policy in the Development Areas will affect the rate of net outward migration,[9] but after taking account of this reduction in net outward migration we shall show that significant net benefits accruing from regional policy remain. Moreover, in so far as net outward migration is reduced there are important indirect economic *benefits* resulting from regional economic policy. These take the form of savings in public expenditure on social infrastructure such as schools and hospitals as well as in housing and in other public services.

From the point of view of the balance of payments two

things have to be taken into account. Firstly, because regional policy combined with counterpart measures raises the level of national output imports will increase. Secondly, regional policy measures can stimulate exports and import substitution when Development Area manufacturers are made more competitive than previously by regional financial incentives.

In a national policy context an increase in imports normally requires compensating measures such as a depreciation of the exchange rate to increase exports and restore external balance. With the economy at or near to full employment such an adjustment to the exchange rate involves resource costs because labour resources are diverted from other uses to produce the additional exports. But if the external balance is restored by the use of a regional policy measure such as the regional employment premium, additional exports will be generated in areas of high unemployment where labour resources are not so scarce. In this case because unemployed resources are being brought into use there is no resource cost involved to produce the increase in exports. The question is whether these additional exports will be greater or less than what is required to balance the additional imports. In the latter case the resource cost will be negative—in the former case, positive. These gains or losses must be considered alongside the resource benefits already outlined.

The above serves to provide a framework for evaluating the economic consequences of regional policy. Of central importance to this framework is first the distinction between the specific effects of policy measures on the regions and the appropriate counterpart macro-economic measures and second the distinction made between the 'income' and 'diversionary' effects of regional policy instruments on the pressure of demand in the fully employed areas and on the balance of payments.

The Net Effects of Regional Policy, the Distribution of Income and the consequences for the Public Sector Accounts

(a) How Regional Policy Works and the Appropriate Demand Management Action Required

There is a substantial body of evidence to support the contention that regional policy in the United Kingdom has caused a sizeable diversion of demand to the Development Areas which, in the absence of regional policy, would have been generated in the fully employed areas.[10] Our earlier published work[11] suggests that this diversion effect may be about 200,000 jobs between 1963 and 1970 and these results are broadly confirmed by other recent research work.[12] Taken by itself the effect of this diversion, brought about by regional policy, is to reduce the pressure of demand in fully employed areas below what it would otherwise have been.

On the other hand the income effects of regional policy increase the pressure of demand in all regions including the fully employed areas. Two different types of income effect must be distinguished. First there are those income effects which derive from Exchequer outlays associated with regional financial incentives to Development Area manufacturers. These find their way into profits, wages or prices which leads to increased expenditures and employment.

The second income effect arises from the increase in income of those employees (including company profits generated) who would otherwise have been unemployed but for regional policy. To the extent, therefore, that a regional policy instrument (including IDC) is successful in generating new jobs in Development Areas this income effect occurs. In the case of those employees previously receiving unemployment or supplementary benefits the increase in income is considerably less than the wage in employment, but for the previously unregistered unemployed (mainly women) the increase in income will be equal to the wage in employment. The effect of regional policy on the rate of net outward migration will also determine the overall size of this income effect in that those employees who would have migrated in the absence of regional policy would have been in employment in the fully employed areas.

As is shown below it is a reasonably straightforward exercise to estimate the order of magnitude of both these income effects. What clearly emerges is that the additional demand for labour falling on fully employed areas on account of these two income effects is very much less than the fall in the demand for labour in these areas brought about by the diversionary effects of regional policy. The net effect of regional policy has therefore been to *reduce* demand in the fully employed areas and this relaxation in the pressure of demand has permitted general measures of an expansionary kind through fiscal and monetary policy. The appropriate demand management action is a reduction in general tax rates so that the pressure of demand in fully employed areas is maintained unchanged. This conclusion may seem at first sight to be paradoxical but it is entirely consistent with the accepted principles of demand management. The unique contribution of regional policy is to provide an opportunity for hitherto unemployed resources to be brought into use by traditional reflationary methods.

Whilst this conclusion emerges for the 1960s regional policy package as a whole it would be dangerous to conclude that it was equally true for each individual regional policy instrument. This is because the income and diversion effects of individual measures are likely to vary widely and it is conceivable that a policy instrument resulting in large income effects but small diversion effects would need to be accompanied by general tax increases. However, such evidence as we have suggests that all the major policy instruments recently used in the United Kingdom have diverted some demand to Development Areas. This is offset to varying degrees by income effects falling back on to fully employed areas. The income effects of Exchequer outlays on the regional employment premium are, for instance, high in relation to those for the IDC policy where Exchequer outlays (apart from the cost of administration) are zero.[13] For each regional policy instrument the direction and extent of the appropriate demand adjustment in terms of general tax rate changes depends on the net outcome on the pressure of demand in the fully employed areas of the income and diversion effects. Our analysis suggests a strong presumption that the reduction in general tax rates appropriate for the regional policy package as a whole in the 1960s is also appropriate for each of the major policy instruments taken separately.[14]

(b) The Distribution of the Benefits from Regional Policy

Whilst the increases in output and employment are confined entirely to the Development Areas (since output and employment are largely unchanged in the fully employed areas where the pressure of demand has been maintained) a reduction in general tax rates (not differentiated by region) brings about an increase in real disposable income in both the Development

Areas *and in the* fully employed regions.[15] Thus benefits arising from regional policy in the form of an increase in real income accrue to *all* regions when the counterpart measures are allowed for. Hence the general taxpayer in the fully employed regions, far from having to 'pay' for regional policy, receives a small tax bonus instead.

This is a challenging result because the contrary view is often expressed that taxpayers in the South must pay for regional policy to the benefit of Development Areas.[16] This view can be presented persuasively both in terms of changes in tax rates and the counterpart changes in the flow of goods and services between fully employed regions and Development Areas. This is based on the presumption that the income effects of regional policy on the fully employed areas are greater than the diversion effects. If this were correct the appropriate counterpart demand management measure would be an increase in general tax rates. This would result in a reduction in real disposable income in the fully employed areas in order to free the resources to produce goods and services which are 'exported' to Development Areas. The Development Areas would thus be better off because of increased consumption made possible by higher imports of goods and services from fully employed areas. Thus the taxpayers in the South could be said to be 'paying' for regional policy in the same way that the general taxpayer has to pay higher taxes to make possible an increase in national exports (at a given level of output) to correct an international deficit on the balance of payments.

If as we argue the diversion effects exceed the income effects, a general reduction in tax rates is required, and far from being worse off the fully employed areas are able to increase their consumption through higher imports from the Development Areas. This deterioration in the 'balance of payments' position of the fully employed areas (*vis-à-vis* the Development Areas) does not require remedial action as would be the case for a deterioration in the United Kingdom balance of payments. This is because such a deterioration in the national balance of payments (which also allows an increase in real consumption) must be short lived and will require correction at the expense of a loss in consumption at a later date. But the deterioration in the fully employed areas 'balance of payments' with the Development

D

Areas is wholly to be welcomed—indeed this is what an effective regional policy must do, since in raising national output, it brings into use the unemployed labour resources of Development Areas, thus making possible the 'export' of more goods and services to the fully employed areas. At the same time Exchequer transfers into Development Areas (e.g. unemployment benefits), which could be regarded as financing their overall balance of payments deficit with fully employed areas, are reduced as a consequence of regional policy.

(c) The Effects of Regional Policy on the Public Sector Accounts

We now explore further this seemingly paradoxical proposition that regional policy although initially requiring *increased* Exchequer expenditures leads to all regions realising an increase in real income through a general *reduction* in tax rates and no sacrifice of output or employment by any region. We maintain that in contrast to most items of public expenditure, it is a mistake to assume that Exchequer outlays on regional policy have a net resource cost which needs to be provided for by additional taxation or the curtailment of other public expenditure.

Any item of public expenditure will have one or both of two effects. On the one hand it may pre-empt resources so that an increase in Government expenditure leads to an increase in demand for labour resources.[17] On the other hand some items of Government expenditure change the productive potential of the economy in either of two directions (i.e. they either increase or decrease the amount of labour and material resources which are available to the economy). Raising the school leaving age for example, not only pre-empts resources through the requirement for more schools, books and teachers, but also reduces— at least in the short run—the productive potential of the economy by taking many thousands of young people out of the labour force.

Exchequer outlays on regional policy are, however, one of the few types of Government expenditure which *raise* both the short and long run productive potential of the economy and so more than compensate for the extra demand they place on resources with what is in effect an extra supply of resources. We have shown that the net effects of regional policy is to bring more labour resources into use and therefore to increase national output and real incomes. In resource terms regional policy expenditures are not only costless but result in substantial benefits for the economy as a whole, and to a varying degree, in all its regions.

In order to examine the implications of regional policy for the public sector accounts, we propose a definition of the Exchequer cost of regional policy which will tell us the net impact of regional policy on the public sector deficit or surplus in the medium term.

The definition of the net Exchequer cost of regional policy is a compound of the following items (i) initial Exchequer outlays on regional incentives, (ii) net of any directly recoverable items,[18] (iii) net of the change in tax yield necessary to maintain the pressure of demand in fully employed areas, and (iv) net of changes in tax revenue resulting from increased employment,[19] output and income brought about by regional policy.

Preliminary Estimates of the Economic and Exchequer Implications of Regional Policy 1963–1970

In this section we give the results of a first attempt to estimate the size of the benefits arising from regional policy. In presenting these figures we aim only to indicate broad orders of magnitude.

Two sets of results are presented in Table 1. The difference between the two sets of estimates, A and B, is the degree to which it can be assumed that a successful regional policy reduces the rate of net outward migration from Development Areas. In version A it is assumed, following the work of A. J. Brown, that the creation of 260,000 jobs in Development Areas reduced outward migration of the labour force by 35,000 (perhaps 100,000 people). In version B the same regional policy effect is assumed to reduce net outward migration of *workers* by the much larger number of 100,000 (say 300,000 people). In each case the remainder of the 260,000 additional jobs must therefore be filled from the ranks of the registered and unregistered unemployed. A detailed explanation of how the figures in Table 1 have been arrived at is given in the Appendices.

Looking at the effects in the country as a whole (i.e. fully employed and Development Areas together) the differing migration assumptions do not affect the picture very much.[20] In version A total employment increases by 291,000 and in version B by 254,000. The additional annual output in the United Kingdom

(GDP) would therefore be £400–£500m per annum higher by 1970 if the productivity of the additional employment was similar to the national average. The additional output therefore amounts to approximately 1 per cent of GDP as at 1970.[21] This is a benefit which continues each year, and if an active regional policy continues to be pursued in the future this benefit is likely to show a gradual increase. Moreover if regional policy were now abandoned a large part of the gain in output and employment would continue into the future since many of the jobs diverted to Development Areas by the policy of the 1960s will remain in being, some of them for many years.

It is possible that our analysis summarised in Table 1 has made insufficient provision for any increase in the demand for investment goods required to produce the additional output made possible by regional policy. The extent to which additional investment demand occurs is governed by two main factors. Firstly the existence of spare capacity, particularly in Development Areas may reduce the requirement for additional investment. Secondly, some activities diverted to Development Areas may be less capital intensive than they would have been had they been located in a region of labour scarcity.

Some allowance for additional investment demand has been catered for in Table 1. Firstly the increase in output will both require and stimulate the production of investment goods and therefore part of the demand for capital equipment will have been satisfied. Secondly in estimating the income effects of Exchequer outlays some expansion of investment demand was also allowed for. Thirdly some of the investment demand will be met from increased imports rather than from domestic output but the potential resource costs of these imports may well be offset by additional exports stimulated by regional policy. We have estimated that if no allowance is made for increased utilisation of spare capacity or labour capital substitution and if in addition we assume that the incremental capital output ratio is as high as the capital stock output ratio then the maximum possible investment demand generated will still leave the gains in output and employment intact and leave room for a small reduction in general tax rates.

In Table 2 we show the overall consequences of regional policy for the Exchequer. The main conclusion is that if regional

TABLE 1

The effects of regional policy on employment inside and outside Development Areas before and after restoring the pressure of demand in the fully employed areas. Orders of magnitude for the period 1963–70

| | A Employment change in (1) | | B Employment change in | |
| | Fully employed Areas | Development Areas | Fully employed Areas | Development Areas |
		000s		000s
(a) Before restoring pressure of demand				
Income effects of initial Exchequer outlays (inc. multiplier effects) Average for the period	+25	+9	+25	+9
Income effects deriving from the increase in employment and profits. Average for the period	+25	+9	+18	+6
Employment creation in and diversion to DAs (inc. multiplier effects)	−195	+260	−195	+260
Sub-Total	−145	+278	−152	+275
(b) After restoring pressure of demand				
Employment generated by Government expenditure associated with migration	−20 (2)	+14	−67	+47
Total increase in employment required to restore pressure of demand	+131	+33	+121	+30
Total Employment Change	−34 (3)	+325	−98	+352
Change in labour supply arising from reduced net outward migration from DAs	−35	+35	−100	+100

Notes to Table 1

(1) A minus sign indicates a decline in the demand for labour, a positive sign indicates an increase in the demand for labour.

(2) The net effect on employment in the fully employed areas is zero because the decline in the demand for labour is exactly matched by the increase in the demand for labour required to restore the pressure of demand.

(3) The total employment change is negative because the given pressure of demand in the fully employed areas is in relation to a marginally reduced supply of labour arising from migration.

TABLE 2

Summary of Exchequer Flows—Orders of magnitude 1963–70

	Annual Average 1963–70 £m	
	A	B
Exchequer outlays on regional incentives gross of directly recoverable items	−155	−155
Directly recoverable items	+30	+30
Reduction in tax rates required. Yield of tax system to maintain pressure of demand in fully employed areas at a given income	−133	−122
Change in tax and social security receipts after restoring pressure of demand in fully employed areas at given rates of tax	+156	+133
Net reduction in infrastructure expenditure and public services	+6	+20
Net change in increase in budgetary deficit (−) increase (+) decrease	−96	−94

policy is effective the budgetary deficit must always be higher (or the surplus lower) if the pressure of demand in the fully employed areas is to be maintained unchanged. In terms of the regional policy package of the 1960s we estimate that the budget deficit has been increased by the order of £100 million. This increase in the budget deficit will be largely financed by additional net savings (i.e. by an increase in demand for additional financial assets resulting from increased output and income) and therefore has minimal monetary implications.

An increase in the public sector deficit emerges for two reasons. Firstly, tax and social security net receipts (after restoring the pressure of demand in the fully employed areas) approximately offset the initial non-recoverable Exchequer outlays on regional incentives, although the offsetting benefits will only accrue to the Exchequer after some years' delay. Secondly, assuming full employment in the non-Development Areas the general level of taxation would be lower by over £100m than what would have been necessary in the absence of regional policy.

Conclusion

We believe that the analysis presented in this paper has important policy implications.

Normally changes in Government expenditure are viewed in relation to the expected claim they make on scarce labour resources. We maintain that Government expenditures on regional policy should not be seen as making such a claim on resources. This is because, unlike most other forms of public expenditure they bring about an increase in the overall utilisation of labour resources (i.e. an increase in productive potential) which is beneficial to the whole economy in terms of increased employment and output. Further in no sense is there a cost associated with these regional policy expenditures. Expenditures on regional policy should not be regarded as competing with other public or private expenditure and therefore increases in regional policy expenditures do not require sacrifices either in terms of other public expenditure or in terms of higher taxation. On the contrary *all* regions enjoy an increase in real disposable income because real output is higher and general taxation is lower (or public expenditure higher) than would have been the case in the absence of regional policy.

Finally, the view is frequently expressed that a solution to the regional problem lies in an unprecedented and sustained increase in the rate of growth of the national economy. Under such conditions it is argued that regional policy expenditures would be superfluous and wasteful. We would argue that such a sustained expansion is constrained by the pressure of demand in the fully employed areas (and by the balance of payments) and that it is in precisely such periods of expansion that an active and effective regional policy is needed to divert the pressure of demand to Development Areas so that additional resources are brought into use to make the general expansion more easily sustainable.

APPENDIX A

Income Effects

(a) Income effects of Exchequer outlays on regional incentives (see Table 1)

The income effects of Exchequer outlays are an average for the period as a whole though in practice it should be recognised that income effects were higher in more recent years.

For REP we assumed that 40 per cent of the annual payment was used to reduce prices, 40 per cent to increase profits and 20 per cent to increase wages. This was consistent with the findings of our industrial enquiry.

For investment incentives and grants under the Local Employment Acts we assumed the whole amount was received initially into profits. After corporation tax and the conventional 40 per cent distribution to dividends, we assumed that retained profits were used partly to increase investment and partly to reduce prices.

Finally, for largely recoverable items under the Local Employment Acts such as loans and Government built factories, we assumed that one-third of these was a net Exchequer outlay the balance being repayment of loans and factory rents which are automatically received back into Exchequer.

The direct[22] and indirect[23] income effects on employment are estimated at 34,000 jobs.

(b) Income effects deriving from increased employment and profits in Development Areas

This derives from the difference between unemployment and supplementary benefits received (for those registered as unemployed) and the average wage. For the unregistered (mainly women) unemployed the additional income is equal to their wages. There is no income effect for those who would otherwise have migrated to work elsewhere. There is also a small income effect deriving from increased profits.

The direct and indirect income effects on employment are again equal to 34,000 jobs on assumption A (low migration effect) and 24,000 jobs on assumption B (high migration effect).

All the jobs arising from income effects will be spread fairly evenly throughout the country. We therefore allocated one-quarter to Development Areas and three-quarters to non-Development Areas.

APPENDIX B

Employment creation in and diversion to Development Areas by regional policy measures 1963–70

Employment creation in Development Areas is estimated at 260,000 jobs. This figure is based on earlier work on the number of manufacturing jobs created in Development Areas by regional policy[24] incorporating more recent research into the effects of policy in the Merseyside Development Area but excluding the effect in Northern Ireland. A multiplier of 1.4 was again used.

It was argued in the text that a substantial amount of employment generated by regional policy in Development Areas represented a *diversion* of economic activity from fully employed areas. Some of the 185,000 *manufacturing* jobs generated in Development Areas between 1963 and 1970 may not have involved a reduction in demand in fully employed areas prior to restoring the pressure of demand in these areas, e.g. the 'creation' of new jobs arising from foreign companies which would otherwise have expanded outside the United Kingdom; new firms starting in Development Areas which would otherwise not have existed at all; and employment in firms winning export orders from foreign competition because of REP.

The precise contribution of 'diversion' and 'creation' is not known but the evidence suggests that 'diversion' is much the larger. We have assumed that one-quarter (65,000) of the jobs arising from regional policy were 'created', i.e. would not have been in the United Kingdom at all in the absence of regional policy and that three-quarters (195,000) have been diverted from the non-Development Areas.

In the case of employment newly created in Development Areas there are no negative service multiplier effects in fully employed areas.

TABLE A1

Exchequer cost of special regional assistance to manufacturing industry over and above that available nationally

Great Britain (£m)

| Years | Recoverable or mainly recoverable items | | | Non-Recoverable Items (5) | | | | | | | | |
	Government factory building (1)	Loans	Total	Grants under Section Four (1)	Building grants (1)	Plant and machinery grants (1)	Special Operational grants (1)	Investment grants (2)	Free depreciation (3)	Regional Employment Premium (4)	S E T Premium (4)	Total
46–7	5.7	0.2	5.9									
47–8	12.5	0.3	12.8									
48–9	11.0	0.5	11.5									
49–50	6.5	0.6	7.1									
50–1	5.0	0.8	5.8									
51–2	5.0	0.8	5.8									
52–3	3.7	0.3	4.0									
53–4	3.1	1.1	4.2									
54–5	4.5	1.7	6.2									
55–6	5.9	0.4	6.3									
56–7	4.9	0.3	5.2									
57–8	2.7	0.1	2.8									
58–9	1.5	2.1	3.6									
59–60	5.6	3.1	8.7									
60–1	21.0	23.5	44.5	2.7	3.3							6.0
61–2	5.5	16.4	21.9	1.2	1.1							2.3

Year												Total
62–3	5.4	4.6	10.0	1.8	4.4	2.0						6.2
63–4	5.6	19.0	24.6	0.7	3.0	6.8						5.7
64–5	12.7	10.4	23.1	0.6	10.0	6.1			3.0			20.4
65–6	12.4	9.6	22.0	0.5	13.8	6.3			45.0			65.4
66–7	14.4	13.2	27.6	0.4	21.1	1.3			25.0			52.8
67–8	11.5	13.7	25.2	1.3	18.5	0.5		72.0	4.0	34.1		131.2
68–9	13.9	17.7	31.6	1.3	21.6	0.1		85.0	—	101.0	25.0	234.4
69–70	18.0	28.1	46.1	1.3	26.3	0.2	10.2	90.0	—	105.0	25.0	257.9
70–1	7.9	28.0	35.9	1.2	30.1		2.8	90.0	—	110.0	—	234.3

Sources.

(1) Annual Reports of the Local Employment Acts
(2) Investment Grants—White Paper—D T I Journal Vol. 10 No. 4 25 January 1973
(3) Department of Economic Affairs and H M Treasury Progress Report No. 55 August 1969
(4) Financial Statistics—C S O
(5) A small figure of about £3m per annum should be added to cover Development Area Training Grants

APPENDIX C

The Effects of Regional Policy on inter-regional migration
and the consequential changes on the demand and supply of
labour in the regions

*(a) The Effects of Regional Policy on net outward migration
from Development Areas*

The increase in Development Area employment arising from
regional policy can be expected to narrow regional differentials in
unemployment rates compared with the non-policy alternative position. The effect of this will be to reduce the level of net outward
migration from Development Areas to fully employed areas.

The causes of migration are extremely complex and not limited
to economic factors. There is therefore considerable uncertainty as
to how far an effective regional policy reduces the rate of net outward migration from Development Areas. For this reason we
thought it wise to undertake two sets of calculations. The first
estimates (version A) are based on recent empirical work on regional
migration published by A. J. Brown.[25] These results indicate that
'a rise of one percentage point in the regional unemployment rate
relative to the rest of the country goes with an increase of about
three per thousand in the net outflow of men of working age in the
region'. On this basis we estimate that regional policy reduced the
level of net outward migration from Development Areas to other
parts of the country by about 35,000 *employed* persons between
1963 and 1970.

In the calculations labelled B we assumed that the creation of
the 260,000 jobs in Development Areas would reduce net outward
migration by 100,000 employed persons.[26] We regard this as an
upper limit based on the rather special case of a sparsely populated
area in Central Wales.

*(b) The consequential changes in the supply and demand for
labour*

Under assumption A the effect of regional policy on migration
is to increase labour supply in Development Areas by 35,000 and
to reduce labour supply by the same amount in the fully employed
areas. Assumption B increases the regional changes in the labour
supply to 100,000.

On the demand side two effects are distinguished. Firstly, there are those effects which result from the switching of personal consumers' expenditure when people migrate from one region to another. A. J. Brown has calculated that 'a hundred occupied persons moving in conditions of slack demand might carry between 18 and 30 jobs with them'.[27] Secondly, whenever people move from one part of the country to another this can affect both the geographical distribution and/or the overall amount of public sector social capital expenditure (e.g. housing, schools and hospitals) and associated current public service expenditure. Thus if net outward migration from Development Areas is reduced, some employment associated with public expenditure is diverted to Development Areas (depending on the utilisation and quality of existing public service provision). But other employment associated with public expenditure that would have been required in fully employed areas at the higher rate of net outward migration may now not be necessary. We have assumed that half the expenditure is diverted to Development Areas and the remainder is not required at all.

Estimates of the social capital requirements of migrants and employment generated in providing these public services were made using information on average requirements derived from the National Income and Expenditure Blue Book. We adopted a marginal rate of public service provision equal to half the average requirements.

APPENDIX D

Estimating by how much taxes are lower if the pressure of demand is maintained in the fully employed areas

We have estimated that as a result of Government regional policy in the 1960s aggregate demand must be expanded by the equivalent of 164,000 jobs (on assumption A) and by the equivalent of 151,000 jobs (on assumption B) to leave the percentage unemployment in the non-Development Areas unchanged. This potential reflation enabled by regional policy can be considered as deriving from a reduction in taxation, an increase in public expenditure, or expansionary monetary policy. We consider only the first of these possibilities.

On the assumption that a 1 per cent addition to employment will add 1 per cent to GDP if the pressure of demand is held constant, we calculate the GDP equivalent of the additional employment assuming that short run multiplier effects have had time to work through. We assume that the reduction in yield of taxes is brought about half from changing the standard rate of income tax and half from an across the board reduction in purchase tax. We estimate that taking income tax and purchase tax together a reduction in these taxes of £100 generates an increase in expenditure at factor cost of £75. The required tax change was thus calculated for each year as the regional policy effect increased and an annual average figure obtained for the period as a whole.

APPENDIX E

Increase in tax receipts (reduction in social security payments) after restoring pressure of demand in fully-employed areas

In Table E1 we summarise the estimated additional revenue which would have accrued to the Exchequer between 1963 and

TABLE E1
Exchequer clawbacks from regional policy 1963–70
£m (current prices)

	Migration Assumption	
	A	B
Employers and employees national insurance contributions	185	161
Corporation Tax (1)	221	201
Tax on distributed profits	44	38
Income Tax	268	235
Indirect taxes	322	281
Sub Total	1040	916
Reduction in unemployment benefits (2)	207	145
Grand Total	1247	1061
Annual Average 1963–70	156	133

(1)   Included Corporation Tax of 40 per cent on that part of R E P received into profits.

(2)   Including national assistance and supplementary benefit paid to unemployed persons. Under assumption A it is assumed that the registered unemployed are reduced by 150,000. Under assumption B the reduction in registered unemployed is 105,000.

1970 as a result of the increased employment and output brought about by regional policy. The various tax revenues are calculated using ratios for each year based on the National Income Blue Book.

The estimates are based on a cumulative series of the additional output and employment generated by regional policy in each year and an annual average was then taken.

In a conventional appraisal of the flow of costs and benefits arising from an item of public expenditure a discounting procedure would normally be adopted. This should be done in due course but in any event the overall conclusion that regional policy leads to negative resources costs is not likely to be affected although the measure of the benefits will be. On the one hand the benefit will be reduced in so far as the Exchequer outlays and income effects precede the clawbacks and diversion effects of regional policy. On the other hand, the benefits as we have measured them (increased output in the years 1963–70) are underestimated in that, even if regional policy were to be abandoned, much of the benefit in terms of increased output would continue for many years into the future.

APPENDIX F

The effects of regional policy on the balance of payments

If it was the case that the effect of regional policy was to increase imports more than exports this external imbalance would have to be corrected by a change in the terms of trade and some resource cost would result. In reality however we think that the balance of payments effects are small and broadly neutral.

The increased output arising from the operation of the investment incentives and the I D C policy will lead to increased imports and thus worsen the balance of payments. In so far as investment incentives make Development Area firms more competitive than they would otherwise have been and attract foreign firms which would otherwise not have come to the United Kingdom at all, there will be offsetting benefits to the balance of payments. The overall effect on the balance of payments is probably unfavourable.

R E P on the other hand, because it makes Development Area firms more competitive than previously, particularly if it enables prices to be held below what they would have been, will stimulate exports and encourage import substitution. The net effects on the balance of payments of this measure is probably favourable and little or no resource cost emerges if the terms of trade are adjusted by use of of an R E P type of policy instrument because a large part of the additional exports are produced in Development Areas where unused resources are available.

We estimate the additional imports generated by regional policy to be of the order of £40–£50m per annum for the period 1963–70. This is not likely to be fully offset by exports generated by R E P from 1967 onwards which we estimate at about £40m per annum 1967–70. However the balance of payments position is improved when regional policy attracts foreign firms to the United Kingdom which would otherwise have gone elsewhere. The inflow of foreign investment improves the capital account and the excess of additional exports over imports generated specifically by these firms improves the current account.[28]

SECTION THREE

The Implications of European Monetary Integration for the Peripheral Areas[1]

JOHN WILLIAMSON

Introduction

M o s t British economists who have addressed themselves to the question of European monetary integration have expressed hostility to the enterprise, primarily on the grounds that loss of the instrument of exchange rate policy would threaten the prosperity of the peripheral areas. The aspect of monetary union which they have considered central is exchange rate union, rather than the integration of capital markets, and this judgement will not be challenged in the present paper. The paper will examine the implicit models that have been used in deriving this conclusion by the critics of monetary integration and the modifications that have been suggested by proponents, and will argue that none of them can be considered adequate. A more comprehensive model is then constructed by assembling elements from the various models examined. It is argued that this more general model justifies a greater agnosticism than has been customary.

The Pearce theory

Professor Ivor Pearce[2] has asserted that adoption of a common currency destroys the 'money illusion' that otherwise allows different real wages to co-exist in different regions.[3] He argued that such differential real wages play a vital economic role in off-setting different productivity levels, thus allowing the areas where productivity is relatively low to compete successfully with those where productivity is higher. It is generally taken for granted that the low-productivity regions tend to be the peripheral ones, and there are *a priori* reasons—notably the existence of transport costs—for this expectation, which reinforce the casual empirical observation that at least in Europe it is the peripheral regions

(Ireland, Scotland, North Norway, South-West France, Southern Italy) which are the least prosperous ones. It follows that peripheral regions (at least those whose geographic disadvantage is not offset by a favourable resource base) would be unable to maintain a tolerable level of prosperity if a common currency were to lead labour to demand and obtain equal money wages (which would imply equal real wages in so far as prices were equalised by the customs union).

In support of his contention Pearce constructed two tables which demonstrated that wages differed as between different European countries. One of these showed hourly wage rates in 1970 in twenty-three narrowly defined occupations in up to seven European countries, where wage rates were converted to United Kingdom pence at 1970 exchange rates. The percentage difference between the highest and lowest wage rates in each occupation varied from 27 per cent to 230 per cent and averaged 69 per cent. His second table compared relative wages in different countries, by deflating hourly wage rates in each occupation by the wage rate for unskilled labour in the construction industry in the same country. He found that the wage differentials so constructed ranged up to 76 per cent and averaged 31 per cent.

As Pearce concedes, this evidence simply establishes that there are absolute and relative wage differentials between European countries. It does not establish that monetary unification would reduce, let alone eliminate, those differentials.[4] This crucial stage of the argument, which Pearce takes for granted, seems highly dubious on *a priori* grounds: the demand and supply of labour can differ between regions, and it is not axiomatic that unions will both desire to, and be able to, override these differences. At the very least, there is need for a demonstration that wage differentials are absent within monetarily integrated areas. To test this proposition it is natural to search for figures which would provide comparisons between the wages paid in different regions of a single country which are similar to Pearce's international comparisons. I have not succeeded in finding such data for any European countries, but there are some North American data which are broadly comparable. Unfortunately these contained only two job classifications that would appear to be comparable to Pearce's. The relevant comparisons are shown in Table 1.

TABLE 1

Percentage Difference Between Lowest and Highest Wage Rates
in Two Occupations

Occupation	(1) Europe	(2) United States	(3) United States
Truck drivers	48		
local trucking		19	
in manufacturing			45
in non-manufacturing			28
in transport, etc.			13
in wholesale trade			54
in retail trade			47
Construction: unskilled labour	31		
Building: helpers and labourers		68	

1. *Source.* Pearce (1972), Table 1. The comparisons involve 6 and 5 countries respectively.
2. *Source. Handbook of Labor Statistics,* U S Department of Labor, Bureau of Labor Statistics, 1971, Table 90. The data relate to average minimum union hourly wage rates in large cities, and cover 9 regions.
3. *Source.* ibid., Table 100. The data relate to average hourly earnings in metropolitan areas, and cover 4 regions.

It is no doubt dangerous to draw conclusions from a sample of two, but there is scant support for the hypothesis that wage differentials do not exist between the regions of a monetarily integrated area. However, the more extensive comparison shown in Table 2 suggests at least weak support for the more modest hypothesis that wage differentials tend to be smaller between the regions of a monetarily integrated area. This is particularly true in view of the fact that the North American data generally relate to more broadly-defined occupations (e.g., 'manufacturing : machinists') than do Pearce's (e.g., 'machinery manufacturing : fitters'), so that some of the inter-regional variation in the former case may be attributable to variations in industrial composition as between different areas.

This crude examination of the facts therefore suggests that Pearce's theory must be rejected in the extreme form that he presented it, since wage rates can and do differ between the regions within a monetary union. However, there is some suggestion that wage differentials tend to be smaller within a monetary union.

TABLE 2
Comparison of International and Inter-Regional Wage Differentials

Area	Minimum Differential %	Average Differential %	Maximum Differential %
Absolute differentials			
Europe (up to 7 countries, 23 occupations)	27	69	230
United States (9 regions, 7 occupations)	19	37	68
United States (4 regions, 38 occupations)	5	29	59
Canada (up to 9 regions, 15 occupations)	27	58	100
Relative differentials			
Europe (6 countries, 23 occupations)	–	31	76
United States (9 regions, 7 occupations)	–	43	48
Canada (9 regions, 11 occupations)	–	21	50

Sources. For Europe and the United States, see notes to Table 1. For Canada, *Employment, Earnings and Hours*, Ministry of Industry, Trade and Commerce, Labor Division, Ottawa, January 1972, Table 3.

The Oppenheimer theory

A second theory, recently articulated by Peter Oppenheimer,[5] recognises that wages in each country may continue to be different after monetary unification, but assumes that wage rates can be treated as exogenous. 'Situations which call for an exchange-rate change arise basically because national cost levels have a life of their own . . .';[6] the rate of change of wage rates is regarded as determined by essentially sociological forces, i.e., independently of the excess demand for labour. If each country devotes its demand management policy to the maintenance of internal balance, it is only by an improbable coincidence that all countries would maintain payments equilibrium.

If this theory were valid as between the different regions of a single country one would expect to observe wage rates in different regions drifting further apart over time. I am not aware of any examples of this having occurred, while there is clear evidence that it has not occurred in Canada in recent years.[7] While wage rates are not equalised between regions, there must be forces which limit the growth of inter-regional wage differentials, and these must be accounted for by a satisfactory theory.

The Fleming/Corden theory

A third theory, which probably represents the most widely-held view among British economists, was first clearly expounded by J. Marcus Fleming[8] and has subsequently been propounded by Max Corden.[9] It is based on the assumption that each area has its own particular Phillips curve, whose position may be influenced by 'sociological forces'. Exchange-rate flexibility permits each region to select its preferred position on its own Phillips curve, whereas monetary union compels each region to accept a common rate of inflation. In equilibrium the regions with the stronger inflationary tendencies—i.e., those with less favourable Phillips curves—do not have more inflation, but more unemployment.

This theory has considerable virtues. It is consistent with the observed persistence of inter-regional wage differentials within a monetary union, while providing an explanation for the fact that wage differentials do not increase without limit. It also provides an explanation for the fact that prosperity varies as between different regions. Specifically, it predicts that unemployment will be lowest in those areas where Phillips curves are most favourable, as can be seen from an inspection of Figure 1. Except in so far as there are systematic differences in such factors as turnover rates which lead to different levels of frictional unemployment, unfavourable Phillips curves will be associated with strong wage-push pressures.

The difficulty with this theory is that it provides no reason for expecting the peripheral regions to be the ones with the highest unemployment, since the theory does not offer a rationale for supposing that the peripheral regions will be prone to suffer more serious wage-push pressures than the others. This is a serious shortcoming, because, as mentioned previously, it is generally accepted that the peripheral regions do tend to suffer higher unemployment.

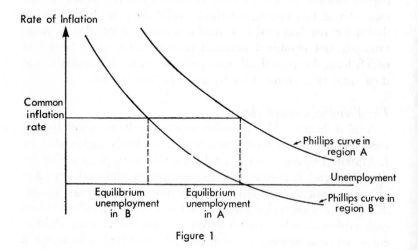

Figure 1

The Parkin theory

The Fleming/Corden theory has been criticised by Professor Parkin[10] in the course of a defence of European monetary union. Parkin's criticism is based on the thesis that the rate of inflation is not a function of the rate of unemployment alone, but that the Phillips curve is shifted vertically upward by the expected rate of inflation. If expectations of inflation are determined by an adaptive expectations mechanism, this implies that any gains from being able to hold unemployment at a level other than its 'natural level' are inherently transitory. Once inflationary expectations have been equalised throughout a monetary union (as they would be by virtue of the common rate of inflation), the separate Phillips curves portrayed in Figure 1 will, *ceteris paribus*, coincide.

There is by now substantial evidence that inflationary expectations do influence the determination of the actual inflation rate, and that expectations are determined in large part adaptively, although there still remains doubt as to whether the coefficient on the expected rate of inflation in the (reduced form) price change equation is unitary, especially for modest rates of inflation.[11] And it is only with a unitary coefficient, as Fleming[12] emphasised, that the Fleming/Corden theory is qualitatively destroyed. Even in the extreme case it can still be argued, as Laidler[13] has in effect done, that the process of adjustment of expectations is sufficiently slow so as to leave exchange rate flexibility a real role in easing adjustments to structural shifts in demand or supply; but the spectre of regions permanently, let alone progressively, pricing themselves into a depressed state would seem to be banished by this theory. Indeed, the very strength of the claims made casts doubt upon the theory, for if regional Phillips curves necessarily coincided in long-run equilibrium it would be impossible to explain the persistence of regional problems. Parkin's reply to this is to claim that regional problems are caused by real, structural factors, rather than monetary ones; but this claim is not accompanied by an analysis of what these factors are and how they lead to persistent depression in peripheral regions.

The Johnson theory

Professor Johnson has offered an embryonic theory intended to account for this.[14] It attributes the higher rate of unemployment typically found in the peripheral regions to consumption and production possibilities. Leisure is an attractive use of time in peripheral areas because consumption possibilities provided by money are limited, and the low level of productivity leads to a low opportunity cost of leisure.

This theory was advanced in the specific context of explaining the high unemployment rate in the Canadian maritime provinces. If it were correct one would expect to find similarly high unemployment rates in other areas where structural problems are similar. Presumably these would include the other remote communities that border the North Atlantic. Average unemployment rates for such areas over the years 1968–71 are as follows:[15]

Canada (Atlantic Provinces)	7.8 per cent
Iceland	1.5 per cent
Ireland	6.9 per cent

Northern Ireland   7.2 per cent
Northern Norway (1968–70 average) 1.8 per cent
Scotland   4.5 per cent

Perhaps it is coincidental that the area with an independent monetary policy shows the lowest unemployment rate, rivalled only by the area where the peripheral region is largest relative to the rest of its monetary union. However, the differences are striking and at least suggest that the level of unemployment in peripheral areas may be related to the size of the monetary area of which they are a part.

More generally, the theory predicts a negative relationship between the level of unemployment and the (real) wage rate in different areas. (This prediction is counter to that which is suggested by the Fleming/Corden theory, in so far as the latter regards the key difference between regions as being the strength of local cost-push forces. For, if this was the only difference between regions, equilibrium would require that both unemployment and relative wages be high in areas with strong cost-push pressures.) It is therefore of interest to examine whether the inter-regional association between unemployment and wages within existing monetary areas is inverse or positive. A number of regressions were run to examine this question, with conflicting results. In the United States the relationship appears to be positive and significant; in Canada it is negative but insignificant (but it becomes significant if British Columbia, an area of strong seasonal fluctuations in highly-paying industries, is omitted); in the United Kingdom it is negative and significant; in France it is positive but insignificant; in Germany it is negative but generally insignificant. (These results are described in somewhat more detail in the Appendix.) These results are not consistent with the Johnson theory. (Neither do they confirm the Fleming/Corden theory; but it is possible that inter-regional productivity differentials mask the effects of variations in cost-push pressures.)

Alternative explanations

One alternative explanation of the fact that unemployment tends to be highest in the peripheral regions of monetary unions might be based upon the type of demonstration effect that was postulated, in an extreme form, by Professor Pearce. In determining wage demands and the vigour with which they are pursued, labour is influenced by the position of its reference groups. In the low-productivity areas labour pursues wage *increases* more aggressively precisely because of a consciousness that wage *levels* are lower. The result is that the lower productivity is reflected not only in lower wages but also in higher unemployment.[16]

A second explanation might be cast in terms of the existence of significant fiscal transfers between the regions of a monetarily-integrated area. Fiscal transfers to areas of high unemployment imply that the full costs of an aggressive pursuit of increased wages are not borne by the inhabitants of the region concerned. Or, to translate this into Johnson's terminology, the existence of fiscal transfers to the unemployed serves to reduce the opportunity cost of leisure.

A formal model

The theory developed in the course of the preceding discussions can be assembled in a formal model. Consider the ith region of the Community and assume that it is sufficiently small to be unable to influence the trend rate of inflation, p, of the Community. If one abstracts from cyclical effects one can assume p to be constant and equal to the trend rate of wage increase (w_c) minus the trend growth of productivity (q_c) of the Community. The price level P is assumed to be common to the whole Community by virtue of the existence of a common market. (Capital letters are being used to denote levels, and the corresponding lower-case letters to denote proportionate time rates of change.) Expectations are assumed to be adaptive, so that in equilibrium p^e, the expected rate of inflation, is equal to p.

The ith region is postulated to have an exogenous growth rate of productivity (q_i) and a Phillips curve which incorporates both the demonstration effect of relative wages and the expected rate of inflation with a coefficient a anywhere between zero and unity:

$$(1) \quad w_i = f_i \left(U_i, W_i/W_c \right) + a\, p^e, f_{11} \leqq 0, f_{12} < 0, a\, \varepsilon\, [0, 1],$$

where U_i = unemployment in region i. Assuming the pursuit of a constant-employment policy in the Community as a whole, the equilibrium level of regional unemployment may be expected to depend positively on the level of unit labour costs, W/Q, in the region relative to that in the Community as a whole. However, because changes in regional employment depend on decisions regarding the location of industry rather than simply on fully utilising the existing productive capacity of the region, unemployment will generally adapt to its equilibrium level only slowly. One therefore postulates:

$$(2) \quad \dot{U}_i = \beta \left[U \left(\frac{W_i Q_c}{W_c Q_i} \right) - U_i \right], \quad U^i > O.$$

Unless they are the beneficiaries of an abnormally favourable resource base, peripheral regions are characterised by sub-normal productivity, i.e., by $Q_i/Q_c < 1$.

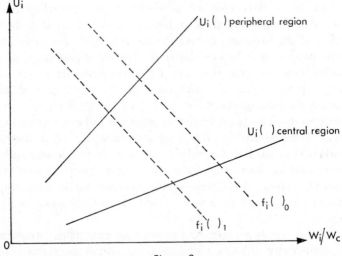

Figure 2

The equilibrium properties of this model may be examined in terms of Figure 2. The equilibrium unemployment level in equation (2) is represented by a curve $U_i (\quad)$ which is positively sloping, because higher relative wages ultimately raise the region's unemployment, and is higher the lower the relative productivity of the region, so that it tends to be high in peripheral regions. When relative wages are in equilibrium the level of unemployment will by definition be constant (except in so far as there is any gradual change due to structural change), which implies, by (2),

$$w_i - q_i = w_c - q_c.$$

Of course, $w_c - q_c = p = p^e$, so substitution into (1) yields

$$(3) \qquad q_i + (1 - a) p = f_i (U_i, W_i/W_c).$$

This equation can be depicted by a downward-sloping curve, labelled $f_i(\ )$. The height of $f_i(\ )$ is determined by the left-hand side of (3): i.e., an increase in regional productivity growth, or a decrease in the extent to which price expectations influence wage increases, will tend to reduce the height of $f_i(\ )$ from, say, a position like $f_i(\ )_0$ to $f_i(\ )_1$. The slope of the curve is determined by the extent to which high relative wages are a substitute for high unemployment in restraining wage growth to the equilibrium rate: $f_i(\ )$ would be horizontal if relative wages have no such effect. Equilibrium regional unemployment and relative wages are given by the intersection of the relevant $U_i(\ )$ and $f_i(\ )$ functions. (This equilibrium will change over time if $q_i \neq q_c$.)

The effects of formation of a monetary union can be examined by considering the displacement of the $f_i(\ )$ function in Figure 2, as is done in Figure 3. The $f_i(\ )$ function will steepen, on account of the increased importance of wage emulation in determining wage pressures, presumably pivoted on its intersection with the $U(\ )$ function of the central region, since the central region will not be subjected to an increased demonstration effect from more affluent neighbours. Figure 3 shows the full phase diagram, and therefore enables one to trace the gradual movement of the peripheral region from its initial equilibrium at I to its new equilibrium, characterised by higher wages and unemployment, at point II.

Consider the consistency of this model with the apparent facts that were adduced (admittedly with no great certainty) in earlier sections of this paper.

(i) 'Wage rates vary between regions.' Nothing in the model requires equilibrium at the same W_i/W_c for all i.

(ii) 'The inter-regional variation of wage rates is reduced by formation of a monetary union.' The model explains this in terms of the influence of joining a monetary union in introducing, or strengthening the effect of, W_i/W_c in the $f_i(\quad)$ function, which tilts, or steepens, $f_i(\quad)$, as shown in Figure 3.

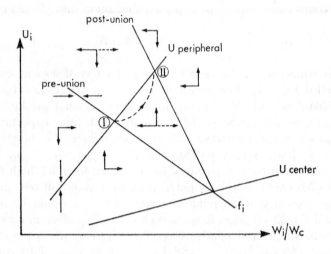

Figure 3

(iii) 'Unemployment is higher in peripheral (low productivity) regions.' Given that the $f_i(\quad)$ function is independent of the *level* of productivity (and despite the fact that it depends on the *growth* of productivity), this follows immediately from Figure 2.

(iv) 'There is no systematic association between relative wages and unemployment across regions.' When the $f_i(\quad)$ functions are negatively sloping, the distribution of regional equilibria need display no correlation: consider the four intersections shown in Figure 2.

(v) 'Unemployment in a low-productivity region rises by its being part of a monetary union.' This again follows from the tilting, or steepening, of the $f_i(\quad)$ function, as shown in Figure 3. Note that it remains true even in the Parkinian case of $a = 1$; the only effect of the latter is to make the regional unemployment rates, and relative wage rates, independent of the rate of inflation in the Community as a whole.

Implications

The preceding section presented a comprehensive model utilising the insights of the various authors whose writings have been considered, the predictions of which are consistent with the apparent facts. It remains to consider what this model implies regarding the advisability of a peripheral, low-productivity region entering a monetary union.

Within the monetary union the region will lose its monetary independence and be obliged to accept the common rate of inflation. This will directly influence the level of unemployment in the long run only if expectations are not fully reflected in inflationary pressures.

The second effect will be that of adding higher-paid populations to the reference group taken into account in the formulation and pursuit of wage claims. This will tend to lead to an increase in the level of wages in the region, but at the cost of a permanent rise in the level of unemployment. The region's disadvantage will be manifested to a greater degree in above-average unemployment and to a lesser degree than before in below-average wages. This will be disadvantageous to the Community as a whole, since output in the peripheral region will fall and there will not be a symmetrical rise in output in the high-productivity regions at the centre if demand management policy is dominated by a concern to avoid overheating in the central regions. The peripheral region will, however, experience a terms-of-trade gain that will partially (but probably only partially) compensate it for its output loss.

However, there may also be a third effect arising from the fiscal transfers that generally accompany monetary union.[17] Such transfers, when well designed, enable a low-productivity region to gain some of the benefits of a devaluation so far as unit labour costs are concerned, without the accompanying terms of trade losses. A system of fiscal transfers that partially compensated for productivity differentials, in conjunction with a demonstration effect as discussed in the previous paragraph, might leave the peripheral areas either better off or worse off than before monetary union. It is therefore the central regions rather than the peripheral ones that seem likely to bear the major costs.

Conclusion

An assessment of the advisability of European monetary integration depends on a weighing of three probable effects. The first concerns the efficiency advantages of monetary union in terms of the greater ease in effecting transactions, the absence of exchange risk, the access to a wider capital market, the greater possibility of stabilising monetary conditions when flows of short-term capital are equilibrating rather than disequilibrating, and so on. The second is the loss of output in the lower productivity regions. The third is the greater equality in the inter-regional distribution of income.

Most economists who have written on this subject have declared it obvious that such an assessment yields an overwhelming case either for or against monetary union. I can only confess that the evidence at present in hand does not seem to me to justify their dogmatism, and I continue to find a cautious strategy for approaching European monetary integration, such as that sketched in Magnifico and Williamson[18] attractive. The attitude there adopted was that partial monetary integration, which would safeguard the ability to neutralise differential cost changes by parity changes, could safely and advantageously be adopted in the short run,[19] but that full monetary union involving the permanent freezing of exchange rates should await evidence that this would not lead to intolerable regional problems, rather than being forced by some arbitrary target date. The necessary evidence is not yet in, but it is hoped that the present paper will contribute to the search for it.

APPENDIX

The Inter-Regional Association of Unemployment and Wages

A number of simple linear regressions of the form of $U = a + bW$ were run in order to examine whether the inter-regional association between unemployment and relative wages is typically positive (as implied by the Fleming/Corden model) or negative (as implied by the Johnson model). A summary of the results obtained is given in this Appendix.

United States

A weak positive relationship was found in a regression covering the 50 states (and the District of Columbia). The typical equation was :

$$U = 0.50 + 0.13 \text{ W} \qquad \bar{R}^2 = 0.19$$
$$(3.57)$$

where the figure in parenthesis is the t-ratio, U is the unemployment percentage in 1970, and W is the average hourly earnings of production workers on manufacturing payrolls in 1970. Variants of the reported equation utilised end-year data, data for other years, and data for specific industries. The results of these variants were generally consistent with the reported equation, although 5 of the 7 coefficients for individual industries were insignificant.

The finding of a positive relationship between unemployment and wages in the United States is consistent with findings of R. E. Hall, 'Why is the Unemployment Rate so High at Full Employment?', *Brookings Papers on Economic Activity*, 1970(3), p. 380, and A. Holen and S. A. Horowitz, 'The Effect of Unemployment Insurance Laws and Administration on Unemployment Rates', unpublished, 1973, p. 10a.

Data sources :

  Employment and Earnings, U S Department of Labor, various issues.

E

Handbook of Labor Statistics 1971, U S Department of Labor.
Manpower Report of the President, March 1972.

Canada

The typical equation for 9 provinces of Canada was :

$$U = 0.12 - 0.18 \text{ W} \qquad \bar{R}^2 = 0.00$$
$$(0.97)$$

where W is an annual average of hourly earnings of hourly-rated
wage earners in manufacturing in 1970. Variants of the equation
were tried for an industrial composite using weekly earnings, for
other years, for 10 provinces and for 5 regions, with similar results.
In specific industries 6 of the 8 regressions were insignificant; both
significant coefficients were negative.

When British Columbia was omitted from the data the typical
equation became :

$$U = 0.21 - 0.52 \text{ W} \qquad \bar{R}^2 = 0.40$$
$$(2.4)$$

Different years gave significant coefficients; other variations all
gave negative coefficients, but only 6 out of 12 were significant.
Data sources :

Employment, Earnings and Hours, February, July 1972.
Man-hours and Hourly Earnings, various issues.
Bank of Canada Review, March 1973.

United Kingdom

The typical equation for 11 regions of the United Kingdom
was :

$$U = 0.24 - 0.63 \text{ W} \qquad \bar{R}^2 = 0.24$$
$$(2.0)$$

where W is average weekly earnings of manual men in all industries and services in April 1971. Variants of the equation were run
for non-manual men, all men, and hourly earnings; 2 of the 6
coefficients were insignificant. Industry regressions yielded 8 negative and 4 positive coefficients, none of which were significant.
Data sources :

Department of Employment Gazette, November 1971, January,
February 1972.

Digest of Statistics, Northern Ireland, March 1973.
Monthly Bulletin of Statistics, United Nations, June 1972.

France

The typical equation for 21 regions of France was:

$$U = 0.15 + 0.11 \ W \qquad \bar{R}^2 = 0.00$$
$$(0.81)$$

where W = average annual earnings of wage earners in 1968.
Seven variants all showed positive but insignificant coefficients.
Data sources: *Collections de l'Insée,* December 1971.

Germany

The typical equation for 8 landern of Germany was:

$$U = 0.12 - 0.97 \ W \qquad \bar{R}^2 = 0.00$$
$$(0.38)$$

where W = gross hourly earnings of industrial workers in 1970.
Variants covered other years and other groups of employees. All
coefficients were negative, but the only significant results were
registered for sales and technical staff.
Data sources:
Statistisches Jahrbuch für die Bundesrepublik Deutschland,
1970–72. Tables VIII.2, VIII.7, XII.3.

Regional Policy in the European Community

PAUL ROMUS

Introduction

CONCERN with regions is a relatively recent feature in the economic policy of states; even more so in that of international institutions.

At national level the first legislation in connection with regional matters dates from 1934 in the United Kingdom. At international level it was only in 1952 with the creation of the European Coal and Steel Community and in 1958 with that of the European Economic Community that there was provision for regional policy affecting several States.

This does not mean that regional problems did not appear well before the application of regional policies. To take one example within the European Community, it is generally accepted that problems affecting the Italian Mezzogiorno go back to the time of Italian unification a century ago. Generally speaking one may say that the European nations are made up of regions which have known a very varied fate in the past without the public authorities responsible making any special effort to rectify the varying degrees of fortune which those regions have experienced.

If therefore a regional dimension in the economic and regional policies is a relatively new factor, it is the same novelty which explains the internal character of these policies, their frequent experimental character and doubtless the relatively unsatisfactory results which they have achieved. Additionally while regional policy is part of economic policy it is also equally political and this means that pressures exist which are not always dictated by economic motives. What then is one to say of a regional policy which aspires to be European but in which States are emphatic that they must be principally if not solely responsible for conditions in their regions and object to the Commission having more than subsidiary powers compared to those which they themselves possess? One is here in the presence of ambiguity with regard to 'European regional policy'; that is in so far as this may be conceived as other than a simple complement to State action. Nevertheless it is with this European regional policy that the following reflections are concerned. That they reflect what exists must be my excuse. They can indeed only reflect what is contained in the Treaties establishing the European Communities. We shall deal successively with the following points: regional imbalances, regional policies considered nationally, European regional policy since it started and lastly the outlook for a new European regional policy.

Regional Imbalances

Since the existence of regional imbalances or differences and the desire to reduce or to remove them lies at the origin of all regional policy it is logical to start with this aspect of the problem. Taking the three criteria of population, employment and income, there are two large-scale regional groups within the European Community which may be geographically described as inner and outer.

On the one hand there is a wide area between approximately the Pennine Chain and the Rhine Valley which covers rather less than one-third of the territory of the Community but which, having a population of approximately 130 millions, comprises half its total population. With a relative density of 300 inhabitants per square kilometre this regional grouping is by far the most populated within the Community. It is the main recipient of the currents of migration coming from other regions of the Community. This regional grouping is proportionately little dependent on agriculture although it is agriculturally speaking the most productive area of the Community. It contains the greater part of the industries and services of the Community and six of the nine capitals of Member States. It has the highest income per head of population in the Community.

On the other hand there is within the Community a wide area which may be described as peripheral, meaning that it lies on the outer frontiers and which has in fact all that is not comprised within the central region described above. Here we have to deal with a very wide regional area covering almost two-thirds of the surface area of the Community including half its total population with a relative density of 120 inhabitants per square kilometre. Considered as a whole this area experiences a population loss through emigration either towards third countries or towards the central area of the Community. Regions which lose most through emigration are above all the Mezzogiorno, Ireland and Scotland. Included within this regional grouping are those regions which are most dependent on agriculture and, proportionately, with less industry and fewer service activities. Its income per head of population is the lowest within the Community.

Looking at the matter as a whole there are therefore substantial differences between the level of population, the level of activity and the level of development within the Community. If one goes to the regions themselves one will note still greater differences which in income terms may be at the level of one to five as between the least and the most developed regions of the Community. This synthesis is necessarily a simplification of regional structures and differences. One must add certain clarifications, as to the origin of these differences with reference to certain exceptions in the general picture and the way matters have evolved.

It may be noted that regional differences as between the central and peripheral areas are only accidentally a consequence of geography. In fact the main resources which led to the industrial revolution are to be found in the central regions. It was also relatively more easy to develop this area on account of its physical characteristics and the existence of major rivers and estuaries which helped to build the largest harbours in the world. By comparison, the peripheral regions had far fewer resources and their physical features made it much more difficult to develop their territory.

There are however some notable exceptions to this synthesis. It is a fact that not all the central regions are prosperous and neither are all the peripheral regions impoverished. It is also a fact that the central regions contain those areas which were in the front line of economic progress in the nineteenth century and are now experiencing a decline in their economy. Contrariwise the peripheral regions are not all under-developed because of their dependence on agriculture. For instance, Denmark is one of the most advanced countries of the Community and there are notable exceptions in several regions of Great Britain.

So far as statistics permit generally speaking it is possible to follow the evolution of regions within the European Community in the light of their population, of employment and of income, over the last ten to twenty years. In this connection one may note considerable diversity in regional evolution. Taken all in all however the difference in the respective levels of each region have not experienced fundamental change. Doubtless certain of the less prosperous regions have experienced a rate of growth higher than the Community average but even this has not been enough to ensure any significant closing of the gap in development levels. On the other hand the most developed regions of the Community have continued to attract both population and economic activity to a greater degree than the less prosperous regions.

The continuation and indeed in certain cases the increase in regional imbalances threaten in many ways to impede progress towards Economic and Monetary Union; for example, because of their inflationary results. Despite the achievements, which in certain instances are by no means negligible, of Member States and European institutions in reducing the gaps between development levels of regions in the Community, there must be action of a far more substantial character if balanced regional development is to be achieved.

National Regional Policies

In order to understand European regional policy it is indispensable to have knowledge of regional policies conducted by the Member States of the Community. We may consider these policies from the angle of aims, of regions concerned, of means available and of results. Generally speaking national regional policies aim to achieve a more balanced distribution of the population and of economic activity and have the following targets :

1. Development of predominantly agricultural regions which suffer from unemployment, under-employment, emigration and low incomes;

2. The reconversion of long established industrial regions

which are at present experiencing unemployment, emigration and fall in income;

3. The development of regions suffering from unemployment for other reasons than those indicated above;

4. The development of frontier regions which are either on the borders of the Community and from this fact are at a disadvantage because of their proximity to certain third countries, or which are inside the Community and are penalised by imbalances which still exist between Member States;

5. Preventive measures to limit concentration in certain urban areas and in some instances decentralisation from those areas;

6. Development of the tertiary (services) sector in certain urban areas of medium size.

The geographical area affected by national regional policies covers about half the surface area of the Community and one-third of its population (eighty millions). If one also takes account of the area affected by preventive measures in force in the regions of London, Paris and Amsterdam, 60 per cent of the territory and 43 per cent of the population of the Community are affected by these policies. While one would expect that regional policies should normally deal with exceptional situations it is to be noted that in practice they are dealing with a very large and important proportion of the Community. On the other hand it is to be noted that most States have laid down a system of priorities in degrees of aid in accordance with the seriousness of regional problems or in the light of development possibilities in certain centres.

The means employed by national regional policies may be classified as preventive measures and development measures. Preventive measures are intended to discourage fresh investment in certain major urban areas and indeed to encourage undertakings to transfer out of those centres into other areas. Control of the location of economic activity is mainly to be found in force in London and Paris. Development measures are intended to encourage the creation, the extension or the modernisation of undertakings in 'development areas'. They take the form of financial aid or tax privileges to undertakings, which may vary between 10 and 60 per cent of the total cost of the overall investment concerned. These aids cover a very wide field of encouragement for investment: premiums on, or subsidies for, capital, participations in the capital of undertakings, loans at a reduced rate of interest, interest rebates on loans granted to undertakings, various tax remissions, the sale or renting of industrial buildings, premiums on employment, financing certain social security payments, payment of expenses for professional training.

The results of national regional policy are hard to assess and to compare and are too often published in a fragmentary manner. An assessment of results of these policies in the light of regional trends in population, employment and income leaves the impression that they have not succeeded in closing the gap in imbalances between regions.

European Regional Policies since they originated

European regional policy has a place and a justification in the Treaties establishing the European Communities. The aims of this policy are there defined in a relatively summary manner but above all are concerned with the basic notion of balance. In the context of the European Coal and Steel Community the aim has been to maintain employment, to avoid basic difficulties and to aid production to adapt to new conditions. These aims have taken precise form in reconversion measures in coal producing, mining or steel producing regions in decline.

In the context of the E E C the aim has been to promote harmonised development within the Community, that is to say, a comprehensive policy affecting each region of Community territory and more especially a reduction in the gap between the various regions by raising levels in the least prosperous of these regions. The powers of the European Communities apply to the following fields : co-ordination of national regional aid, means for financing regions, regional studies. It should be emphasised that whatever their scope, the powers of the European Communities are complementary or subsidiary to those exercised by Member States.

CO-ORDINATION OF REGIONAL AID

The co-ordination of regional aid is the first function of the European Communities in connection with regional policy. This co-ordination derives directly from the Treaty of Rome which forbids aid in the light of the principle of free competition to be observed. There is however an important exception which allows for aid to regions in so far as this aid may contribute to solving regional problems, characteristics of which may be an abnormally low level of living or serious under-employment. Given the difficulty of interpreting these criteria on a European scale, the Commission has been obliged to authorise numerous national rules of regional aid which by the nature of things have become competitive and are the source of continual bargaining by Member States. The Commission also decided as from 1 January 1972 to co-ordinate the various national rules for regional aid. This co-ordination must be progressive; it is not applied from the start to the whole territory of the Community but only to the 'central area' of the Community, defined as equivalent to the territory of the Community excluding the following regions:

1. In France: all Western France;
2. In Italy: the Mezzogiorno;
3. In Germany: the Eastern frontiers area (Zonenrandgebiete);
4. In the United Kingdom: North and West;
5. In Ireland: the whole territory;
6. In Denmark: the North West and South East (special development regions).

All other regions, except North and West of the United Kingdom, have been declared peripheral. Within the 'central area' a ceiling has been fixed which is a cumulative equivalent to all subsidies by way of regional aid. The Member States are not authorised to exceed this ceiling. This co-ordination implies the possibility of comparing regional aid between one State and another which would involve suppressing certain aids which cannot be quantified.

FINANCIAL MEANS AVAILABLE

The second field of Community activity concerns the financial mechanisms which may be used for regional development. These are five in number and have clearly defined objectives.

1. The first financial mechanism to which the European Communities have had recourse in their history has taken the form of funds actually owned by the High Authority of the European Coal and Steel Community. These have allowed for loans to be granted to any undertaking located within regions where the re-employment of labour made redundant in the coal

and steel industry raises regional problems. To date these loans have contributed directly and indirectly to the creation of some 100,000 new jobs.

2. The European Investment Bank may be considered as a regional development bank since its task is to finance projects in less prosperous regions and in reconversion regions, or projects which are jointly undertaken by several Member States. From 1958 to 1972 the Bank granted loans totalling 2.5 milliards of units of account, of which 75 per cent were for projects located in the less prosperous regions.

3. The Guidance Section of the EAGGF (European Agricultural Guidance and Guarantee Fund) may give subsidies for restructuring agricultural undertakings either in sectors concerned with production or in those marketing agricultural products. Funds expended to date total 150 millions of units of account.

4. Professional retraining (taking the various forms of indemnifying workers waiting for new jobs, of rehousing and of expenses for professional retraining) is supported by subsidies deriving either from the former European Coal and Steel Community Fund or from the European Social Fund. These subsidies represent half the cost of expenses incurred, the other half being paid by the Member State concerned. The European Social Fund has, since it started, distributed 265 millions of units of account.

5. Lastly the European Communities have resources available for financing regional studies covering numerous aspects of regional problems with which the Community is faced.

CONCLUSIONS

Since 1952 in the context of the European Coal and Steel Community and 1958 with regard to the E E C, European institutions have been positively active on behalf of regional development. In certain cases they even showed the way for Member States in leading them to introduce provisions into their national laws which did not previously exist and in connection with certain aspects of regional policy.

However the European Executives (the High Authority and the Commission until 1968 and the Commission solely since that time) as guardians of the European Treaties have been aware that the total of the measures adopted do not make for a European regional policy.

Various proposals have been made over the years either by the Commission or by the European Parliament with a view to a wider notion of regional development and to undertaking action on a wider scale. These proposals derive support in particular from the fact that regional imbalances have hardly disappeared at all since the creation of the Common Market. But up until 1972 they encountered reserves from Member States in principle with regard to giving powers to the Commission and additional funds for regional development.

The Outlook for a New European Regional Policy

It would appear that a turning point was reached, with the Conference of Heads of State or of Government held in Paris in October 1972, with regard to European construction and, in particular, with regard to regional policy. The final communique of that Conference accepted that a high priority should be given within the Community to the aim of correcting the structural and regional imbalances which might affect the realisation of Economic and Monetary Union. It may logically be thought that European regional policy will from now on go forward more rapidly than beforehand.

In concrete terms the Paris Conference gave new mandates to European institutions both with regard to organisation and to scope and concerning finance for regional development and the co-ordination of national regional policies.

FINANCE FOR REGIONAL DEVELOPMENT

The new mechanism proposed for financing regional development is a European Fund for Regional Development. According to the present proposals of the Commission this Fund should:

1. Be a complement and not a substitute to action by States. It is understood thereby that it should allow for action beyond that which is taken by Member States;

2. Act with substantial flexibility which means that it should be able to deal with very varied regional situations;

3. Participate in investment in so far as this lies within the framework of regional development programmes.

The Fund, which will start work at the beginning of 1974,

should receive a credit of 2.25 milliards of units of account, of which 500 millions u.a. will form part of the Community's budget for 1974, 750 millions u.a. for 1975 and 1 milliard u.a. for 1976. Regions qualified to receive contributions from the Fund should be selected from those in receipt of national regional aid and where the gross domestic product is lower than the Community average. Furthermore they should include regions characterised either by agricultural preponderance or by industrial change or by structural under-employment.

Finance from the Fund should be accorded :

1. Either to industry or to service activity in receipt of national regional aid; but the amount of the contribution should not be more than 15 per cent of the individual investment and 50 per cent of the quantity of national regional aid;

2. Or to infrastructure undertaken by public authorities. Here the contribution should not exceed 30 per cent of the investment and might take the form of an interest rebate of 3 per cent on the loans of the European Investment Bank.

Contributions from the Fund are to be fixed in the light of the relative degree of regional imbalances and of its impact on employment.

Investment seeking contributions from the Fund should already form part of regional development programmes. It will be notified by Member States to the Commission and it should comply with principles that have been laid down.

Requests for contributions from the Fund should be sent by States to the Commission which will decide in each individual case on the degree of participation or comprehensively in the case of certain amounts required. The Commission will make payment to States.

Lastly one part of the resources of the Fund should be used to promote or to undertake regional studies.

Since these proposals were made in 1973, a European Regional Development Fund has been created and entered into force in 1975 with rules slightly different to those abovementioned. The principal difference is the volume of the Fund, now fixed at 1,300 million units of account.

CO-ORDINATING NATIONAL REGIONAL POLICIES

Parallel with the establishment of the Fund it is proposed to create a Committee on Regional Policy. This will be an institution both of the Commission and of the Council and its members will represent both Member States and the Commission. This Committee will be called upon to promote the co-ordination of regional policies of Member States in the widest sense since its tasks will include the study of aims and means of regional policy, of regional trends within the Community, of regional programmes, of finance available for regional policy and its impact, of rules applying to regional aid, of preventive measures in regions of high concentration and of better information for public and private investors. It should be noted that the Committee may seek the opinions of regional organisations and of trade unions and professional organisations.

Ireland in the Enlarged EEC:
Economic Consequences and Prospects [1]

DERMOT McALEESE

Introduction

T H E results of the May 1972 referendum on Irish entry into
the E E C were decisive to a virtually unprecedented degree. A
high percentage poll and a low proportion of spoilt votes were
accompanied by a massive 83 per cent majority in favour of
amending the Constitution to permit E E C entry. The spatial
distribution of the votes indicated a remarkable consensus
throughout the country. All constituencies, without exception,
returned a majority 'YES' vote; only two constituencies had
majorities of less than 75 per cent; and the lowest majority in
favour (recorded in South-West Dublin) amounted to 73 per
cent.[2] This apparent unanimity of view between all sections of
the population, urban and rural, no less than the size of the
overall majority, took even the most optimistic supporters of
E E C entry by surprise.

Doubtless there were many complex factors, political, social
and economic, which motivated people to vote in such large
numbers in favour of entry. Five considerations could, I think,
be singled out as being of particular importance.

First, high growth rates (by past Irish standards) of G N P
and exports during the sixties, allied with a continuing influx of
foreign investment and the progressive reduction of import
restrictions under the terms of the Anglo-Irish Free Trade Area
Agreement, had instilled confidence in Ireland's capacity to
maintain economic growth, to withstand foreign competition on
the home market and to increase its share of foreign markets—
in a word, to hold its own in a highly competitive European
environment.

Second, E E C entry offered the prospect of a lessened degree
of economic dependence on the United Kingdom. Already some

diversification of market outlets for manufactured exports had occurred during the sixties and membership of the Community was seen as a way of consolidating this trend. In the case of agricultural exports, however, Ireland was still overwhelmingly dependent on the British market, the terms of access to which were mainly determined by the United Kingdom Government. Participation in the Common Agricultural Policy held out the promise of higher prices and more secure outlets in the British market, as well as of guaranteed access to the European market.

Third, the results of the negotiations between the E E C and the non-applicant European Free Trade Area countries, together with the limited concessions offered to New Zealand in the United Kingdom market up to 1978, fortified the widespread belief that little consideration for Ireland's agricultural export needs could be expected if the country remained outside the Community—our small size, relative poverty and historic 'special position' in the British market notwithstanding.

Fourth, there were the terms of entry themselves. In addition to providing immediate participation in the C A P, with its attendant benefits to the Irish farmer and Exchequer, a number of special concessions were made to facilitate entry. On the industrial side, an extended transitional period was granted in respect of motor vehicle imports. On the delicate issue of fisheries, Ireland retained exclusive fishing rights within a six-mile limit and partial protection in the six to twelve mile zone, for ten years, after which the matter would be renegotiated.[3] In addition to these other minor concessions, a Special Protocol was negotiated which involved a commitment by the E E C to take particular account of Ireland's economic problems. In practice, this meant that Ireland could continue to operate its grant scheme for new enterprises, could honour its commitments already undertaken in respect of export tax reliefs and also could continue to grant these reliefs to new firms manufacturing for export up to 1990. It was also accepted that, should modification of the investment incentive scheme be required, any revised incentive scheme would have to be equally effective in promoting industrial development.

The terms of entry, therefore, were such as to offer reassurances regarding the Community's flexibility of response to particular national needs and the ability of the Irish government to obtain a hearing in Brussels for what these needs were. More-over, membership of the E E C on these conditions offered a number of immediate short-run gains, and short-run guarantees against economic loss, against which the possibilities of long-run loss, stressed by some opponents to entry, appeared exceedingly remote and intangible. In this respect, Ireland's position was exactly opposite that of the United Kingdom, whose fully predict-able and concrete short-term economic losses had to be weighed against speculative 'dynamic' long-term economic gains.

A final, and purely political, factor was the enthusiastic sup-port given to E E C entry by both major Irish political parties. This aspect of the referendum is heavily emphasised by Garvin and Parker who interpret the results as being as much an indica-tion of the strength of party loyalty in Ireland as of popular commitment to E E C entry.[4] While the authors probably over-state their case, voters must undoubtedly have been impressed by the common position adopted by the two parties on an issue of such immense national importance. The electorate must also have been impressed by the fact, much stressed by Dr Garret Fitz-Gerald, that the political power structure of the E E C is heavily biased in favour of small nations. Ireland's viewpoint on Com-munity issues would therefore carry a weight well in excess of its proportion of the E E C's population or G N P. It must also be remembered that Ireland's choice, in sharp contrast with that of the United Kingdom, was not one between maintaining the *status quo* and entering the E E C. Rather the choice was between entering the E E C alongside the United Kingdom and staying out of the E E C while our major trading partner, the United Kingdom, went in. Either way, a fairly radical change in our environment was going to be required.

Thus, Ireland became, as and from 1 January 1973, a full member of the enlarged E E C. The main objective of this paper is to spell out, and where possible to quantify, the economic implications of this fact.[5] The industrial sector is examined first, after which the effects of E E C membership on the agricultural sector are investigated. Results are summarised and conclusions drawn in the final section of the paper.

Industry and Foreign Investment

THE VIABILITY OF IRISH INDUSTRY

'If on 1 January, 1973 Ireland were to have plunged head-
long into the Common Market and its firms put on a strictly
even footing with competitors in other countries, it is unlikely
that the Irish economy could effectively have withstood the
shock: the gains for agriculture could not have made up for
the disadvantages suffered by manufacturing industry. Hence the
vital nature of the transition period into which Ireland has now
entered prior to her full entry into Common Market competitive
conditions.'[6]

This unflattering assessment of Irish industry's current position
might be contested, not least by those who supported Ireland's
decision to apply for entry way back in 1961! The Examiners'
comments none the less serve as a convenient starting point for
this section. Although opinions might differ as to Irish industry's
capacity to meet foreign competition, there is no disagreement
over the fact that, up to a short time ago, most Irish industrial
establishments were effectively insulated from any such poten-
tially unpleasant experience. The level of the average effective
tariff in Irish manufacturing industry was estimated at about 80
per cent in 1966, which placed Irish industry as one of the most
heavily protected in Western Europe.[7]

On a more optimistic note, however, account must be taken
of two features of Ireland's industrial progress during the last
fifteen years which would, at least superficially, suggest the existence of a much more healthy manufacturing sector than the
O E C D Examiners allow.

The first of these is the very rapid growth of Irish manufactured exports during the last two decades. These have increased at an average annual growth rate of more than 19 per
cent in current value terms. Correspondingly, the share of manufactured exports in total merchandise exports has increased from
6 per cent in 1950, to 19 per cent in 1959 and reached the un-
precedently high proportion of 35 per cent in 1971. Recently
published figures show a rise of 33 per cent in the value of manufactured exports during the year 1972 alone.[8]

The second feature is the rapid diversification of market outlets which accompanied this export growth. Thus, during the
last decade alone, the proportion of Ireland's manufactured

TABLE 1

Composition and Geographical Distribution of Ireland's Foreign Trade 1971

		EXPORTS % Distribution by Area of Destination:					IMPORTS % Distribution by Area of Origin:			
SITC DESCRIPTION	Value £m	UK	EEC (6)	Other EFTA	All other Areas	Value £m	UK	EEC (6)	Other EFTA	All other Areas
0. Live Animals and Food	236,85	78.3	4.2	1.1	16.4	82.26	36.0	9.0	1.7	53.3
1. Beverages and Tobacco	14.79	63.5	4.7	0.4	31.4	11.31	13.8	32.7	3.4	50.1
2. Raw Materials	29.66	38.7	33.0	4.4	23.9	40.34	21.0	28.4	8.3	42.3
3. Mineral Fuels & Lubs.	6.26	92.7	1.7	4.9	0.7	68.31	39.2	4.9	0.3	55.6
4. Ani./Veg. Oils and Fats	2.53	72.1	21.3	–	6.6	4.35	13.3	14.3	11.1	59.3
Total Sections 0–4	290.10	73.7	7.3	1.5	17.5	206.58	32.5	8.9	6.7	41.9
5. Chemicals	21.13	43.4	22.9	2.0	31.7	70.40	58.3	27.6	6.7	10.9
6. Manufactured Goods Classified by Material	71.19	72.2	8.0	2.5	17.3	158.27	61.0	17.9	8.7	12.4
7. Mach. & Transport Eq.	32.57	58.0	11.6	3.3	27.1	203.77	51.2	23.8	6.2	18.8
8. Manuf'd Goods n.e.s.	58.88	62.0	14.6	2.6	20.8	65.28	72.9	12.1	3.3	11.7
Total Sections 5–8	183.77	63.1	12.4	2.6	21.9	497.72	58.9	21.0	6.2	13.9
TOTAL Sections 0–9	527.90	65.7	9.8	2.2	22.3	754.91	49.5	16.7	6.2	27.6

Source. Computed from *External Trade Statistics* 1971. Figures in the last row of the Table include trade of the Shannon Free Airport.

exports destined for the United Kingdom market fell from 83 per cent in 1959 to 63 per cent in 1971. At the same time, Ireland's share of total United Kingdom manufactured imports has managed to increase during this period. Thus, Ireland's dependence on the United Kingdom market as an outlet for manufactured exports has been reduced not because of a failure to maintain market shares in Britain, but because of the extraordinarily rapid growth in manufactured exports to areas other than the United Kingdom, in particular to the E E C (Six) and the United States.

The apparent inconsistency between doubts as to the present viability of Irish industry on the one hand and the existence of a healthy manufacturing export sector on the other can be at least partially resolved if account is taken of the 'dualistic' structure of Irish industry. It is now generally accepted that throughout the sixties two types of manufacturing establishment existed in Ireland. The first was the older established firm which exported only a small proportion of its output, was more often than not badly managed, produced an overdiversified range of products and was characterised by low levels of capacity utilisation. The second was the modern enterprise set up under the auspices of the Industrial Development Authority, more often than not foreign-owned, and exporting 75 per cent or more of its total output. It has been fairly clearly established that most of the last fifteen years' export growth, and the attendant diversification of export markets, is attributable to these new grant-aided enterprises. Thus, nearly half of Ireland's manufactured exports in 1970 are estimated to have come from firms which were established since 1959.[9]

The exceptionally rapid increase in manufactured exports over the last few years of course raises the question of whether the dichotomy between older established and newly established firms is as sharply drawn now as it was in the past decade. Certainly the incentives to export are strong. The carrot of complete tax remission on profits earned on exports on one side is combined with the stick of a virtually inevitable domestic market share loss on the other.[10] E E C entry itself can be expected to strengthen the trend towards increased exports at a firm level, both by making competing imports more competitive and by further facilitating the growth of exports.

TABLE 2

Effects of EEC Entry on Irish Manufactured Imports

Area	Imports 1971 £m	Average Nominal Tariff %	Removal of Irish Tariff on Imports £m	Change to Common External Tariff on All Other Areas Imports £m	Discrimination against All Other Areas £m	Removal of Discrimination in favour of UK £m	Total Effect in Irish market (Cols. (3) to (6) inclusive) £m	Percentage Increase in Imports at 1971 prices %
	(1)	(2)	(3)	(4)	(5)	(6)	(7)	(8)
UK	293.21	10.0	+40	0	+8	−33	+15	5
EEC (Six)	104.30	30.0	+36	0	+3	+25	+64	62
Other EFTA	30.88	30.0	+11	0	+1	+8	+20	65
All Other Areas	69.33	30.0	0	+19	−12	0	+7	10
Total	497.72	—	+87	+19	0	0	+106	21

Notes.

1. Data of Col. (1) are obtained from *External Trade Statistics 1971*.
2. Derivation of estimates is explained in the text and Appendix I.
3. Percentage figures in Col. (8) for EEC and Other EFTA differ solely because of rounding errors.

EFFECTS ON IMPORTS

Membership of the enlarged E E C involves, in the case of manufactured imports : (i) the elimination of Irish import restrictions on E E C (Six) products by 1978, in five instalments of 20 per cent beginning April 1973, (ii) the continuation of tariff and quota reductions on imports from the United Kingdom as scheduled under the terms of A I F T A (which implies virtually complete free trade in industrial products with the United Kingdom by 1976), (iii) the removal of the Irish tariff on imports from E F T A and the Associated Territories, plus concessionary tariff rates for imports from Spain, Israel and other countries with which the E E C has special trading arrangements, (iv) the alignment of the Irish tariff to the level of the Common External Tariff on non-member countries other than those mentioned above, and (v) the adoption of the Community's system of generalised preferences for the L D C's, by 1978 or before.

Not all manufactured imports will, of course, be affected by these changes. Special provisions extending the transitional period to 1985 were made in respect of motor vehicle imports. Moreover, certain manufactured products (many types of machinery and transport equipment, for example) which were not subject to either Irish import restrictions or the C E T, will not be affected. Similarly, since most industrial raw materials are permitted duty-free entry under both tariff regimes, the impact of entry on these products will also be minimal.

To estimate the consequences of enlargement, we utilise the comparative static method commonly employed in *ex-ante* studies of this kind.[11] Estimates of import demand elasticities are combined with nominal tariff averages to predict the effect of tariff reductions (and the 'tariff-equivalent' of quota reductions) under the *ceteris paribus* assumption that this is the only price effect taking place and that 'dynamic' effects can be ignored, etc.

Estimates of average nominal tariffs on manufactured goods for 1971 by area of origin are presented in Table 2. These estimates derived from earlier tariff computations relating to the year 1966, are not as precise as we would wish.[12] Nevertheless the suggested tariff averages of 10 per cent for the United Kingdom and 30 per cent for non-United Kingdom areas are accurate enough for present purposes. These figures take account of the 50 per cent reduction in tariffs on imports from the United

Kingdom in conformity with the terms of A I F T A. They also serve to underline the rather high levels of nominal protection obtaining in Ireland prior to the A I F T A reductions, as well as the high degree of preference afforded to British suppliers in the Irish market as a result of the Agreement.

The aggregate price elasticity of demand for Irish manufactured imports is assumed to be -1.5. Leser's figures based on import data up to 1963 suggest a high elasticity of -1.86, but McAleese's study, using more recent data (albeit with a different import classification), points to a lower degree of price sensitivity.[13] In the absence of directly estimated elasticities of substitution for Irish imports, we follow Kreinin in using an estimate of -2.7.[14]

With these assumed values of the tariff and elasticity parameters and applying the conventional formulae,[15] we are able to estimate the various effects of E E C enlargement on Ireland's imports, as indicated in Table 2. Attention is drawn to a number of aspects of these calculations in the following brief commentary.

First, the elimination of import restrictions on United Kingdom E E C (Six) and Other E F T A products will bring about an £87m increase in total manufactured imports from these areas at 1971 import prices.

Second, the reduction of the Irish tariff to the Common External Tariff level of 7.5 per cent,[16] will involve an increase in imports from All Other Areas of £19m. The main beneficiary will probably be the United States. There are, of course, some products whose Irish tariff is less than the C E T (e.g. newsprint, wattle extracts for tanning, aluminium), but these are quite exceptional cases.

Third, E E C enlargement involves discrimination against non-members (other than those with which the E E C has special agreements, such as E F T A), this discrimination being equal to the height of the C E T. Hence a diversion effect on £12m can be expected against All Other Area imports and in favour of imports from the United Kingdom, E E C (Six) and Other E F T A in proportion to their shares of total Irish imports.

Fourth, membership of the enlarged E E C implies a loss by the United Kingdom of its special preferential trading position in the Irish market. The value of this preference in 1971 is calculated as [130/110 =] 18 per cent, which, gives a substitution elasticity of -2.7, implies a change in the ratio of non-U K/U K imports equal to [$-2.7 \times 18=$] 49 per cent. In value terms, the United Kingdom's loss is estimated as £33m, which is, in turn, converted into a gain of £25m for the E E C (Six) and £8m for Other E F T A.

The calculations, therefore, point to a significant increase in imports of £106m, occurring over the next few years. In percentage terms, this amounts to an increase in imports of 21 per cent over their 1971 base level.[17]

The main beneficiary of this increased penetration of the Irish market will be the E E C (Six) exporter. He will gain directly through the elimination of the high Irish tariff, and indirectly through the erosion of Britain's highly preferential position in the Irish market and through increased discrimination against All Other Area imports. The enlargement effect on imports from the E E C is estimated as £64m, an increase of 62 per cent. A percentage gain of similar magnitude will accrue to Other E F T A exporters for the same reasons.

A glance at Table 1 shows the inherent plausibility of this forecast. The share of the E E C (Six) in light consumer (Section 8) imports and to a lesser extent in intermediate (Section 6) imports appears exceedingly low, in absolute terms as well as by comparison with other sections. It is scarcely fortuitous that these products are also the most heavily protected of all imports into Ireland.

In a recent study, McAleese and Martin stressed the significant role played by A I F T A up to 1970 in determining the level of demand for United Kingdom manufactured goods on the Irish market.[18] The United Kingdom share of manufactured goods imports, it was noted, had been steadily declining throughout the last two decades, but the A I F T A tariff reductions had succeeded in slowing down the pace of the United Kingdom's market share decline. The authors predicted an even more pronounced effect over the years 1971–76, during which tariffs on United Kingdom imports were to be progressively reduced to zero. While trade creation effects will indeed continue to be felt, it is clear that any trade diversion effect experienced up to the mid-seventies will quickly be reversed as tariffs on E E C and E F T A imports come down.

To complete the discussion, we must also consider the effects of the transition from the Irish to the E E C generalised preference system for imports from the Less Developed Countries. Ireland's system, which came into effect at the beginning of 1972, provided for a reduction of 33 per cent in the rate of duty normally applicable to the L D Cs, for an unlimited quantity of imports but subject to a number of exceptions, principally textile goods. The E E C system allows duty-free importation from the L D Cs subject to quantitative ceilings. To judge from past experience in the E E C it is unlikely that these quantitative ceilings will be set at a level which is likely to cause much embarrassment to Irish industry.

Taking a long-run view, however, it must be admitted that a substantial part of Ireland's older established industrial sector— for example, the footwear, shirt-making, woollen and worsted, and toy industries—may prove highly vulnerable against low-cost competition from the L D Cs. Further concessions to the L D Cs, however desirable in themselves, might therefore well prove highly embarrassing to the Irish government. While trade liberalisation with the L D Cs might well stimulate their demand for capital-intensive and technology-intensive goods imports from the enlarged E E C, this would not be of much consolation to Ireland, given our present industrial structure. In other words, the members who stand to lose most heavily from further concessions to the L D Cs would not be the same as those who gain the most from the resultant increase in the L D Cs' demand for Western funds. There is an important potential conflict of interest here which, even at this early stage, must be faced.

EFFECT ON MANUFACTURED EXPORTS

Free trade, as we have seen, will involve both an increase in total imports and a change in their geographical composition. A matter of critical importance is the extent to which intensified competition on the home market is counterbalanced by an improved competitive position in export markets. We begin our examination of this subject by applying the same comparative static methods as before.[19] What we wish to quantify in this instance is: (a) the effects of the removal of E E C and Other E F T A tariffs on Irish exports and (b) the effects of the elimination of Ireland's preferential position in the United Kingdom

TABLE 3

Effects of EEC Entry on Irish Manufactured Exports

Irish Sales to:		Exports 1971 £m (1)	Average Nominal Tariff (%) (2)	Removal of CET and Other EFTA Tariffs £m (3)	Removal of Preferential Position in UK market vis-à-vis EEC (Six) £m (4)	Total Effect Cols. (3) + (4) £m (5)	Percentage Change in Exports at 1971 Prices (%) (6)
UK	1971	115.96	0	0	−12	−12	−10
	1978*	322			−33	−33	
EEC (Six)	1971	22.79	9.1	+8	—	+8	+33
	1978*	83		+28		+28	
Other EFTA	1971	4.80	6.2	+1	—	+1	+23
	1978*	20		+5		+5	
All Other Areas	1971	40.22	n.a.	0	—	—	—
	1978*	154					
TOTAL	1971	183.77	—	+9	−12	−3	−2
	1978*	579		+33	−33	0	0

Notes.

1. Col. (1) data are computed from *External Trade Statistics*, 1971.
2. Average nominal tariffs on exports to EEC are taken from McAleese and Martin 'Ireland's Manufactured Exports to the EEC and the Common External Tariff', *Economic and Social Review*, July 1972. The EFTA tariff is computed from the GATT estimates provided in the June 1972 issue of *European Community*.

*Projected on basis of extrapolation of 1963–71 trends.

market.[20] This involves the estimation of nominal tariff averages and export demand elasticities.

The average (post Kennedy Round) nominal tariff levied on Irish exports to the E E C was estimated by McAleese and Martin as 9.1 per cent.[21] This is rather higher than the overall E E C average of 7.5 per cent estimated by G A T T and reflects the fact that many products bearing low E E C tariffs are not, and are unlikely to be, produced and exported from Ireland. The Other E F T A tariff average of 6.2 per cent was computed from the G A T T estimates for each of the six Other E F T A countries.[22]

Unfortunately, no estimates of the elasticity of demand for Irish exports have been computed direct from Irish data. However, studies of price elasticity of demand for manufactured imports into the E E C and E F T A markets have yielded estimates in the range -2.5 to -3.0.

Given the high proportion of Irish manufactured exports falling into the price-sensitive S I T C 6 and 8 categories, it seems reasonable to assume that the Irish export elasticity is at least as high as this. In fact, if allowance is made for the improved competitive position of Irish exports *vis-à-vis* those of All Other Areas in the enlarged E E C market, the presumption is that the price elasticity would be even higher. Accordingly, a value of -4 for the price elasticity of Irish exports in that market is assumed.[23]

In order to assess the effects of reduced preference in the British market, an estimate of the elasticity of substitution between Irish and E E C/Other E F T A exports to the United Kingdom has to be obtained. Empirical studies have placed the elasticity of demand for total United Kingdom manufactured imports at about -2.5.[24] Given that the elasticity for Irish exports to the United Kingdom is approximately the same, the elasticity of substitution between Irish products and those of other suppliers to the British market must by definition be even higher still. Accordingly, a value of -4 was assumed.

The results of our calculations are presented in Table 3 and may be summarised as follows:[25]

First, the effects of entry on sales to the E E C and Other E F T A countries emerges as being small in absolute terms. In percentage terms, however, the effect is quite significant, involving a 33 per cent and 23 per cent increase in exports to the two markets respectively. The small absolute size is not really sur-prising in view of the very small base from which the compara-tive static effect is being estimated. As already noted, manu-factured exports have been growing at more than 19 per cent per annum on average during the last two decades and exports to the E E C and E F T A have increased at a much faster rate still. If pre 1973 trends continued to 1978, the extrapolated projections in Table 3 show how the percentage increases in E E C and Other E F T A sales would be translated into much larger magnitudes of £28m and £5m respectively.[26]

Second, in addition to the benefits of more liberal access to the continental markets for Irish exports, E E C entry at some time involves, on the negative side, a significantly reduced degree of preferential treatment in the British market. The United Kingdom tariff, estimated as 9.4 per cent in 1973, is one of the highest among the industrialised countries of Western Europe. The loss of Ireland's preferential position is estimated to cost £12m, or 10 per cent of current Irish manufactured exports to the United Kingdom. The size of this negative effect in the United Kingdom market relative to the positive effects in other markets comes as something of a surprise. However, when one considers the comparatively high degree of preference now en-joyed by Irish exporters to the United Kingdom market and the fact that nearly two-thirds of Ireland's total manufactured exports are destined for the United Kingdom, it is easy to see how a small adverse competitive effect in that market can be just as important as a large favourable competitive effect in the E E C and Other E F T A markets.

Third, the net effect of E E C entry on Ireland's manufactured exports emerges as slightly negative if 1971 is taken as base—a decline of £1.6m or 2 per cent—and as zero if a crudely esti-mated 1978 base is used. The benefits of improved access to the E E C and Other E F T A markets, in other words, are wiped out by the deterioration in our competitive position in the British market *vis-à-vis* the E E C (Six). This conclusion would emerge even more clearly if account were taken of the high import content of the increased exports.

While the present exercise indicates the direction and rough order of magnitude of trends at an aggregate level, it does not enable us to identify the actual products which are likely to be affected by Ireland's loss of preference on the United Kingdom market or by our improved competitive position in the E E C market etc. While the range of *ex ante* information is not sufficient to make any further research along these lines useful at this stage, it is worth emphasising that the practical importance of increased or reduced degrees of preference in export markets has been substantiated in almost every *ex post* empirical study of the integration effects of the E E C and E F T A.[27]

EFFECTS ON FOREIGN INVESTMENT

To complete this section, the effects of entry on private foreign investment in manufacturing must be considered. To a private investor, the change in the tariff position facing his prospective sales depends both on the alternative investment locations he is considering in addition to Ireland (since tariffs are levied according to country of origin) and also on the geographical composition of the market he intends to serve. A comparison between the pre-entry and post-entry situation of Ireland from a foreign investor's viewpoint (taking only tariffs into account) shows little significant change. This point is illustrated schematically in Table 4.

TABLE 4

Effects of E E C entry on Foreign Investment

Alternative Locations \ Prospective Market	U K	E E C (Six)	Other E F T A	All Other Areas
Ireland or :				
U K	0	0	+	0
E E C (Six)	−	+	0	0
Other E F T A	0	0	0	0
All Other Areas	0	+	+	0

0 = No change in competitive position.
+ = Improvement in competitive position.
− = Deterioration in competitive position.

Beginning with the first row, the table shows that Ireland's attractiveness relative to the United Kingdom as an investment location does not change if the investor intends selling on the United Kingdom market (both locations would have enjoyed duty-free access to this market before and after entry), on the E E C (Six) market (prior to entry, both locations would have attracted the C E T; after entry, both enjoy free access) or on the All Other Areas market.[28] A slight gain in competitiveness relative to a United Kingdom location is however obtained in the case of an investor selling solely to Other E F T A. Prior to E E C entry, exports from Ireland to Other E F T A would have been liable to Other E F T A duties, whereas exports from the United Kingdom would have been duty-free. This bias against exports from Ireland would be eliminated after E E C entry.

Three other *plus* signs can be observed. Two relate to Ireland's improved competitive position relative to All Other Area locations and one refers to the advantages we gain *vis-à-vis* E E C (Six) locations by virtue of the C E T's removal on our exports to the E E C market.

The single *minus* sign shows that Ireland loses some of its attractiveness over E E C (Six) locations in so far as our privileged access to the United Kingdom market must after entry be shared with products originating in the E E C.

Although we have no means of estimating the quantitative importance of these various effects, the balance of probability is that the response to improvements in Ireland's competitive position will outweigh the potential negative effects. One gets the impression that few of the I D A-sponsored firms have set up in Ireland primarily to serve the British market from a privileged location. Moreover, the positive effects are likely to be considerably more significant than might at first sight appear. The elimination of an average C E T of 9 per cent, for example, given a profit/final output ratio of between 6 and 8 per cent, could increase the profitability of exports by anything from 110 to 150 per cent.[29] This factor could make all the difference to a foreign investor as he reckons up the pros and cons of alternative locations. Also, the enlargement of the E E C is bound to attract an increased volume of extra-E E C foreign investment into the area. Both British and Irish commentators have placed emphasis on the potential benefits arising from this factor.

Another implication of E E C entry is the certainty and security of market access that membership brings. Although the free trade arrangements between Other E F T A and the E E C theoretically offer the same concessions, foreign investors would simply not have regarded the two situations as equivalent. This point has been strongly emphasised by Ireland's Industrial Development Authority on a number of occasions. The position of an E E C member in the enlarged E E C market is seen by out-siders as something altogether more secure and stable than that of a member of E F T A.[30] Furthermore, a prospective investor might well feel that efforts to reduce non-tariff barriers on intra-E E C trade will be pursued far more vigorously than in the case of trade between E E C and other trading blocs. Thus, while E E C entry may not have brought about any improvement in Ireland's competitive position *vis-à-vis* the United Kingdom, the position relative to Other E F T A countries has been strength-ened in a manner and to a degree not allowed for in Table 4. It also follows that exclusion from the E E C could have exercised a sharp negative effect on foreign investment, which again Table 4 does not take fully into account. This brings us back to the view expressed earlier that Ireland's entry into the E E C in-volved a choice between two utterly changed situations, not one between entry and the *status quo*.

Of second-order importance, but perhaps still worthy of men-tion, are the consequences of E E C membership for domestic input costs. Some reduction in input costs may be expected in so far as the efficiency of the services sector is improved, due to a closer scrutiny of costs on the part of industrial users.[31] Against this, an increase in input costs can be expected as the higher food prices of the C A P are translated into demands for higher wages. There is, however, no way of knowing what the net impact of these two factors will be on foreign investment.

The increased inflow of foreign investment ascribable to E E C membership will, of course, have important implications for the balance of payments, initially on capital account and afterwards on the current account as the enterprises get estab-lished and begin to export. We have no way of knowing the precise magnitude of these effects. It is, however, highly un-likely that the extra foreign investment will be sufficient to offset the comparative static deficit of about £100m revealed in Tables 2 and 3.[32] Thus, we conclude that the net impact of E E C entry on Ireland's balance of payments in manufactured goods will be unfavourable. This point is not in any way incompatible with the fact that to have stayed out of the E E C would have made the balance of payments situation even worse. In that eventuality, it is clear that a drastic revision of the A I F T A Agreement would have been necessitated. The overall conclusion—that free trade in manufactured goods would place a severe strain on Ireland's balance of payments in manufactured goods—is surely not all that surprising, given the high level of protection of the industrial sector up to a few years ago.

Agriculture in the Enlarged Community

RESULTS OF PREVIOUS ESTIMATES

The prospect of substantial gains in the agricultural sector was one of the most powerful forces propelling Ireland towards E E C membership. The increase in Irish export earnings due to higher C A P prices was reckoned by various authors to lie between £65m and £100m on the basis of an unchanged volume of agricultural exports. When allowance was made for price-induced increases in output, these estimates were raised by a further £120m to £160m.[33] Considered against a background of sluggish growth of farm production, disappointment with the agricultural provisions of the A I F T A and unfavourable world demand conditions for dairy products, the attractiveness of this potential C A P bonanza to the Irish farmer, no less than to the Irish economy, can readily be appreciated.

Previous estimates of the gains from E E C entry were all based on price data for the years 1968 to 1970. The question naturally arises : what if price data for a more recent year were used? In the case of the industrial sector, this issue would not be of interest, since the widespread use of fixed *ad valorem* tariff rates means that the differential between Irish export and E E C internal prices remain equal to the tariff rate irrespective of movements in absolute prices. The E E C's use of the variable levy system to protect agricultural products, by contrast, means that the differential between Irish export prices and internal E E C prices is likely to be constantly changing. Hence the desirability of revising past estimates and the virtual necessity of making some rough price projections, if meaningful assessments of the gains from participation in the C A P are to be obtained. This

TABLE 5
Irish Agricultural Exports 1972

SITC Description	£ million				Percentage Distribution			
	UK	EEC (6)	All Other Areas	Total	UK	EEC (6)	All Other Areas	Total
00 Live Animals	66.8	16.2	3.1	86.1	77.6	18.8	3.6	100
01 Meat and Meat Products	61.8	22.2	12.8	96.8	63.8	22.9	13.2	100
02 Dairy Products	35.3	—	6.4	41.7	84.7	—	15.3	100
	163.9	38.4	22.3	224.6	73.0	17.1	9.9	100
03 Fish and Fish Products	2.7	3.7	1.4	7.8	34.6	47.4	18.0	100
04 Cereals and Cereal Products	2.6	—	1.3	3.9	66.7	—	33.3	100
05 Fruit and Vegetables	5.6	0.4	1.4	7.4	75.7	5.4	18.9	100
06 Sugar and Sugar Products	2.2	0.5	1.2	3.9	56.4	12.8	30.8	100
07 Cocoa, Chocolate Products	9.8	—	2.3	12.1	81.0	—	19.0	100
08 Animal Foodstuffs	9.0	—	1.8	10.8	83.3	—	16.7	100
Total	195.8	43.0	31.7	270.5	72.4	15.9	11.7	100

Source. Irish Export Board, *Annual Report* 1972 (Statistical Appendix).
Note. Figures for S I T C 09 exports distributed by area of destination were not available at the time of writing. (Exports of the goods amount to £2.8m.)

F

aspect of the problem appears to have been completely ignored in Ireland's various White Paper estimates of the benefits of entry.

The above argument may be given point by updating some of the past estimates of gain with the assistance of more up-to-date price data. The method we use is the same as before and involves calculating the price effect of entry and then applying the relevant supply elasticity.

Irish agricultural exports amounted to roughly £270m in 1972 (see Table 5). The British market absorbed 72 per cent of these exports and the E E C (Six) 16 per cent: thus, roughly 88 per cent are sold to members of the enlarged Community. Exports of the first three product groups listed in Table 5—live animals, meat and meat products, and dairy products—account for over 80 per cent of the total, and it is on these products that our analysis will be concentrated. Any favourable effects which the E E C entry may have on the remaining product groups included in Standard International Tariff Classification divisions 03 to 08 are assumed to be approximately offset by unfavourable effects on the import side. Thus, for example, potential gains in mutton and lamb exports, sugar and fish would have to be set against potential losses due to trade diversion in the case of cereal and fruit imports.

COMPARATIVE BEEF AND MILK PRICES

Estimates of the difference between E E C and Irish beef prices used in the various White Papers, pamphlets, and articles which preceded E E C entry, ranged from 50 to 60 per cent.[34] These estimates accord reasonably well with those of studies of the divergence between E E C and world market prices of beef.[35] The conformity is scarcely surprising, since world prices of many agricultural products were reflected in or dictated by those operating in the United Kingdom market. The latter, in turn, exercise a dominant influence on Irish export prices.

A useful indicator of the course of prices in the intervening period is provided by a comparison between the E E C guide price for beef and the Irish price of fat bullocks. Although the absolute gap between these two prices is not the most reliable measure of differences in absolute price levels between Ireland and the E E C,[36] it represents the general order of magnitude of

TABLE 6
Irish and EEC Prices of Beef and Dairy Produce 1969–72

Year	Beef[1] (£ per live cwt.)			Butter[2] (£ per ton)			Skim Milk Powder[2] (£ per ton)			Dairy Produce[3] (Composite Index) (£ per 5,120 gallons of milk)		
	EEC	Irish	EEC/ Irish %	EEC	Irish	EEC/ Irish %	EEC	Irish	EEC/ Irish %	EEC	Irish	EEC/ Irish %
1969	14.40	8.90	62	734	227	223	174	136	28	1060	482	120
1970	14.40	9.61	50	734	269	173	174	130	34	1060	512	107
1971	15.20	10.61	43	754	464	62	199	197	1	1127	833	35
1972	16.19	13.60	19	873	486	80	253	255	–	1347	964	40

Notes.

1. EEC guide price is compared with the Irish price of steers, 10–11 cwt. The two prices are not strictly comparable but are reliable indicators of trend.

2. EEC intervention price compared with average Irish export (unit value) price.

3. Computed from the formula 5,120 gallons of milk (3.6 butter fat content) = 1 ton butter + 1.873 tons skim milk powder.

Sources. Irish Statistical Bulletin, March 1973 and 1971; Department of Agriculture; An Bord Bainne.

these differences and should certainly succeed in pinpointing the direction of trend. As Table 6 shows, one of the most significant aspects of price trends since 1969 is the reduction in the gap between E E C and Irish prices from about 60 per cent in 1969 to 19 per cent in 1972. The absolute size of the gap has been narrowed due to the extremely rapid increase in the Irish price. Although the recent devaluation of sterling has resulted in a sharp rise in the E E C guide price for beef (measured in terms of sterling), the divergence between the Irish and E E C prices is still below 30 per cent.[37]

We can, therefore, assume that Ireland would have received a 20 per cent higher price on her beef exports to the enlarged Community had she been fully participating in the C A P in 1972. This implies an overall rise in earnings in cattle and beef exports of £26m, at current production levels, over their current value of £132m. Such a sum lies well below the corresponding estimates made a few years ago. Even if 1971 export volume figures are used instead of the exceptionally low 1972 figures, the price effect would still amount to only £31m.[38]

A downward trend in the difference between E E C and world market prices is also evidenced in the case of dairy products. Thus, in 1969, the E E C guide price for butter was more than three times higher than the average export price for Irish butter received in the world market. By 1972, the divergence had declined to 80 per cent. Similarly in the case of skim milk, the disparity between E E C and Irish export prices has fallen from 28 per cent to zero over the past three years. A composite price index is calculated in Table 6 which takes account of the technical joint-product relationship between skim milk and butter production. This also shows a decline in relative prices from 120 per cent in 1969 to 40 per cent in 1972. The 'composite' price is useful in that it enables us to attach accurate weights to the prices of skim milk and butter respectively.

The Irish export price as reflected in the dairy product composite index, cannot, however, be taken as a satisfactory indicator of world market price. This is because the British, prior to E E C entry, imposed a minimum import price on these products in a deliberate effort to keep the British price high and hence soften the adverse cost-of-living impact of the C A P. Thus, the British butter price significantly exceeded the world market price on several occasions, particularly during 1970 when the E E C Six's 'butter mountain' was being disposed of. This naturally affected the price Irish exporters received also.

EFFECTS OF PRODUCTION

So far the gains from the C A P have been estimated in the context of fixed 1972 production levels. If account were taken of the positive supply response to these price increases, it is obvious that the effects on exports would be even further increased. Evidence on Irish supply elasticities has been provided by Josling and Lucey and by O'Connor.[39] O'Connor finds a supply elasticity of cattle output equal to 0.8 with respect to milk price, but a much lower elasticity of 0.1 with respect to calf price. Josling and Lucey, on the other hand, estimate a long-run price elasticity of supply for beef and veal equal to 0.4. The elasticity of milk output with respect to milk price these authors estimate at 0.35.

Given price effects of 20 per cent in the case of beef and 50 per cent (at the very minimum) for dairy products, and assuming a supply elasticity of roughly 0.5 in accordance with the Josling and Lucey estimates, increases in output of the order of 10 and 25 per cent respectively can be anticipated. Export volume will, however, rise at a much faster rate than this since domestic market demand will not keep pace with the rise in output. If we assume that *all* the extra output is exported, then export volume would be expected to increase by twice the rate of output increase. This implies increased agricultural export receipts for dairy products and beef of £31m and £32m respectively, representing the value of the production effect of E E C entry. By adding the price effects to these amounts, we come up with a total effect of about £109m. This sum represents a lower bound estimate of the amount of extra export receipts which would have been obtained had Ireland been a full participant in the C A P in 1972 and had adjustment to the increased prices been instantaneous.

The direction of future trends in the relationship between E E C and world agricultural prices is of course a matter of much greater significance than the above analysis of the implications of existing price differences. It is at the same time a vastly more hazardous exercise. Experts in this area, however, seem to be broadly in agreement that:[40]

(*a*) world supplies of beef are unlikely to expand sufficiently to satisfy world demand even at the high price levels of 1972–73. Hence beef prices both outside and within the enlarged E E C will continue to rise. There is consequently no reason to expect any widening in the E E C/world beef price differential.

(*b*) although world supplies of milk products are also likely to be insufficient to meet world demand, the tendency is towards large surplus production in the O E C D (plus Oceania). Excess demand by the L D Cs, which is projected to absorb this surplus, may not be translated into effective purchases for a variety of reasons. Thus, world dairy product prices are likely to remain depressed.

(*c*) export availabilities of grain projected for the O E D C plus Oceania would be more than adequate to offset the import requirements projected by the F A O for the rest of the world. Hence world grain prices will be subject to heavy downward pressure from their present exceptionally high levels.

The implications of these last two trends for the enlarged E E C are far from clear. While the United Kingdom will undoubtedly argue strongly for a closer alignment between world prices and C A P prices, the close technical relationship that exists between cattle and milk production in the enlarged E E C will make it impossible for the British to insist on reductions in the price of milk without having to face the consequences of even higher beef prices. Cattle and milk are, especially in a European context, akin to joint products and a fall in the price of one necessarily entails a rise in the price of the other if production is to remain constant. The importance of this relationship in Ireland is apparent from O'Connor's already cited estimates of supply elasticities for cattle output, where milk prices are found to have much greater influence on cattle stock than calf prices. The consequences of trends in world grain prices are even more difficult to disentangle. On the one hand, a decline in these prices would eventually lower cattle prices as input costs fall; on the other hand, by inducing a shift from tillage to dairy farming, a decline in grain prices could easily place further pressure on dairy product prices which in turn would tend to raise beef prices.

Perhaps the most likely eventuality is that milk and grain prices will be kept at their present levels in absolute value and may mean a further increase in the gap between the E E C that the E E C will rely on inflation to keep the real burden of the agricultural price supports at a generally acceptable level. This and the world price of dairy products. But the outlook for dairy product prices in real terms looks unfavourable either inside or outside the Community.

Summary and Conclusion

This paper has attempted to estimate the economic implications of E E C entry for Ireland, using comparative static analysis and taking the years 1971–72 as base. The 'effects of entry', as defined in this paper, must however be interpreted carefully. Thus our measure of the E E C effect takes as its basis of comparison a situation which was itself bound to change. The 'effects of entry' consequently include the effects of the tariff reductions on United Kingdom imports even though these were scheduled to take place in any event. Similarly, possible adverse effects on agricultural exports and foreign investment of remaining outside the Community are not taken into account in our estimates. The estimates are not therefore intended primarily as a retrospective contribution to the E E C entry *v.* no-entry debate (although it is to be hoped that they are of some indirect relevance to that debate), but rather as an indication of the likely trade and balance of payments effects associated with, even if not directly caused by, Ireland's membership of the Community. As already noted, Ireland in contrast with the United Kingdom did not have the option of maintaining the *status quo*.

Our analysis of the effects of E E C enlargement on the Irish balance of payments indicates: (*a*) an increase in imports of £106m attributable to the elimination of Irish import restrictions, (*b*) a negligible net change in manufactured exports, the positive effects of the C E T's elimination on Irish exports being cancelled by the negative effects of the loss of Ireland's preferential position in the United Kingdom market *vis-à-vis* E E C (Six) exporters, (*c*) a favourable but non-quantifiable effect on foreign direct investment in Ireland, with correspondingly favourable repercussions on capital account and exports and (*d*) an increase in agricultural exports of at least £109m. The overall comparative static effect is therefore at worst neutral, and very likely positive, in the sense that balance of payments equilibrium at this higher level of trade can be maintained at the existing exchange rate.[41] Furthermore, underwriting the increased agricultural exports directly attributable to entry, we have the prospect of further substantial independent increases in world and C A P meat prices. Ireland's balance of payments position is, therefore, expected to remain strong. This implies that the so-called 'dynamic' gains from E E C entry will not be choked off by restrictionist economic policy measures dictated by balance of payments problems and crises. It is indeed fortunate for Ireland that the movement towards trade liberalisation in manufactured goods is coinciding with high prices for agricultural produce.

To what extent has E E C entry *per se*—as opposed to alternative trading arrangements—contributed to this favourable conclusion?

On the industrial side, it is fairly certain that Ireland would have been able to negotiate a free trade agreement with the E E C similar to those reached with the E F T A countries. This would have implied free access to the markets of Western Europe and the United Kingdom for practically all industrial goods, including processed foods, by 1978. For certain 'sensitive' products, the transitional period would have been lengthened to seven and even eleven years, but these would not have affected us to any great extent. It is unlikely that the 'indicative ceilings' placed on certain Portuguese textile and clothing products would have been extended to us. Also an examination of the list of 'sensitive' products shows that only a negligible fraction of existing Irish exports would fall under that umbrella.[42]

Thus, in or out of the E E C, Ireland would still have enjoyed free access to the European market. Does it follow from this that the anxiety expressed by bodies such as the Industrial Development Authority about the necessity of E E C entry for the continued expansion of foreign industrial investment was misplaced? On balance, we think not, for the simple reason that foreign investors would not regard the two situations as equivalent. Membership of the Community carries with it a security of access which no trade agreement can quite replicate. The gradual harmonisation of economic and social policies to which the E E C aspires, with the ensuing removal of many non-tariff barriers to trade must also appeal to the foreign investor. As has often been stressed before, uncertainty and incomplete information constitute no less serious an obstacle to international exchange than tariffs and quotas.

Regarding agriculture, there is likely to be a further narrowing of the present comparatively small differential between E E C and world prices. Does this mean, as some have argued, that an intelligent exploitation of this price trend by the Irish farmer could have succeeded in obtaining for the economy the same, if not more, economic gains outside the E E C as would accrue to us as a member?[43]

An implication of this paper is that earlier estimates of the gains from E E C entry in agriculture were almost certainly overestimated as a result of the failure to take account of world price trends in meat and meat products. The stress laid on this factor by the opponents of entry is, therefore, seen to have considerable justification.

The crux of the matter, however, from the Irish point of view is the likely trend in world milk prices. Membership of the E E C has brought with it the expectation of high milk prices (in absolute terms and relative to current Irish milk prices). 'The *existing* E E C price,' a recently published Economic and Social Research Institute study concludes, 'is sufficiently high by Irish standards to stimulate a continued rapid increase in the dairy herd, which is the principal source of calves for the beef cattle industry.'[44] It is highly unlikely that this price will be reduced over the next few years in absolute terms. A more likely outcome is that the C A P price in real terms will be eroded by inflation. But even this modest assurance of absolute price stability could not be extended to world prices of dairy products. Also the importance of the short-run needs to be emphasised on this issue. What Ireland needs, and what the prospect of high dairy prices appears to be bringing about, is a rapid increase in cattle stocks, implying high rates of investment and saving on the part of the farmers. In a highly uncertain international market for dairy products, it is unlikely that the necessary investment effort would have been forthcoming.

In the very long run, the C A P will have to be modified and the European system of agricultural protection gradually rationalised. Before that time comes, however, Ireland will, it is hoped, have availed of the breathing space afforded by the C A P's protection to build up the cattle herd and to establish a strong selling position in the enlarged Community's market for agricultural produce.

At this stage, more than ever before, attention will have to focus on regional policy. Ireland, as one of the least developed regions of the Community, has a particularly active interest in the evolution of such a policy. But progress has so far been extremely slow and dissatisfaction over this has been expressed by the Irish Government on a number of occasions. Given the tremendous strains under which the enlarged Community is now operating, however, too much cannot be expected in the short-run. Paradoxically, therefore, the strongest long run economic argument in favour of Ireland's joining the Community is based on a policy which does not yet exist.

APPENDIX

Nominal Tariff Estimates

In 1966, two average nominal tariff estimates were computed, one (25 per cent) using domestic production weights and the other (14 per cent) using import weights.[45] Neither estimate is suitable for the present study because (a) the use of domestic production weights tends to exaggerate the height of the average S I T C 5–8 tariff (i.e. goods not produced domestically and therefore excluded under this weighting system are typically those which are not dutiable) and (b) estimates based on import weights referred to *total* Irish imports and hence are biased downwards by the inclusion of the large number of zero-duty items included in S I T C 0–4 imports. Our position is that the 'true' average tariff must lie somewhere between the two estimates and the mid-point is chosen as our 'best guess' estimate.

As they stand, however, the tariffs do not distinguish between area of origin. Fortunately, a separate estimate, based on import share weights, was made for imports from the United Kingdom which came to 12 per cent. By 1971, this would have been reduced to roughly 6 per cent, which provides a definite lower bound estimate to the United Kingdom tariff. The upper bound estimate by contrast is 13 per cent (i.e. one-half of 25 per cent), on the basis of domestic production weights and not differentiating between the preferential United Kingdom tariff and the full tariff. Taking the mid-point as our best guess, this left us with an estimated United Kingdom tariff of 10 per cent, as in Table 2.

Our estimate of the average tariff on imports of non-United Kingdom origin is based on the observation that the full tariff is typically 10 to 20 percentage points higher than the United Kingdom preferential tariff on dutiable imports. However, where a zero duty is levied on imports from the United Kingdom, the corresponding full tariff is also zero. Consequently, we felt that the best procedure would be to add 10 percentage points to the average tariff on

United Kingdom imports as it stood in 1966 (i.e. 20 per cent), to yield an estimate of 30 per cent for the average nominal tariff on imports of non-United Kingdom origin.

SECTION FOUR

SECTION FOUR

The Industrial Development Process in the Republic of Ireland 1953-72 [1]

P. S. McMENAMIN

Introduction

THE aim of this paper is:

(1) to describe the industrial development process in the Republic of Ireland in the period 1953–72,

(2) to indicate the roles played by domestic and foreign firms in this process, and

(3) to show the important evolutionary role played by the Government and public sector.

To achieve these purposes, the paper has been broken down into three main parts. Part I briefly traces developments in the Irish economy, particularly the manufacturing industry sector, over the period 1953–72. Part II shows how the Government's and public sector's role in the process evolved over the period and is still evolving in the light of changing circumstances. Part III includes discussion of some issues arising from the paper, which are related to the general theme of the conference, namely, 'The Relation of Small Economies to a Dominant Neighbour'.

The choice of time covered in the paper was dictated by two primary considerations:

(*a*) it was felt necessary to cover a lengthy period to show the extremely significant changes that have taken place in the Irish economy, and

(*b*) the years 1953–72 cover a period of active stimulation of the economy by the Government and public sector by means of a system of incentives designed to encourage expansion in the private sector.

In view of the fact that other papers presented to the conference cover items germane to the overall subject matter of this paper from the theoretical point of view, coverage here has been

severely restricted to the practical side of the industrial development process in the Republic.

Part I
Irish Economy 1953–72
In the six years 1953–58 the Irish economy experienced many
difficulties and problems. At a time when most of Western
Europe was expanding rapidly, the Irish economy expanded at
a very slow rate, or declined. Table I provides details of changes
in Gross National Product.

TABLE 1
Changes in GNP 1953–58 (Constant 1958 Prices)

Year	1953	1954	1955	1956	1957	1958
GNP (£m)	601	607	619	610	614	600
% Change GNP	+1.0	+1.0	+2.0	−1.5	+0.7	−2.3

Source. NIEC Report on Full Employment (Pr 9188).

The economic stagnation of the period is clearly demonstrated
by the fact that GNP in 1958 (£600m) was lower than the
corresponding 1953 (£601m) figure.

In the period, however, GNP per head remained constant
or increased slightly. This was due to a fall in population which
resulted from a substantial rise in emigration. At the same time
the numbers out of work were also on the increase. Table 2
illustrates.

TABLE 2
Trends in Emigration and Unemployment 1953–58 (000s)

Year	1953	1954	1955	1956	1957	1958
Emigration	37	48	49	44	60	34
Unemployment	65	65	62	63	78	73

Source. NIEC Report on Full Employment (Pr 9188).

The economy was also characterised by difficulties in external
payments. The difficulties were particularly severe in 1955 when
a large increase in the import excess in merchandise trade
occurred without a corresponding increase in invisible earnings.
As a result there was a balance of payments deficit on the current

account of £35.5m. Because of the lack of confidence in the economy there was also a net outflow of capital (£11.8m) which, combined with the balance of payments deficit already mentioned, resulted in the country's external reserves falling by £47.3m.

PROGRAMME FOR ECONOMIC EXPANSION

Partly as a result of these problems and to ensure orderly control of the economy, the Government published a 'Programme for Economic Expansion' in 1958. This in fact was an outline of the more important contributions, direct and indirect, which the Government proposed to make to economic development.

The main objective of the Government policy in relation to private enterprise was to create the conditions in which it would be stimulated and encouraged to embark upon new activities. Industry was expected to be a major contributor to development and the stated aim of the Programme was 'to stimulate a vast increase in private industrial development while maintaining the supply of capital for prospective State enterprise'. The proposed target for growth in GNP was a modest 2 per cent per annum.

By 1963 GNP had increased by 24 per cent in constant 1958 prices or an average of over $4\frac{1}{2}$ per cent per annum. Exports increased by 90 per cent. Between 1961–62 and 1962–63 there were increases in population—in marked contrast to the fall in population experienced during the fifties. Perhaps, however, the major contribution of the Programme was to restore confidence in the economy.

Second Programme for Economic Expansion

The outcome of the First Programme encouraged the Government to formulate a further programme. This was called the Second Programme for Economic Expansion. It was more detailed and covered a longer (7 year) period. The main objective of the programme was to raise real income by 50 per cent in the 1960s, in line with the target for real income increases decided upon by the OECD. The other main aims were to reduce emigration to 10,000 per annum and to achieve an increase in overall employment during the decade of 78,000. The Programme stated that 'the main contribution to future expansion of GNP both by way of increased employment and increased production, is expected to be from industry'. For this purpose the Programme set in train measures to facilitate adaptation of existing industry and the attraction of new foreign industry. Later sections in this paper deal in greater depth with these measures.

The targets for industry were a 7 per cent annual increase in output, to be achieved through annual productivity increases of 4 per cent and employment increases of 3 per cent. The net increase of industrial employment over the decade was expected to amount to 86,000.

In 1968 a review of progress was published which examined the achievements during the first half of the Programme's projected time table. Table 3 provides details.

TABLE 3

Average Annual Growth Rates (% per annum) 1964–67

	Projected	Actual
Output	4.3	3.3
Imports	4.6 – 7.3	7.1
Exports	4.9 – 7.9	8.1
Investment	4.4	3.2
Employment	1.0	−0.1

Source. Review of Progress 1964–67 (Pr 9949).

Exports exceeded expectations, but disappointingly, employment fell well below target. The industrial sector, however, made substantial progress despite a slowdown which occurred in 1965 and 1966. Industrial exports moreover expanded at a rate of 18.4 per cent per annum in constant price terms.

During the course of the Second Programme the Government-sponsored National Industrial and Economic Council published a number of papers examining the Irish economy and its problems. In 1967 it published a seminal work on what was required to achieve full employment.

This report was not a plan for full employment. Rather it attempted to point out the main problems which would arise in seeking full employment, 'to assess their dimensions, suggest the principal elements in a broad stategy by which full employment might be pursued, to examine some of the main obstacles which lay in the way of its achievement and generally to state the choices which all sections of the community must face and make'.

The importance of this report lies not so much in the exact strategies it suggested but rather in its identification of the conditions and sacrifices necessary to achieve full employment. Subsequent Government planning and employment policy has been influenced by the report.

When it became clear in 1967 that the Second Programme targets for 1970 were not going to be achieved, a new shorter Third Programme for Economic Expansion was published for the years 1969–73.

The Third Programme for Economic Expansion 1969–73

The Third Programme was a general document which took into account not only issues which had a direct bearing on economic development, but also such inter-related areas as Science, Social and Regional Policies.

The Programme's stated objective was to achieve a 17 per cent national growth rate (GNP) over the four year period. The associated rise in employment (16,000) was expected to reduce emigration to an annual average of 12–13,000.

The target for GNP was a 3.8 per cent increase per annum and the out-turn was 3.3 per cent. As regards sectoral output, agriculture came close to achieving its modest target but industry fell short. The output performance of industry was affected by difficulties in foreign markets and the impact of the Northern Ireland situation.

The biggest disappointment was in employment which was below target for the three main economic sectors.

Trends in External Reserves since 1967

A feature of the general development of the economy, in particular the industrial sector, in recent years has been rising external reserves. Every year between 1967–72, with the exception of 1967 there has been a deficit in the balance of payments current account. However, with the exception of 1968, the net capital inflow has been more than adequate to offset this and cause an increase in external reserves. A spectacular year was

1971 when despite a deficit of £68m, the external reserves increased by £90.8m.

Much of these inflows have been associated with foreign subscriptions to National Loans, borrowings abroad by semi-state companies and direct foreign investment in industry. Undoubtedly these capital inflows originating from various sources for different purposes are indicative of confidence in the economy.

OUTSIDE INFLUENCES

The impact of outside influences on our development is most obvious in relation to exports and foreign investment.

The importance of the United Kingdom market for our exports is discussed in the second part of this paper. It is worth mentioning here, however, that this importance was clearly exemplified by our reaction in the mid-sixties when the United Kingdom authorities imposed an import levy scheme. Immediately the Irish Government found it necessary to adopt measures to help Irish exporters by subsidising interest charges which the exporters incurred when making the required deposits in London. The import levy scheme of the United Kingdom Government did have one benefit from the Republic's point of view—it gave further impetus to the efforts of Coras Trachtala Teo. (the Irish Export Board) to diversify exports to other than United Kingdom markets.

Foreign industrial investment has been of obvious importance for our development. The major sources of foreign investment have been the United Kingdom, Germany and the U S A. However, during 1970–71 only four projects with total employment of just over 300 or 4.7 per cent of total projected new job opportunities created in new industry for that year, came from the United Kingdom. This fall-off in United Kingdom investment in Ireland, caused in part by the slowdown of the United Kingdom economy, the Northern Ireland situation and the deterioration of Anglo-Irish relations, emphasised the necessity of attracting new foreign industry from other sources.

MANUFACTURING INDUSTRY

The following sections deal in more detail with manufacturing industry which is and will be, for some time, the primary and principal generator of economic growth in the Irish Republic.

EMPLOYMENT

Between the years 1954 and 1971 employment in manufacturing industry has increased by 50,344 or 34.5 per cent. Of this increase 76 per cent occurred after 1961. During this whole period, unemployment remained at very high levels. In fact despite expansion in manufacturing, the unemployment rate remained over 4 per cent. This was caused in the main by a very large outflow from agriculture. In recent years an increase in redundancies in industry has added to this problem.

The rates of increase in employment have varied according to industrial groups and this has resulted in changing the relative importance of some of them. Table 4 shows in fact that our traditional industries have become less important and our newer type industries, especially chemicals, metals and engineering and 'Others' have expanded.

OUTPUT

The volume of production in total manufacturing industry more than doubled between 1953 and 1971. Data relating to volume of production are given in Table 5.

Between 1953–56 expansion was relatively slow in all main industrial groups, while some actually declined. Expansion was recorded in all industrial groups in the following five years.

The next ten year period was characterised by substantial increases in production: in each of the main groups and in volume terms, all except one (Drink and Tobacco) expanded by at least 50 per cent and some by even more.

One outcome of the varying rates of growth in output of the main industrial groups is that our traditional industries, Food, Drink and Tobacco, Textiles, Clothing and Footwear, have declined in relative importance. Similar to their performance in employment terms our newer industries increased in both absolute and relative importance. These industries included Chemicals, Structural Clay and Cement, Metals and Engineering and Other Manufactures.

Productivity in manufacturing industry increased from an index of 86 in 1953 to 148 in 1971. The relevant data are presented in Table 6.

Between 1961–66 productivity increased by about 3.6 per cent per annum. In the following five years it averaged 5.2 per cent.

TABLE 4
Employment in main Industrial Groups as % of Employment in Total Manufacturing Industries, 1954–71

	1954	1956	1961	1966	1971
Food	23.9	23.3	23.0	22.5	21.9
Drink and Tobacco	7.1	7.1	6.3	5.9	5.4
Textiles	12.4	13.1	13.4	12.5	12.4
Clothing and Footwear	14.7	14.8	14.0	12.6	11.8
Wood and Furniture	5.9	5.7	4.5	4.4	4.0
Paper and Printing	9.2	9.7	9.3	8.5	8.3
Chemicals	3.0	3.2	3.5	3.9	4.1
Structural Clay and Cement	3.9	4.0	3.8	4.7	5.2
Metals and Engineering	15.0	14.5	16.7	18.9	19.6
Others	4.7	4.6	5.3	6.0	7.0
Total Manufacturing	100.0	100.0	100.0	100.0	100.0
Actual Numbers	145,656	145,036	157,600	174,900	196,000

Source. Review of 1972, Outlook for 1973 (Prl 3090.) Trends in Employment and Unemployment 1958 (Pr 5179.) Trends in Employment and Unemployment 1961 (Pr 6720.)

TABLE 5
Volume of Production, 1953–71 (Base year 1953 = 100)

Industrial Group	1953	1956	1961	1966	1971
Food	100	84	105	129	163
Drink and Tobacco	100	106	108	112	145
Textiles	100	121	174	218	356
Clothing and Footwear	100	100	121	148	173
Wood and Furniture	100	102	105	141	189
Paper and Printing	100	121	157	179	239
Chemicals	100	117	183	297	437
Structural Clay and Cement	100	123	144	253	426
Metals and Engineering	100	112	179	261	317
Other	100	112	203	324	549
Total Manufacturing Industry	100	104	135	175	240

Source. Review of 1972, Outlook for 1973 (Prl 3090.)

As regards productivity of industrial groups, increases were lower in the more traditional manfacturing industries i.e. Food, Drink and Tobacco, Clothing and Footwear. The only exception to this was the Textile industry.

TABLE 6
Productivity in Manufacturing Industry 1953–71
(Base year 1960 = 100)

Year	(1) Vol. of Output	(2) Employment	(3) Productivity
1953	80	93	86
1956	83	95	87
1961	109	105	104
1966	142	116	122
1971	193	130	148

Source. N I E C Report on Full Employment (Pr 9088). Review of 1972, Outlook for 1973 (Prl 3090).

From 1963 State grants were made available to assist industry to adapt and re-equip itself by means of Adaptation and Re-equipment Grants. These are discussed further elsewhere in this paper.

OTHER SECTORS

In the previous section headed 'Employment' the importance of manufacturing industry within the industrial sector as a whole was discussed. This is further highlighted when the importance of industry as a whole in the economy is examined.

In Table 7 the breakdown of the labour force between sectors is outlined. What emerges from this table is that while employment in agriculture fell continuously, the majority of new jobs were created in industry. After 1966 expansion of the services sector improved and this sector is expected to become increasingly important in the future. This is recognised by the Industrial Development Authority and is discussed further elsewhere in this paper.

MARKETS

Between 1953 and 1971 exports of manfactured goods increased by almost 650 per cent, from £56.7m to £365m. During the same period diversification by area and product of manufactured exports also occurred. In 1952, 88.3 per cent of total manufactured exports went to the United Kingdom, while in 1971 the comparative figure was 66.7 per cent. Full details are in Table 8.

In 1961 the most important industrial export was Food, which contributed more than 57 per cent of total manufactured exports. If we include Drink, Tobacco, Clothing and Footwear and Textiles, this figure increases to 78 per cent. By 1971 the relative contribution of Food had fallen to 45 per cent. Drink and Tobacco, Clothing and Footwear also declined in relative importance while Textiles increased slightly.

During this ten year period, the exports of other sectors increased dramatically. These included, for example, Chemicals (.8 per cent of total manufactured exports in 1961 to 5.2 per cent in 1971) and Other Manufacturers (7.9 per cent to 13.5 per cent).

SUMMARY

Between 1958–72 the Irish economy has continuously expanded with only two major downturns. During the period, G N P has

TABLE 7

Sectoral Breakdown of Total at Work (000s)

	1951		1956		1961		1966		1971	
	No.	%	No.	%	No.	%	No.	%	No.	%
Agriculture etc.	496	40.8	430	38.2	379.5	36.1	333.6	31.3	282.0	26.3
Industry	283	23.3	269	23.9	257.2	24.4	293.7	27.6	328.0	30.6
Services	438	35.9	426	37.9	415.8	39.5	438.6	41.1	461.0	43.1
Total	1217	100.0	1125	100.0	1052.5	100.0	1066	100.0	1071.0	100.0

Source. N I E C Report on Full Employment (Pr 9088). Review of 1972, Outlook for 1973 (Prl 3090).

TABLE 8

Area Analysis of Manufacturing Exports (%) 1952-71

Year	1952	1956	1961	1966	1971
U K and N I	88.3	83.6	74.7	69.5	66.7
E E C (Six)	2.8	5.4	5.7	10.3	9.0
N America	4.4	3.5	12.8	9.7	13.2
Other Areas	4.4	7.5	6.8	10.5	11.1
Total	100	100	100	100	100

Source. Coras Trachtala Annual Reports

risen from £600m (1958) to £2,237m in 1972. At the same time, growth in manufacturing industry has been particularly dynamic in terms of output (which increased by 150 per cent to a value of £1,377m in 1972) and exports (£83.8m in 1960 to £436m in 1972). Employment in the manufacturing industry grew substantially from 141,800 in 1958 to 198,000 in 1972, while productivity increases were recorded in all main industrial groups. Thus the Irish industrial base has been both widened (through the creation of new industry) and strengthened (because of improvements in technology). Part 2 describes how the Government, through the agency of a State organisation—The Industrial Development Authority—encouraged the development of the manufacturing industry sector by a system of incentives.

Part II
The Industrial Development Authority
The Industrial Development Authority was founded in 1949 as an agency of the Department of Industry and Commerce. With the implementation of the Industrial Development Act, 1969, it became an autonomous state sponsored organisation in April 1970. This Act merged two organisations within the public service, The Grants Board and the Industrial Development Authority into a new and larger I D A. The former was established originally under the Undeveloped Areas Act, 1952, and at the time of the merger, had the functions of administering new industry and adaptation grants, and of developing industrial estates. The original I D A was first set up as an industrial

DONEGAL

Northern Ireland

NORTH-WEST

NORTH-EAST

WEST

MIDLANDS

●Galway

●Dublin

EAST

MID-WEST

Limerick/
Shannon

SOUTH-EAST

SOUTH-WEST

Waterford●

Cork●

Designated Areas
(Previously called undeveloped Areas)

advisory and promotion agency. Its main functions included the initiation of proposals for the creation of industries in certain specified fields and the attraction of foreign industrialists to the country, either to establish new enterprises or to participate in the development of existing industries.

The 'Undeveloped Areas'

The Grants Board was empowered by Acts of 1952 and 1957 to make grants towards the establishment or extension of industry in what were described as the 'undeveloped areas' i.e. the counties of Donegal, Sligo, Leitrim, Mayo, Galway, Roscommon, Kerry, West of Clare and parts of West Cork. (See Map 1.) For good reasons these areas could be extended on occasion by the Minister for Industry and Commerce who could declare a place outside these areas named 'undeveloped' for the purpose of qualifying for a grant. These grants were outright and were available up to the full cost of the factory site and the buildings and fifty per cent of the cost of plant and machinery. The origin of these Acts lay in the recognition that the West of Ireland had failed to benefit from the general industrial development programme to the same extent as other parts of the country, and that emigration from the West was far heavier than from other parts of Ireland. These Acts signified the emergence of a regional attitude towards industrial planning.

Areas outside the 'Undeveloped Areas'

The Industrial Grants Act, 1956, which empowered the IDA to give grants for new industrial projects located outside the undeveloped areas, had two broad objectives viz., the arrest of the rising trend in emigration through the balanced expansion of industrial employment, and the improvement of the external balance of payments position through imports substitution and increased exports. Supplementary measures, introduced about the same time, included tax concessions for profits derived from exports.

The Industrial Grants Act, 1959, provided that industrial grants could be given towards the establishment or development of projects located outside the undeveloped areas where there were sound reasons why the projects could not be established in the undeveloped areas, where they would be of exceptional potential and where the need for financial assistance by way of grant, as distinct from other forms of financial aid, could be established. It also transferred the administration of these grants from the I D A to The Grants Board, which was already administering the grants scheme for the undeveloped areas. The act provided, for the first time outside the undeveloped areas, that an existing concern could qualify for a grant in the same way as if it were a completely new enterprise.

The Industrial Grants (Amendment) Act, 1963, and the Undeveloped Areas (Amendment) Act, 1963, resolved many of the divergencies between the treatment of the so-called 'undeveloped areas' and the rest of the country. They marked a re-orientation of the industrial grants scheme by (i) making it somewhat easier for promoters to qualify for grants in respect of projects located outside the undeveloped areas; (ii) revising the employment test for large scale capital intensive projects; and (iii) making training grants hitherto available only in the 'undeveloped areas', available nationally.

Adaptation Grants

In order to encourage existing Irish industry to adapt to free trade conditions, special grants were made available under the Industrial Grants (Amendment) Act, 1963. Industrial Adaptation Councils were established to co-ordinate rationalisation on an industry-wide basis. By early 1965, Adaptation Councils had been set up in twenty-four industries. Time limits were set for making application for an adaptation grant. Under the provisions of the Industrial Grants (Amendment) Act, 1966, the limit expired on the 30th September 1967, while the time within which the Board could approve a grant expired on the 30th June 1968, under the provisions of the Industrial Grants (Amendment) Act, 1968. Over the whole period of the Adaptation Grants Scheme (i.e. February 1963 to March 1968) a total of 1,423 grants were approved totalling £21.6m. Related total projected investment in existing industries was £96.9m. In 1968 these Adaptation Grants were replaced by Re-equipment Grants which are discussed again elsewhere in this paper.

Industrial Estates and Provision of Advance Facilities

Originally, Shannon Free Airport had been statutorily desig-

nated as a customs-free airport as far back as 1947, when legislation was enacted to facilitate transit traffic and to enable the
establishment at the airport of manufacturing, processing ware-
housing and entrepôt trade generally. Little progress was, however, made with the development of the area as an industrial
centre until 1957–59 when the Shannon Free Airport Development Company was set up and later given the power to promote
and develop an industrial estate at the airport.

The 1966 Industrial Grants (Amendment) Act provided for
the development of industrial estates other than at Shannon and
to date two major estates have been developed at Galway and at
Waterford. In 1973, 933 were employed on the Galway estate
and 773 in Waterford. The Authority has also commenced a
programme of (*a*) Advance Factory construction at over 30
selected centres and (*b*) advance acquisition of land for industrial development.

Small Industries Programme

In 1967 a special Small Industries Programme was introduced. The aim of this programme was to facilitate the establishment and expansion of small scale industries. Nearly 900 projects
have been approved and grants paid to date amount to £4.0m.
Total projected employment at full production in these projects
is over 6,500.

A.D. Little Reports and the Industrial Development Act, 1969

Two reports commissioned by the I D A from A. D. Little Inc.,
were published in 1967. These reviewed (i) the Structure of the
I D A and (ii) the range of Incentives for Industry available in
Ireland, and formed the basis for the legislative provisions embodied in the Industrial Development Act, 1969, which provided for the dissolution of The Grants Board and the transfer
of its functions to an expanded and re-organised I D A as
already mentioned.

This act increased the range and scale of incentives, grants
and other financial measures, for industrial development; gave
to the I D A the function of fostering regional industrial development; and enabled the Authority to provide advance factories,
sites and services for anticipated industrial development throughout the country, including housing for key persons employed in

industry. The Act also re-defined the 'Undeveloped Areas' as 'Designated Areas'. It forms the basis of present-day activities and the full scope of its provisions will be more readily appreciated on reading the sections of this paper which cover the Role, Functions and Organisational Structure of the IDA.

Summary

From this brief historical review of state industrial development policy up to and including the 1969 Act, it is possible to identify a number of objectives which were basic to the whole philosophy underlying the various legislative enactments. These are as follows:

(i) to increase industrial employment opportunities as a whole;

(ii) to encourage the location of new industries away from Dublin, so as to secure a more balanced distribution of population and employment throughout the country;

(iii) to encourage the expansion of existing industry, particularly by the development of exports;

(iv) to assist our balance of payments position by substituting home-manufactured for imported goods and by increasing export earnings;

(v) to attract industrial development from abroad, in the form of capital and technology, to supplement domestic resources.

These objectives reflect a growing concern for a more comprehensive regional approach to national industrial development and an increasing need to evolve a viable and properly integrated industrial structure based on a major input of foreign capital, technology and entrepreneurship to supplement native resources.

ROLE AND FUNCTIONS OF THE IDA

The present development powers of the IDA concentrate on the following range of activities:

(i) The preparation and implementation of Regional Industrial Plans which accord with national, social and economic goals as laid down in various Government policy statements.

(ii) Making grants to manufacturing industry towards the cost of fixed assets, re-equipment, manpower training, research and development of new products and processes, reduction of loan interest and factory rentals.

(iii) Guaranteeing loans and where appropriate taking equity participation in industrial enterprises.

(iv) The encouragement of diversification through associations, licensing agreements and joint ventures.

(v) The carrying out of promotion and publicity campaigns at home and abroad.

(vi) Securing the provision of physical infrastructure for industrial development i.e. land, services, factories and housing.

Operational programmes related to these activities have been devised :

(i) to assist the development of new large and medium sized industry by both home and foreign based enterprise;

(ii) to modernise, strengthen and expand existing industry in Ireland;

(iii) to develop existing and new small industries (i.e with up to fifty employees and £100,000 in fixed assets in designated areas of the country and up to thirty employees and £60,000 in fixed assets in non-designated areas).

(iv) to provide industrial estates, advance factories and housing for key industrial workers.

The IDA is financed by grants-in-aid from the vote of the Department of Industry and Commerce and currently has an annual revenue budget of £1.4m and disposes of an annual capital budget of £25–£30m. The capital budget finances actual payments of current IDA grant commitments as well as direct capital expenditure by the IDA on industrial estates and advance factories.

Organisational Structure

The IDA's headquarters organisation is made up of 9 divisions corresponding to the major functional areas of the IDA's work. Diagram 1 illustrates this (page 183).

Overseas offices of the IDA which are located in London, Paris, Brussels, Cologne, New York, Chicago, San Francisco, Los Angeles, Toronto, Sydney, Tokyo and Copenhagen, provide the points of direct promotional contact between the IDA and overseas industrialists. The offices undertake promotional work through other channels which influence industrial investment

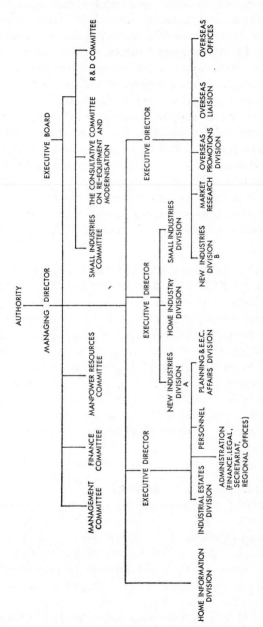

I.D.A. ORGANISATIONAL STRUCTURE

decisions, such as banks, accountancy and management consultancy firms, and financial journalists. They also work closely with the Department of Foreign Affairs representatives abroad.

The I D A's regional offices, which were established in January 1971, supply a wide range of services for existing and new industries in their regions, including information and advice on I D A grants and services, site and factory availability, labour resources, water supples, housing communications and educational and training facilities. The regional offices also provide an after-care service for new industries in their regions and are responsible for monitoring industrial trends in their regions, particularly with reference to impending commercial difficulties. The offices work closely with the regional development organisations, county development teams, local authorities and voluntary development organisations in their regions.

CO-ORDINATION WITH OTHER ORGANISATIONS

The complex range of development activities discharged by the I D A form only a part—though a central part—of the total industrial development process. Other state agencies, as well as Government departments, have responsibility for activities which critically affect, or depend upon the activities of the I D A. The whole system of inter-dependencies represented by the industrial development process is such as to require that continuous and wide-ranging consultation occurs in day-to-day contacts, but in certain key policy areas, there are also formal I D A committees which include representatives of various co-operating development agencies.

OPERATIONAL FRAMEWORK

This section deals generally with the overall I D A operational framework as set out in Diagram 2, and in particular with individual elements of the industrialisation process as set out in Diagram 3. All operational activities are best appreciated in the context of the job targets established for the current year which are set out in Diagram 4 on a divisional and place of origin basis.

The I D A's direct involvement in the Industrial Development Process breaks down into two main divisions: the attraction of

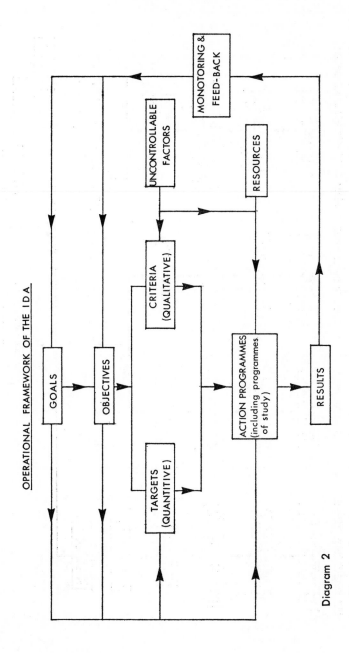

OPERATIONAL FRAMEWORK OF THE IDA

Diagram 2

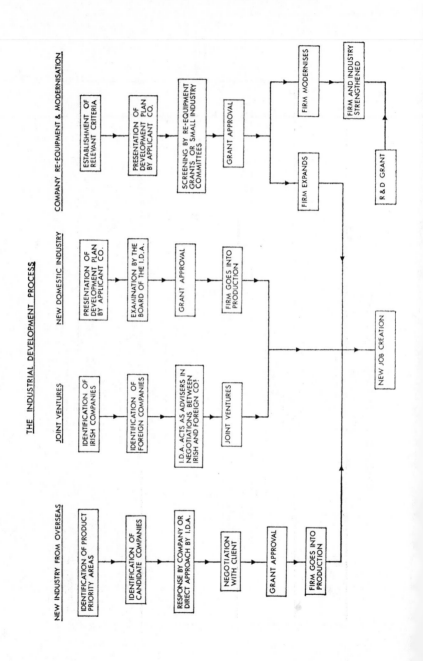

THE INDUSTRIAL DEVELOPMENT PROCESS

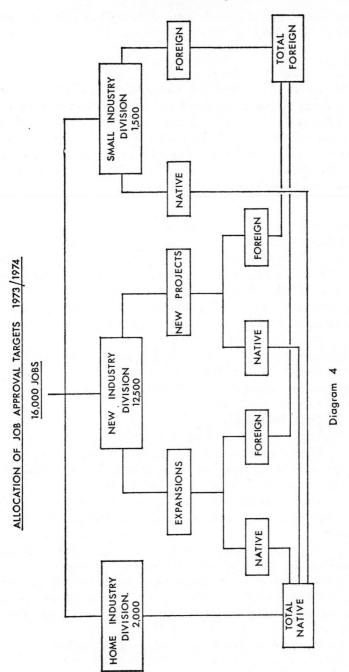

ALLOCATION OF JOB APPROVAL TARGETS 1973/1974

16,000 JOBS

Diagram 4

new foreign industry (both large and small) and the expansion and modernisation of domestic industry.

OVERSEAS JOB PROMOTION
The Industrial Development Authority, in its efforts to attract new foreign industry has developed a 'direct approach strategy' which is outlined below. Essentially this consists of (i) establishing basic selection criteria for product priority areas (ii) selecting the actual products (iii) screening of company leaders in various product priority areas and then (iv) making a direct approach to the short-listed companies.

Basic Selection Criteria
Criteria have been established to identify product priority areas and projects and related companies which taken together yield high national, social and economic benefits. The information for the identification process has emerged from research carried out by the IDA itself and from a number of studies commissioned from consultancy firms. The basic selection criteria for product areas are:
(1) Exportable by nature with high growth rate of product in international markets. Such growth should be high relative to risk involved and at least 90 per cent of aggregate output should be directed to export markets.
(2) High profitability.
(3) High male labour content.
(4) High dependence on a skilled work-force.
(5) Stability in terms of small probability of technological obsolescence, that is long product life cycle.
(6) High national value added through the use of native resources and raw materials, locally manufactured products or services.
(7) Not too capital intensive or if it is high, substantial possibilities of linkage or spin-off benefits from the product.
(8) Contribute to specific sectoral integration of industrial structure and/or have joint venture possibilities where companies can match complementary strengths to their mutual benefit.
(9) Potential for generating services sector employment.

Product Priority Areas

A ranking is carried out of the product areas which have the greatest potential for conversion into actual projects in Ireland. The list below gives some of the industrial product areas which have been isolated by the I D A research as having priority in future industrial developments. Very few of these product areas have been established, to a substantial level, to date in Ireland.

Food. Nutritional/health products—Processed meat products—Delicatessen products.

Instrumentation. Electronics navigational aids—Medical, surgical, opthalmic instruments—Laboratory and scientific measuring equipment—Video equipment—hand power tools—Process control equipment—Computer peripheral equipment.

Chemicals. Antibiotics (bulk)—Other pharmaceuticals (active ingredients only).

Engineering/Electronics. Environmental control equipment—Office equipment—Commercial/institutional food service equipment—Automobile parts and accessories—Security devices—Mechanical handling/hydraulic equipment.

Other Products. Industrial ceramics and refractories—Adhesives—Bonded fabrics—Sports/leisure equipment—Pleasure boats—Education/teaching products.

The research into priority industrial sectors is only the beginning of a very complex process of identification and selection of new industrial investment possibilities from industrial sectors. The process next leads to industrial companies which are established as leaders in the various priority product areas.

Screening of Company Leaders

The criteria for identification and screening of company leaders in the various product priority areas are :

(i) Commercial soundness as measured by liquidity, general growth and profitability record.

(ii) Company growth potential as indicated by the company's

present strategic positioning for market growth and its likely effectiveness in exploiting this position e.g. company originating from outside the E E C but seeking to establish enterprises within the enlarged community.

(iii) Production capacity pressures in the company.

(iv) Ability of company to fund new investments.

(v) Pressures in the company towards locational mobility.

(vi) Historical policy of the company in responding to advantages of new locations for investment.

(vii) International companies prepared to give an Irish subsidiary a high degree of independence in policy and decision making and with a natural orientation to the Irish situation.

(viii) Likely capacity and commitment to integrate into the Irish economy and to grow in Ireland.

(ix) Likely degree of preparedness to become associated with the scientific and technological infrastructure of the country.

The sifting and short listing of industrial companies on the basis of the above screening criteria is a long and laborious process. A search in a certain product area started with 21,000 companies, and was reduced to 3,325 after the elimination of companies with less than 100 employed, and yielded 1,235 candidates after screening on the above criteria.

International Marketing

Since each company has been selected with an eye to the pressure which its growth performance is putting on existing production capacity and which may be leading the company to decisions on new locations for its activities, the next phase of the process is that of intercepting ongoing investment planning in candidate companies. This is the vital stage of the selection effort in that it seeks to channel scarce I D A marketing resources to where investment planning is at critical stages in companies and therefore, to where the benefits of locating new investment projects in Ireland are likely to be more relevant and attractive.

Contact with prospective clients occurs in many ways. These include direct approach to the companies by the I D A, response by the companies to I D A advertising, and banks, consultants and other experts drawing the Republic to the attention of industrialists.

The marketing environment for this activity is dynamic. There can be radical changes in legislation, political climate or availablity of resources which could radically alter the course, timing and intensity of promotional and selling programmes. Examples of this are the Northern Ireland political unrest, the Nixon Tax measures and the world investment climate. The impact of such external factors means that a programme aiming to further industrial development must be flexible if it is to be successful.

Small Industries

The approach outlined above applies particularly to the attraction of medium and large size firms. However, since 1971 the IDA have adapted this process to attract new foreign small industry. In this context 250 presentations were made in 1972–73 to companies in the Netherlands and Sweden and also to a number of commercial organisations and companies in Denmark, France, Germany and Britain.

DOMESTIC JOB CREATION

The IDA's involvement in the domestic industrial sector has four main elements: (i) the identification and screening of Irish companies capable of major expansion (ii) assisting the restructuring of Irish industry (iii) the promotion of product and process development and (iv) the encouragement of joint ventures.

Major Expansions

Major expansions within the domestic sector are considered as new industries. The 'direct approach strategy' which the IDA developed to attract new foreign industry and which has been outlined above has been adapted to suit domestic conditions.

Essentially the process involves contact with firms which have the capability for undertaking major expansions. Such expansions must be consistent with expected market growth and the firm in question must demonstrate its ability to handle the project in terms of production know-how, financial control and marketing ability.

Re-equipment and Modernisation

Under the Re-equipment and Modernisation Grants Schemes Irish firms can get grants towards the cost of new buildings and machinery (up to 35 per cent in designated areas, 25 per cent in other areas) where the investment is part of a sound plan to re-organise a firm's manufacturing operations. The I D A sees the scheme as an instrument for encouraging firms to work out development/expansion programmes for up to five years ahead. The programme takes account of forecast changes in the firm's product sector.

In contrast to foreign firms setting up, first contact between the I D A and the firm for re-equipment grants is initiated usually by the firm. While there is an acknowledged need for flexibility in dealing with projects of this kind, the I D A has developed certain guidelines to assist in the evaluation of proposals from companies. The selection criteria differ in detail according to the industry, but the following is a list of the more general ones:

(i) The firm's application for assistance under the Re-equipment Grants Scheme must be part of a comprehensive plan of future strategy and development;

(ii) The firm must satisfy the I D A as to the efficiency of its management and the soundness of its financial structure;

(iii) the recent performance of the firm will be considered and is expected to at least equal the average growth in production and return on capital employed in its production section. Thus for example, an applicant from one industry would be expected to have a return on capital employed of around 15 per cent.

(iv) Grants are not approved for expansion which create excess production capacity out of line with the likely future demand for the particular products.

(v) Special criteria are sometimes applied depending on the industries involved and the circumstances. For example, some firms are encouraged to merge, while others are discouraged from producing particular types of product.

These criteria are designed so the firms concerned can survive and expand profitably.

The I D A has not only been tackling the problem of modernisation of industries on a firm by firm basis. A task force was established last year to deal with the wool textile industry as a whole. Following examination and discussions the closure of certain woollen mills was decided upon; the affected areas then received priority as regards the setting up of new firms.

Joint Ventures

Continued attention is being given to partnership investment in the form of joint ventures between overseas and Irish companies with complementary strengths. Conclusions from experience to date are:

(i) the potential for new investment in the form of joint ventures is limited but valuable.

(ii) the principal limitations derive from a mismatch between the respective capabilities and requirements of Irish and overseas companies.

(iii) within the limitations that exist suitable partnerships can be evolved. In the context of our industrial needs joint ventures are a very desirable form of business. It is intended, therefore, to continue to apply resources to this area.

Research and Development in Industry

The I D A in 1970 introduced a scheme to encourage research and development mainly in domestic industry. The scheme is designed to assist the undertaking of projects which contribute to the viability and competitiveness of manufacturing firms by promoting the development of new and improved processes and products, particularly those suited to native materials and local conditions.

Under this scheme in the period 1970–73, total grants of over £400,000 have been made available for eighty-six development projects. A further £120,000 also has been allocated to provide research facilities for eight firms.

Domestic Small Industry

Many of the present activities of the Small Industries Division fall under the broad heading of domestic industry, since its operations were mainly geared towards developing the existing small industry base and assisting the development of new projects by Irish people.

There are three main stages in assisting existing industry:

(i) The organisational and production capabilities of small enterprises are examined.

(ii) In the light of this investigation, a development plan is prepared by the manufacturer in conjunction with his local

County Development Team and the Small Industries Division of the IDA.

(iii) After the approval of the plan, its implementation involves IDA grants and after-care assistance as well as help from various organisations.

The development of management skills, through courses organised by the Irish Management Institute, is of vital importance to the overall small industries programme.

RESULTS TO DATE

Table 9 below gives details of IDA expenditure over the years. This expenditure includes non-repayable cash grants and monies expended on the provision of advance factories and other facilities for industry. The increased rate of expenditure in recent years reflects the more extensive commitments and activities of the IDA. There is also an element of the increased cost of job creation in these figures.

During the period 1954–73 actual jobs created with IDA assistance totalled about 50,000. At the same time employment in manufacturing industry in the state increased by 58,000. These data are in net terms. Because substantial redundancies occurred in recent years, the gross employment increases in

TABLE 9

IDA Expenditure for 1952–73 (£m) Annual Average

1952–61	1961–66	1966–71	1971–72	1972–73
.3	2.6	8.9	26.0	24.7

Source. IDA Annual Reports.

industry have been considerably greater. Nevertheless IDA assisted industries have been the primary source of new industrial employment in the last twenty years.

The main sources of the 50,000 jobs created with IDA aid were projects from abroad and some major expansions by Irish firms. A discernible and very welcome trend in recent years has been the growing emergence of Irish based firms, both as providers of new employment opportunities and greater industrial output. It is estimated that over 40 per cent of employment creation in the year ended 31 March 1973 came from domestic sources.

A significant indicator of this trend has been the increasing amounts that the I D A has disbursed on its Re-equipment and Modernisation Grants. (£14.5m since 1970.)

SOME NEW INITIATIVES
The dynamic nature of the industrial development process renders it imperative to continuously monitor the effectiveness of existing policies and to introduce new initiatives which in the changed circumstances can contribute more effectively towards the aim of creating a viable and integrated industrial structure. The following is a résumé of some important questions relating to the industrial development process in the Republic which are at present receiving consideration within the I D A.

Sectoral Policy
Considerable attention is being given to the application of an overall sectoral policy in Irish manufacturing industry with particular regard to areas of special advantage by virtue of our natural resources.

(i) What industries are suitable for the achievement of a high degree of sectoral integration?

(ii) How confined in a regional geographic area might these industries have to be to develop the required degree of mutual interrelatedness?

(iii) How and at what stage will these industries induce further growth of economic activities and forge strong self-sustaining growth?

(iv) What special forms of social investment are required in order that this necessary industrialisation can commence and continue?

Much further research is needed before actual action programmes can be formulated and implemented in relation to these issues.

The development of key maritime resources is seen as an important medium and long-term instrument of national and regional planning policy in Ireland and has a crucial role to play in the sphere of sectoral policy. Port and Harbour projects and related maritime industrial development are particularly important in this respect. Consideration is now being given to the preparation of practical and co-ordinated plans for certain key natural deep-water bays and estuaries.

This type of approach lends itself to concentration in one or two selected sectors in which it should be possible to identify a few specific industrial groupings for which special incentive 'Packages' could be designed. Related to this concept is the whole question of the existence (or otherwise) of valuable off-shore oil and gas resources and the servicing requirements needed at the exploration and (if successful) development stages.

Services Sector

It is recognised that effective national development involves all sectors of the economy, and that the industrial sector alone cannot provide enough jobs to meet our national requirements. Services employment and in particular office employment has increased rapidly in the last decade. It has, however, in the main been concentrated in the Dublin region.

A well developed services sector is regarded by the I D A as essential to the expansion of manufacturing industry and the Authority has recently taken measures to investigate the scope for attracting certain service type industries to locate export oriented activities in Ireland. A pilot investigation which included discussions with firms involved in chemical and mechanical plant design and construction, and consulting engineering has recently been carried out in three countries, Britain, Holland and Germany. The results of this study are still being analysed but preliminary indications are that a programme along the lines of that used to encourage the manufacturing industry sector could facilitate faster and more effective development of our services sector.

In 1972, the Authority published comprehensive Regional Industrial Plans covering the period 1973–77. These plans which have been endorsed by the Government set out national, regional and local job targets and the I D A has geared itself to achieve these targets. The plans are monitored closely and it is intended to review them at regular intervals.

Ireland and the E E C

Since one of the papers at the conference dealt explicitly with the topic 'Ireland and the Common Market', I have confined comment here to the simple statement that Ireland's accession to the European Community has very important implications for our industrial development process. Naturally our present and future programmes of activity take explicit account of the opportunities and constraints of our membership of the Community.

Part III
Some Conclusions

As can be seen from the data on the progress made in the manufacturing industry sector over the twenty year period (see pages 166–76) and the important part Government incentives played in this expansion (see page 194) the approach adopted has succeeded in the aim of re-organising and expanding the country's manufacturing industry, and thereby creating a more viable and competitive economy in general.

Two striking features of the Government's efforts have been the evolutionary and flexible nature of the measures used. These of course, are not surprising bearing in mind the ever changing and complex nature of the environment in which industry itself operates.

Moreover, while the Irish experience could be used as a guideline by other countries attempting to either develop or strengthen their manufacturing industry sectors, certain unique characteristics of the Irish situation are worth mentioning in the context of the relationship of the Irish economy to that of the United Kingdom.

Except for the short period when the impact of the Northern Ireland political unrest affected relations, economic and political, social and cultural ties between the Republic and the United Kingdom were strong. From the Irish industrial development point of view, these factors were of crucial importance in that (a) Irish industrialists had a market for their exports and (b) United Kingdom companies availed of the Irish labour surplus and industrial incentives. Thus, even yet, over 60 per cent of Irish manufacturing exports go to the United Kingdom and on average, the United Kingdom has been the source of 20 per cent of our new grant-aided employment. The system adopted by the Irish Government in the late 1950s of encouraging the private sector, especially manufacturing industry, with incentives to develop and strengthen itself in the context of international competition was certainly facilitated by this special relationship.

The frequent modulation of our incentives system must also be seen in the light of the size and stage of development of the Irish economy and in particular the manufacturing industry sector. As the smaller firm is normally able to adapt quicker than the larger firm because of a shorter management structure and less commitment of resources to a particular activity, thus it is possible to successfully refine an industrial development programme of incentives for an economy with a small industrial sector more often than for a large economy. For example, in the United Kingdom, a change in a particular Government measure, designed to encourage industry, would have to be assessed in relation to a larger number of firms located in diverse and quite unevenly developed regions, and with substantial linkages with other concerns and large employment implications. In the Republic the scale is totally different. In addition, where the smaller economy is engaged in international trade, quick adaptation to international developments in investment and trade, even when these are slight, is essential and normal.

Also, it must be clearly recognised that the implementation of a programme of industrial incentives is itself a learning process and in the Irish context part of the movement towards the full development of our economy. Accordingly, on the one hand experience suggests new approaches, for example, the development of the marketing approach described earlier, and on the other hand, ultimate achievement of the overall development objectives described on page 181 suggests, for example, the introduction of a more comprehensive sectoral policy for manufacturing industry and the initiation of action in relation to the service sector.

Finally, this paper has attempted to show the flexible and evolutionary nature of the industrial development process in the Republic over the past twenty years. Since 1969 when more extensive powers were vested in the I D A, new initiatives, measures and emphases within the framework laid down by the legislation have been introduced at a rapid rate. One safe forecast can be made about this paper. In certain respects it will be out of date very shortly!

MAIN INDUSTRIAL INCENTIVES

Taxation

15 years complete exemption from taxes on export profits and partial exemption for the remaining years up to 1990. The provision applies to profits earned from exports of manufactured goods and certain services.

Cash Grants

Non-repayable cash grants towards the cost of fixed assets negotiable up the following limits of : 50 per cent in the Designated Areas. 35 per cent in other areas. (Consistent with regional industrial development strategy.)

Grants are provided towards the cost of training workers and managers and towards the cost of instructors and consultants engaged to train personnel.

Non-repayable cash grants towards the cost of approved research and development projects in new industrial products and processes. Maximum : £15,000 or 50 per cent of approved costs, whichever is smallest.

Grants towards the reduction of rentals on factories on the I D A industrial estates and elsewhere.

Other Incentives

Guarantees of loans and subsidisation of interest on loans.

Ready-made facilities on industrial estates at Shannon Airport, Waterford and Galway including advance factories and industrial services.

Industrial housing for workers close to the industrial estates at Waterford and Galway and at other selected centres provided in conjunction with the National Building Agency.

Advance factories at selected centres as part of the regional development programmes now in operation.

An after-care advisory service for newly established industries in the early years of production.

Some Economic Implications of the Various 'Solutions' to the Northern Ireland Problem [1]

NORMAN GIBSON

THERE are no doubt in principle many possible so-called political solutions to the Northern Ireland problem. Only three are considered here: (i) that Northern Ireland remains part of the United Kingdom on the sort of terms laid down in the recent Northern Ireland Constitution Act; (ii) that an independent Northern Ireland is established outside the United Kingdom; and (iii) that Northern Ireland becomes part of a united Ireland. In what follows I try and explore, tentatively and incompletely, some of the macro-economic implications of each of these alternative 'solutions'. Clearly the discussion is inevitably hypothetical and would require major modifications depending upon the precise form of any political solution and the associated economic and other arrangements. To begin with, however, I sketch some of the main features of the present Northern Ireland economy as a background to the primary purpose of the paper.

The Northern Ireland Economy

Probably the most satisfactory way to describe any economy would be to present it in terms of a well specified behavioural model that had withstood the test of time. However, few such models exist and, as far as I know, none exists for the Northern Ireland economy. The best that I am able to do is to select some of the more strategic macro-variables and use them to give some indication of the shape and structure of the economy.

Table 1 shows that gross domestic product and personal income *per capita* have each been rising over the last ten years or so and also as a proportion of the corresponding figures for the United Kingdom as a whole. However, at 72 per cent and 79 per cent respectively of gross domestic product and personal income for 1971 they remain much below the United Kingdom average. Furthermore, since gross domestic product includes interest, dividends and undistributed profits, which accrue to those outside the area, it may give a distorted picture of the product or income available. This may be of particular importance to areas such as Northern Ireland where so much attention is given to attracting industry from outside. On the other hand Northern Ireland like other regions earns income outside its boundaries and this would have to be allowed for in estimating gross regional income or product. To the best of my knowledge no such estimates exist, though if they did they would certainly be most useful. (It would also be highly informative to have a further income measure—*gross regional disposable income*—which is the sum of gross regional income and *net* current transfers to the region.)

TABLE 1

Per Capita Gross Domestic Product (at Factor Cost) and Personal Income for Northern Ireland at Selected Dates and as a Percentage of United Kingdom Figures

	1960	1961	1963	1966	1967	1969	1970	1971
Gross Domestic Product £	273	284	326	396	423	489	547	620
Per cent of United Kingdom	63	62	66	66	67	70	71	72
Personal Income £	296	312	350	427	467	543	602	676
Per cent of United Kingdom	73	72	74	73	76	78	78	79

Source. Ministry of Commerce

It is noteworthy that personal income *per capita* is substantially higher than gross domestic product both absolutely and as a proportion of the United Kingdom figure. The main arithmetic reason for this is that current grants from public authorities as a component of personal income are some 50 per cent more important in Northern Ireland than in the United Kingdom as a whole. Inter-regional income transfers would seem to be a reality and are necessarily a recurring theme in what follows.

The industry of origin of gross domestic product is of interest to our topic and is shown in Table 2.

As might perhaps be expected from the relative growth of gross domestic product *per capita* in Northern Ireland and the United Kingdom, industrial production has in the last ten years or so expanded much more rapidly in the former. Over the thirteen years 1959 to 1972 the rate of growth for Northern Ireland was about 4.9 per cent per year and for the whole United

TABLE 2

Contribution of Specified Industry to Gross Domestic Product
1960, 1965 and 1970

	£m 1960 Actual	%	£m 1965 Actual	%	£m 1970 Actual	%
Agriculture etc.	49	12.7	58	10.5	75	9.0
Food, drink and tobacco			49	8.9	64	7.7
Engineering			50	9.1	76	9.1
Textiles	129	33.4	44	8.0	69	8.3
Clothing			13	2.4	21	2.5
Building and contracting	22	5.7	36	6.5	55	6.6
Transport and communications	15	3.9	31	5.6	53	6.3
Professional, financial and miscellaneous services	84	21.8	115	20.9	180	21.6
Government administration and defence	22	5.7	35	6.4	59	7.1
Other manufacturing industries	*	*	30	5.4	67	6.8
Gas, electricity and water	9	2.3	14	2.5	21	2.5
Distribution	46	11.9	59	10.7	75	9.0
Ownership of dwellings	10	2.6	17	3.1	30	3.6
Total	386	100.0	551	100.0	835	100.0

Source. Digest of Statistics : Northern Ireland No. 39. March 1973. Table 109, and *ibid.*, No. 28, September 1967. Table 134.

Note. Other manufacturing industries includes mining and quarrying and no allowance for stock appreciation has been made. Actual figures are in current prices.

*Included in 129 and 33.4 for 1960.

Kingdom 2.5 per cent. A major contributor to the expansion has been textiles which over the period grew at an average annual rate of 7.5 per cent. This latter figure includes a decline in the linen industry and a dramatic expansion of miscellaneous textiles which is mostly concentrated on synthetic fibres. The important and composite engineering industry which includes shipbuilding, marine, electrical and mechanical engineering, vehicles and aircraft, increased its output by only some 10 per cent over the same thirteen years. On the other hand the construction industry grew at an annual rate of around 6.5 per cent over the same period. The food, drink and tobacco industry expanded at an annual rate of about 2.6 per cent. Between them these four industrial groups account for some 75 per cent of total industrial production.

In the light of the overall expansion of output of the Northern Ireland economy it will come as no surprise that gross domestic fixed capital formation has for a number of years been a relatively high proportion of gross domestic product. Table 3 shows that since 1967 it has been over 30 per cent of gross domestic product. The table also shows for purposes of comparison that since 1965 this proportion has been some 50 per cent higher than that for the whole United Kingdom and that public sector investment in Northern Ireland has generally been a much higher component of gross domestic product than in the United Kingdom as a whole.

Most regional economies, and Northern Ireland is no exception, are open in the sense that their imports and exports represent a high proportion of their gross domestic products by comparison with most, though by no means all, distinct countries. For the past five years or so imports of goods have been between 88 per cent and 99 per cent of gross domestic product and exports between 80 per cent and 89 per cent. Of the imports the equivalent of some 70 per cent of gross domestic product came 'from and through Great Britain' and 24 per cent from outside the United Kingdom. The corresponding figures for exports are 76 per cent and 11 per cent. In trading terms Northern Ireland is clearly highly dependent on the British economy. More particularly every major industry in Northern Ireland relies heavily on the British market both as a source of raw materials and as an outlet for its final products.

TABLE 3

Gross Domestic Fixed Capital Formation as a Percentage of
Gross Domestic Product 1960–71

NI	1960	1961	1962	1963	1964	1965
G.D.F.C.F./G.D.P.	22.0	23.5	25.1	26.3	26.9	29.2
G.D.F.C.F.*/G.D.P.	9.3	9.9	10.9	11.3	11.6	12.0
UK						
G.D.F.C.F./G.D.P.	18.2	19.1	18.7	18.3	20.2	20.4
G.D.F.C.F.*/G.D.P.	7.3	7.5	7.8	8.0	8.9	9.0

NI	1966	1967	1968	1969	1970	1971
G.D.F.C.F./G.D.P.	29.9	30.3	32.4	33.6	33.7	34.0
G.D.F.C.F.*/G.D.P.	14.1	15.4	14.8	13.5	13.9	15.2
UK						
G.D.F.C.F./G.D.P.	20.5	21.0	21.5	21.1	21.5	20.8
G.D.F.C.F.*/G.D.P.	9.6	10.5	10.3	9.6	9.4	9.4

Sources. Northern Ireland Digest of Statistics, Northern Ireland
Economic Report on 1972 and National Income and Expenditure 1971 and 1972 (Blue Books).

Note. Gross Domestic Product is measured at factor cost and Gross
Domestic Fixed Capital Formation at market prices. Thus all
the percentages are slightly overstated in comparison with a consistent pricing basis. No figures exist for Northern Ireland for
allocating taxation on expenditure and subsidies to Gross
Domestic Fixed Capital Formation.

*Public Sector.

Probably the most politically sensitive aspect of the Northern
Ireland economy is the question of employment and unemployment. In the last twenty years or so major changes have taken
place in the industrial distribution of employment. In 1950
about 101,000 were employed in agriculture, and 24,000 in
ship-building and marine engineering but as Table 4 indicates
these figures had fallen to just over 51,000 and 10,000 by 1972.
In contrast other engineering had expanded from some 14,000
in 1950 to over 26,000 by 1972. The numbers employed in

textiles has also declined over the same period, but at least as significant is the change within the industry, especially the fall in employment in the linen industry, which has not been compensated by the expansion of the synthetic fibre industry, carpet making and the like. In fact, despite the massive efforts to increase employment by the expansion of manufacturing industry the numbers employed in 1972 were some 17,000 less than in 1950, though civil employment had grown by about 10,000.[2] The growth in employment that has taken place has been largely concentrated amongst the construction and service industries.

Unemployment has, of course, been a perennial problem with rates running from two to five times as high in Northern Ireland as in the rest of the United Kingdom, with the lower rates being achieved in the last few years. The highest rates of unemployment are found amongst males and tend to be located in the western part of the region. The unemployed are mostly amongst the semi-skilled and unskilled; shortages of skilled labour are quite frequent. A large proportion of the unemployed have been out of work for more than twelve months.

Emigration has also been a feature of the situation with net rates of 6.6 per 1,000 between 1951–61 and 4.8 between 1961–71. The latter rate represents some 42 per cent of the natural rate of increase. The more northerly regions of the United Kingdom would seem overall to have had much the same experience.

Finally, it is necessary to consider briefly the financial relationships between the Northern Ireland and United Kingdom governments. Under the Government of Ireland Act Northern Ireland had few powers of taxation. Those that it had included estate duties, stamp duties, excise duties, motor vehicles duties and more recently selective employment tax. These were known as transferred taxes. But the bulk of the revenue was raised from customs and excise duties, income tax and corporation tax and these were known as reserved taxes, being the prerogative of the United Kingdom government. Under the Northern Ireland Constitution Act the powers of taxation are even fewer and are restricted to the levying of some licences and rates.

For many years the budgetary position has been—broadly speaking—that with parity of taxation in Northern Ireland with the rest of the United Kingdom there should be parity of services and that any short-fall in revenue over expenditure should

TABLE 4
Civil Employment and Unemployment

	1965	% of Total	1970	% of Total	1972	% of Total
Agriculture, forestry and fishing	65.8	11.8	54.3	9.7	51.5	9.3
Food, drink and tobacco	29.0	5.2	29.2	5.2	29.1	5.2
Shipbuilding and marine engineering	13.7	2.5	10.2	1.8	10.1	1.8
Other engineering	27.0	4.8	30.1	5.4	26.5	4.8
Textiles	52.9	9.5	48.8	8.7	43.3	7.8
Clothing and footwear	26.6	4.8	27.0	4.8	26.9	4.8
Construction	48.9	8.8	52.0	9.3	51.7	9.3
Transport and communication	27.2	4.9	24.5	4.4	23.6	4.2
Distributive trades	72.2	13.0	66.0	11.8	62.9	11.3
Professional and scientific services	57.9	10.4	73.5	13.1	81.4	14.7
Miscellaneous services	45.1	8.1	42.8	7.6	41.7	7.5
Public administration and defence	35.3	6.3	39.4	7.0	43.8	7.9
Other employment	55.8	10.0	63.4	11.3	63.1	11.4
Total in civil employment	557.4	100.0	561.2	100.0	555.6	100.0
Of whom						
Males	371.6		368.3		360.3	
Females	185.9		192.9		195.3	
manufacturing industries	181.6		184.0		173.0	
Registered unemployed	28.7		31.7		38.8	
Unemployed as % of Insured Employees		5.7		6.1		7.4

Source. Digest of Statistics Northern Ireland.
Note. All figures relate to June of the particular year. The figures
   are not completely comparable because of changes in classification; for further details see, Digests of Statistics.

be made good by payments from the United Kingdom government. But to put the matter like this is to make it sound decep-
tively straightforward. It is, for instance, extremely difficult to
define parity of services precisely and to determine in total and

in detail the amounts of government revenue and expenditure—both Northern Ireland and United Kingdom—that are raised in and take place in Northern Ireland. These qualifications should be borne in mind in the following discussion and others are indicated below. Table 5 attempts to show net payments to Northern Ireland from the United Kingdom government, that is, after allowing for revenue attributed to Northern Ireland and excluding borrowing transactions.[3]

TABLE 5

£m 'Net' United Kingdom Government Payments to Northern Ireland Excluding Borrowing

	1972–73	1973–74
Health Service Agreement	25	15
Social Services Payments	45	31
Agricultural Acts 1957 and 1970	2	2
Finance Act 1967 : Additional Selective Employment Premiums	11	8
N I Office : Grant in Aid	51	175
N I Office : Law and Order	–	21
National Insurance Funds	22	30
*Other Agricultural Subsidies	25	30
Total	181	312

Sources. Northern Ireland Financial Statements 1972–73 and 1973–74 and Ministry of Finance. See also, Northern Ireland : Financial Arrangements and Legislation, Cmnd. 4998.

*These figures *exclude* milk subsidies received by Northern Ireland farmers through the Milk Fund arrangements since apparently no government payments are involved. The amounts concerned were some £5.6m for 1972–3 and £9.5m for 1973–74.

The figures in Table 5 are in a number of respects incomplete. They make, for instance, no allowance for army and defence expenditure specific to Northern Ireland and more generally for expenditure incurred by the United Kingdom government on defence, foreign and diplomatic services and the like, which would presumably arise if Northern Ireland were not part of the United Kingdom.[4]

Furthermore, there is reason to believe that the amount of revenue attributable to Northern Ireland is over estimated, thus understating the net payments made to it. This occurs mainly because Northern Ireland is credited with 2.7 per cent of the total customs and excise duties and purchase tax for the United Kingdom as a whole since this is the proportion that the population of Northern Ireland bears to the total population of the United Kingdom. It would seem that this probably over-states the amount of such taxes actually paid by the people of Northern Ireland, though there is no straightforward way of determining by how much.

If, however, these indirect taxes were directly related to income then the appropriate percentage would be closer to 2 per cent since both gross domestic product and personal income for Northern Ireland are some 2 per cent to 2.2 per cent of the United Kingdom totals. But since there would seem to be some element of regressiveness in indirect taxes and with Northern Ireland probably a rather more open economy *vis-à-vis* the rest of the world than the United Kingdom as a whole it may be that a percentage of 2.4 per cent or 2.5 per cent, some half-way between 2.2 per cent and 2.7 per cent, would be as good a guess as any. On this basis the over attribution of revenue may have been some £11m to £16m for 1972–73 and some £16m to £21m for 1973–74. Thus in total, and dealing only with actual expenditure as regards Northern Ireland, the figures for 1972–73 may be understated by some £40m to £45m and, assuming army costs about £30m for 1973–74, some £45m to £50m in the latter year. This would raise the 'net' payment figures for the two financial years to around £220m and £360m respectively.

These are massive sums both in relation to Northern Ireland government expenditure and to the gross domestic product. This is not to say, however, that they are simply 'income' transfers. Indeed the payments include, amongst other things, production and price subsidies to agriculture and industry which presumably are of some benefit to the rest of the United Kingdom.[5] In general, public sector expenditure in Northern Ireland in the last couple of years would seem to be running at the rate of over 60 per cent of gross domestic product, which is not to imply that the total expenditure constitutes a demand for goods and services.[6] However, it strongly suggests that government expenditure is of crucial importance to the Northern Ireland economy and of fundamental relevance to the discussion of possible political solutions.

Continued Membership of the United Kingdom

The recent White Paper, Northern Ireland Constitutional Proposals, and the subsequent Northern Ireland Constitution Act, between them provide us with a broad framework for attempting to assess some of the economic implications of Northern Ireland's continued membership of the United Kingdom.[7] This is not to say that alternative frameworks are inconceivable.

I have already indicated that under the Constitution Act Northern Ireland has virtually no powers of taxation other than the power to levy rates. Thus by and large taxation as a fiscal policy instrument, except as modified through regional policy, is not to be available as a means of achieving the specific economic goals of Northern Ireland. And indeed even regional policy is to be determined in relation to the problems of the development areas in Britain. Subject to this last point and compatibility with the overall economic policy of the United Kingdom government and its obligations from membership of the European Community, the Northern Ireland Executive is to have some freedom in how it allocates its expenditure in matters concerning education, health and personal social services, housing, roads, nationalised fuel industries and local environmental services.

Thus on the face of it the amount of fiscal manoeuvrability available to Northern Ireland would seem to be extremely limited. However, this may be an exaggeration if the experience of the last few years can be taken as a precedent when considerable flexibility has been shown in tackling the economic problems of Northern Ireland. I have in mind the establishment and activities of a number of semi-state bodies such as the Northern Ireland Finance Corporation, Enterprise Ulster and the Local Enterprise Development Unit as well as counter-redundancy schemes, the industrial regeneration programme and the like.[8]

Furthermore, the White Paper lays down 'broad objectives by which the financial requirements of Northern Ireland will be judged . . . These are:

(*a*) to accomplish as rapidly as possible, once violence has ended, the task of physical reconstruction and rehabilitation created by the disorders of recent years;

(*b*) to create a sound base for the economy and to encourage external industrial investment;

(*c*) to work progressively towards the achievement in Northern Ireland of those standards of living, employment and social conditions which prevail in Great Britain' (par. 86). The White Paper continues, 'The overall level of public expenditure in Northern Ireland will be determined in the light of these objectives and will be compatible with public expenditure policies for the United Kingdom as a whole' (par. 87).

These objectives are perhaps necessarily rather vague and it maybe worthwhile to make them more specific and try and determine some of their economic consequences. Suppose working progressively towards those standards of living which prevail in Britain is interpreted to mean achieving over a ten year period levels of income *per capita* which are 90 per cent of the average for the United Kingdom as a whole. Thus starting with 1971 as base and assuming that income *per capita* grows at 2.5 per cent per year in the United Kingdom, the required annual rate of growth for Northern Ireland to reach 90 per cent of the United Kingdom figure by 1981 would be about 4.8 per cent. By recent historical standards this rate of growth is high since over the 10 years 1961–71 the actual annual rate of growth of gross domestic product *per capita* was around 3.4 per cent.

The scale of the problem, if looked at in these terms which are admittedly arbitrary but surely not unreasonable, can be further appreciated by considering the amount of capital investment that might be involved in raising living standards to this level. One way of trying to do this is to make some strong assumptions about population growth, similarities between the Northern Ireland and United Kingdom economies and put much weight on the importance of capital-output ratios.[9] Thus at best the whole exercise can only be considered as a crude approximation.

If the population of Northern Ireland is assumed to grow at the same rate, 0.7 per cent a year, between 1971–81 as it grew between 1961–71, then gross domestic product in 1981 would have to reach some £1,620m in terms of 1971 prices, compared to £950m for 1971, to achieve the 1981 target. The question arises what increase in the stock of capital would be required to make this possible. The choice of capital-output ratio is crucial. There is none, as far as I know, available for the Northern Ireland economy. One alternative is to make use of those available for the United Kingdom. It would seem that in recent years the incremental capital-output ratio is of the order 5 to 6, measuring gross capital stock at 1963 replacement cost and using annual gross domestic product data at 1963 factor prices. Now the average capital-output ratio for the United Kingdom would seem to be slightly over four and if this is applied to Northern Ireland it gives a gross capital stock of some £4,000m for the year 1971. Thus to reach the 1981 projected income levels, and using the incremental capital output ratio, the gross capital stock would have to grow to between £7,400m and £8,000m or at an annual rate of some 6.4 per cent and 7.2 per cent respectively. For 1972 this would imply an increase in the gross capital stock of either £260m or £290m.

There remains the question of what this might mean in terms of gross fixed capital formation. It would seem that gross fixed capital formation at 1963 prices for the United Kingdom over the last five years has been about 33 per cent greater than the increase in gross capital stock at 1963 replacement cost. If it can be assumed that the position for Northern Ireland, and in terms of 1971 prices, is similar it would suggest that gross fixed capital formation for 1972 would need to have been of the order of £350m to £390m, depending on whether an incremental capital-output ratio of 5 or 6 is employed. For subsequent years the figures would, of course, have to expand at rates of either 6.4 per cent or 7.2 per cent, according to the assumptions made earlier.

The figures of £350m to £390m for gross fixed capital formation for 1972 are large, especially the latter one, in comparison with the actual figure of £322m for 1971, some 45 per cent of which was public sector investment. Moreover, this is before allowing for grants to the private sector of some £45m.[10] In other words gross fixed capital formation on the scale indicated here would seem to require a substantial increase in the amount of public funds made available, though these are already large in comparison with the rest of the United Kingdom. However, this would seem to be one of the implications of the White Paper, subject, of course, to the particular interpretation of its objectives given above and to the highly tentative nature of the argument. It remains to be seen how the economic proposals of the White Paper will in fact be implemented. Indeed it would be interesting to know what, if any, projections have been attempted by the authorities.

An 'Independent' Northern Ireland

At one extreme an independent Northern Ireland, in opposition to the will of Britain, would presumably imply that all financial aid from Britain would cease. What would be some of the economic implications of such an eventuality? One way to try and answer this question is to employ multiplier analysis. However, it needs to be borne in mind that multiplier analysis is generally incomplete and at best approximate since the models employed tend to be at least implicitly a truncated part of a larger model and essentially static. Furthermore, the actual magnitudes used in the calculation of multipliers are often fairly crude. Both comments apply to the discussion here.[11]

The analysis in the Appendix suggests that the short-run multiplier effects of government expenditure on gross domestic product may vary according to the type of expenditure. Thus transfers to persons may have a slightly larger effect than other forms of expenditure such as capital investment and other current expenditure. The reasons for this are the assumptions built into the model; in particular that import leakages from transfers to persons are very small or non-existent whereas they are quite large from other forms of government expenditure. However, broadly speaking, and assuming that the parameter values employed are not too seriously wrong, a unit change in transfers to persons combined with a unit change in other government expenditure would result in a two unit change in gross domestic product. In other words a unit change in overall government expenditure spread equally between these two categories would result in a unit change in gross domestic product. This of course implies that the multiplier so defined is approximately one which would seem to be roughly in keeping—though it is slightly on the low side—with what is generally known about regional multipliers for the United Kingdom.

If a multiplier of around one is not too wide of the mark then the model suggests that a cut in financial aid from Britain, spread equally between the two broad types of government expenditure, would result in a more or less equal fall in income.[11a] Now some part of British aid is, as already stated, subsidies and is not simply income transfers or direct demands for goods and services. The major subsidies are those to agriculture and are not directly taken account of in the model. Clearly, however, the withdrawal of agricultural subsidies, both production and price subsidies, would have effects on both output and prices. On the face of it one would expect some contraction of output and a rise in prices. Nevertheless, putting the question of subsidies aside there is on an annual basis probably some £250m to £300m in 1973–74 prices which might be withheld by Britain if Northern Ireland became independent against the will of the former.[12] On the arguments in the text and in the appendix this would bring about a more or less equal drop in income unless effective offsetting measures were taken, though as I have already stressed the figures are necessarily highly tentative.

Britain's power over the Northern Ireland economy does not, of course, end here. It has already been pointed out that Northern Ireland is highly 'dependent' on Britain for both exports and imports and indeed more specifically some industries are helped by British government contracts. Pressure could, in fact, be put by Britain on the Northern Ireland economy in a multitude of ways. It is conceivable in extreme circumstances that by a combination of measures which stopped the flow of British government funds to Northern Ireland that its gross domestic product might decline by anything up to one-quarter. Employment might be expected to decline at least in proportion.[13] This could mean an addition of some 120,000 to the ranks of the unemployed, though it could be less if an income multiplier of 0.7 is used, say 80,000 persons.

These conclusions, which hopefully are unlikely to happen, *only* hold on the basis of the model and on the assumption that *no* effective offsetting measures are taken.[14] Clearly, in such circumstances massive offsetting measures would be attempted. My judgement would be, however, that they would be unable to be completely offsetting and that the Northern Ireland economy would experience great disruption.[15]

To write in such cataclysmic economic terms on the implicit assumption that ordinary political processes within Northern Ireland would continue without upheaval is obviously unrealistic. I would expect, in fact, major movements of population and a re-drawing of the geographical boundaries of Northern Ireland to include a much smaller land area. To try and work out the economic consequences of this would require another model which I am not in a position to provide.

Finally, it would clearly be possible to interpret an 'independent' Northern Ireland in terms of 'degrees' of independence and assume that Britain would not cut financial aid in the savage way postulated above. The model, subject to the qualifications already made, would suggest in these circumstances that for each one pound cut in aid income would fall by between 70 per cent to 100 per cent of the amount involved unless the cuts were effectively offset.

A 'United' Ireland

Despite frequent mention of a United Ireland over the years little thought would seem to have been given to either its possible political shape or economic arrangements. However, at one extreme there would appear to be the view that Ireland would have a central government and four regional governments based on the historical provinces and be economically 'independent' of Britain. This seems to me to be so unlikely as not to merit further discussion here. A more plausible, though perhaps somewhat distant, possibility is some form of federal government based on regional institutions in Dublin and Belfast for the respective geographic areas of the Republic and Northern Ireland and supported by some all Ireland bodies with both political and economic responsibilities. It is this sort of structure which I have in mind in what follows.

During the fourteen years 1958–72 the economy of the Irish Republic has experienced marked economic progress by comparison with earlier performance. Output grew at an average annual rate of about 4 per cent, employment in manufacturing industry increased by around one-third to reach a total of almost 200,000 workers and industrial exports expanded rapidly. Despite these achievements gross domestic product *per capita* for 1971 was only about 62 per cent of the United Kingdom average, compared with 72 per cent for Northern Ireland. Furthermore, the expenditure *per capita* on social and welfare services in the Republic was considerably smaller than in Northern Ireland. These points are not mentioned for the purpose of making invidious comparisons but because they are highly relevant to the question of a federal United Ireland. And in any event the higher standards in Northern Ireland are underpinned by the largesse of Britain.

If by some turn of events a federal Ireland became politically acceptable to the different interests it would seem essential to its survival that it did not impose severe economic costs on the people of Northern Ireland. In other words they would probably require strong assurances that whatever political and economic arrangements were entered into this would not reduce their current standard of living and they would probably also want assurances about their future standard of living. As we have seen their standard of living is crucially dependent on 'net' payments to Northern Ireland from Britain. Since the Republic could not in the foreseeable future undertake such payments in total it would seem imperative that initially Britain should do so, though presumably on a declining scale over a period of years.[16] In other words as the 'two' Irish economies grew they would gradually have to dispense with payments from Britain. At the same time if the federation was to be politically meaningful it would be proceeding to harmonise its social and welfare services and agricultural and industrial support systems—all presumably within the framework of the European Community. Clearly, the choice of time period for such developments would be of major importance. One economic factor which would necessarily influence the choice of time period or transitionary period to a 'fully' federal state would be the expected rates of growth of the respective regional economies.

A major task for the two economies would be to absorb over the transitionary period the curtailment and ultimately disappearance of the 'net' payments from Britain to Northern Ireland. For 1973–74 we have seen that these payments are of the order of £300m, though the precise figure is difficult to determine and is a matter of interpretation. Furthermore, just how the task might be split between the Republic and Northern Ireland—on the assumption that for the transitionary period at

H

least each maintains separate exchequers and accounting systems
—would raise very difficult and sensitive political questions.

If for the sake of the argument it is assumed that any reduction in British payments below their current level would be completely compensated by transfers from the Republic then by the
end of the transitionary period the latter would be paying to
Northern Ireland some £300m a year in terms of 1973 prices.
Now the gross domestic product at factor cost of the Republic
for 1973 is anticipated to be about £2,000m. Over a ten year
period with an annual rate of growth of 4 per cent this would
reach £3,000m and over a fifteen year period £3,600m. Thus
even by the end of fifteen years £300m would represent a very
high proportion of gross domestic product and, of course, an even
higher proportion of taxation. With income and expenditure
taxes almost 38 per cent of gross domestic product—roughly
the 1971 precentage—£300m would amount to 22 per cent of
the tax revenue.[17] On these arguments the taking over of British
payments to Northern Ireland by the Republic would be a
formidable task.[18] Moreover, payments of this order might well
have adverse effects on the growth rate of the Republic's
economy, further complicating the establishment of the federation, and give rise to serious balance of payments problems.

There are, however, factors that might work the other way
and be some compensation for a reduction in net payments to
Northern Ireland either below their current level or below what
they might have been if Northern Ireland had stayed part of the
United Kingdom. Northern Ireland would presumably obtain
some measure of autonomy over fiscal, monetary and economic
policy, at least during the transitional period, and subject to
the harmonisation policies of the federation. Just what value
should be placed on autonomy of this kind is very difficult to
assess.[19] However, a suitable combination of tax and monetary
and credit measures might be found to stimulate domestic expansion sufficiently to offset a reduction, perhaps of the order of
£30m to £50m—allowing for some additional capital inflow—
in net payments at current levels to Northern Ireland.[20]

If this argument has some validity then the cost to the Republic of taking over British payments to Northern Ireland might be
somewhat less than suggested above, but would still remain a
very substantial sum. Furthermore, the discussion has been car-

ried on in terms of a net payments figure of £300m which probably understates what is required, if the norm used is what
would be necessary to prevent living standards falling below
what they would have reached, if Northern Ireland had remained part of the United Kingdom.[21]

If these circumstances are at all plausible then it seems unlikely that the Republic could afford progressively to take over
the net British payments to Northern Ireland, over say a fifteen
year period, even allowing for some reduction in those payments
because of the increased fiscal, and economic flexibility generally, available to Northern Ireland.[22] In other words Northern
Ireland would be likely to experience a slower rise in its
standard of living as an emergent part of a federal Ireland than
as a part of the United Kingdom—especially if the commitments
of the White Paper on the Northern Ireland Constitutional Proposals can be interpreted more or less as they were above.[23]
However, major political and constitutional changes of the kind
postulated in this paper are—perhaps rightly—never decided on
the basis of economic considerations alone; but equally it would
be highly irresponsible to ignore such considerations.

Conclusions

This paper has attempted to sketch in broad macro-economic
terms some of the implications of three possible political 'solutions' to the Northern Ireland problem. To venture into such a
hypothetical field is at the least foolhardy and yet it may well
be essential to try and do so if only in the hope that rational
political economy—if it exists—might have some little thing to
contribute to the alleviation of the human and tragic circumstances of the people of Northern Ireland.

In broad terms continued membership of the United Kingdom by Northern Ireland, might be expected, on the basis of
the White Paper Constitutional Proposals, to lead to a faster
rate of growth of output than in the past and rising *per capita*
living standards, closer to the average for the United Kingdom
as a whole. An 'independent' Northern Ireland without financial
aid from Britain or elsewhere would be likely to be economically
disastrous, at least for a considerable number of years, with
income levels falling dramatically and unemployment on a scale
not even experienced in the Great Depression. A 'United' or

emergent federal Ireland would be likely to mean, over say a fifteen year transitional period, a slower rate of growth of output and lower living standards for Northern Ireland than if it remained part of the United Kingdom, granted that the latter makes a determined attempt to raise living standards in Northern Ireland to a level closer to the average for the whole United Kingdom. Both output and living standards in Northern Ireland would probably be substantially higher in an emergent federal Ireland than if the former opted for 'independence'.

Finally, it is clearly unrealistic to assume that the three broad political alternatives are equally likely to occur. It seems clear that after centuries of involvement in Ireland, Britain is determined in due course to disengage. If this is true then it may well be that much greater attention than has been possible here should be given to the question of an emergent federal Ireland and beyond.

APPENDIX 1

Consider the following simplified model where the variables measure *changes*:

$$Y = C + I + \bar{G} + \bar{X} - M - T_i$$
$$C = c(Y_p - \bar{U})(1 - t_{dp}) + \bar{U}$$
$$Y_p = Y - T_{dc} - S_c + \bar{U} + Y_{nd}$$
$$T_{dp} = t_{dp} Y_p$$
$$I = \bar{I} + I_y$$
$$I_y = i_y Y$$
$$M = M_c + M_i + M_g + M_x$$
$$M_c = m_c(C - \bar{U})$$
$$M_i = m_i I$$
$$M_g = m_g \bar{G}$$
$$M_x = m_x \bar{X}$$
$$T_i = t_i C$$
$$T_{dc} = t_{dc} Y_c$$
$$Y_c = y_c Y$$
$$S_c = s_c Y_c(1 - t_{dc})$$
$$Y_{nd} = y_{nd} Y,$$

where Y = gross domestic product at factor cost
C = consumers' expenditure
I = gross private domestic capital formation
G = government expenditure on goods and services
X = exports
M = imports
T_i = net indirect taxes
Y_p = personal income
U = transfers to persons from government
T_{dc} = direct tax on company income
S_c = savings of companies
Y_{nd} = net dividends, property income etc. accruing to persons
T_{dp} = direct tax on persons
I_y = induced investment

M_c = consumption goods imports
M_i = investment goods imports
M_g = government expenditure on imports
M_x = imports for re-export
Y_c = company income before tax.

A bar over a symbol indicates that the variable is treated as exogenous. If the model is solved for Y we find that:

$$Y = \frac{\bar{U}(1-t_i) + \bar{I}(1-m_i) + \bar{X}(1-m_x) + \bar{G}(1-m_g)}{1-c(1-m_c-t_i)[1-t_{dc}\,y_c-s_c\,y_c(1-t_{dc})+y_{nd}](1-t_{dp}) - (i_y - m_i\,i_y).}$$

The way the model has been specified implies that all transfer payments from government to persons, $\bar{U}$, is spent on consumption goods and that none of these is imported. These are clearly strong assumptions that may need some modification. Furthermore, it is assumed that some part of expenditure on investment, exports and government expenditure seeps immediately into imports—a fairly plausible assumption for an economy as open as that of Northern Ireland.

The next problem is to try and attach numbers to the parameters of the model. In doing so I have relied heavily on the work of others and, on occasion, resorted to what can only be described as guess-work.[24] Thus the arithmetic which follows should only be considered as illustrative and not necessarily indicative of magnitudes that are automatically applicable to the Northern Ireland economy. The following is one set of assumed values:

$c = 0.9$ the marginal propensity to consume out of disposable income net of government transfers;

$t_{dp} = 0.25$ the marginal rate of direct tax on personal income;

$i_y = 0.1$ the income induced investment coefficient;

$m_c = 0.4$ the marginal propensity to import consumers' goods in relation to consumption expenditure net of government transfers;

$m_i = 0.5$ the marginal propensity to import investment goods in relation to private investment expenditure;

$m_g = 0.4$ the marginal propensity to import in relation to government expenditure;

$m_x = 0.4$ the marginal propensity to import in relation to exports;

t_i = 0.2   the marginal rate of indirect tax in relation to consumers' expenditure;

t_{dc} = 0.4   the marginal rate of company tax;[25]

y_c = 0.22   the marginal rate of change of company income in relation to gross domestic product;[26]

s_c = 0.46   the marginal rate of company saving from income net of tax; and

y_{nd} = 0   the marginal rate of net property income etc. in relation to gross domestic product.

By substituting these values into the solution above and assuming in each case that all changes are zero except in the one under consideration it is found that:

$$\frac{Y}{\bar{U}} \simeq 1.11; \quad \frac{Y}{\bar{G}} \simeq .83; \quad \frac{Y}{\bar{I}} \simeq .69 \text{ and } \frac{Y}{\bar{X}} \simeq .83.$$

Thus on the assumptions made different types of expenditure have different multiplier effects.

APPENDIX 2

If the assumption that all transfer payments from government to persons, $\bar{U}$, is spent on consumption goods is relaxed and that some of this expenditure does seep into imports then, of course, the multipliers will be affected. It is also plausible to argue that transfer payments are, at least in part, inversely related to income. These modifications, as well as making direct personal taxation payable out of disposable income, are allowed for below. In particular, the following equations are substituted for the corresponding ones in appendix 1:

$$C = c_p (Y_p - U) (1 - t_{dp}) + c_u U$$
$$T_{dp} = t_{dp} (Y_p - U)$$
$$M_c = m_c (C - U) + m_u U \text{ and}$$
$$U = \bar{U} - uY \text{ is introduced as an additional equation. If the}$$
new model is solved it is found that

$$Y = \frac{\bar{U}(c_u - m_c c_u + m_c - m_u - t_i c_u) + \bar{I}(1 - m_i)}{1 - c_p(1 - m_c - t_i) \left\{ 1 - t_{dc} y_c - s_c y_c (1 - t_{dc}) \right.}$$

$$+ \bar{G}(1 - m_y) + \bar{X}(1 - m_x)$$

$$+ y_{nd} \left. \right\} (1 - t_{dp}) - i_j(1 - m_i) + u(c_u - m_c c_u + m_c - m_u - t_i c_u)$$

Using the same parameter values as before except that :

$c_p = c = \quad$ 0.9

$c_u = 0.97 \quad$ the marginal propensity to consume out of government transfer payments;

$m_u = 0.1 \quad$ the marginal propensity to import consumers' goods in relation to government transfer payments;

$u = 0.2 \quad$ the short-term variation in transfer payments associated with income changes;[27]

and assuming $y_{nd} = -0.05$, it is found that

$$\frac{Y}{\bar{U}} \simeq 0.84; \quad \frac{Y}{\bar{G}} \simeq 0.73; \quad \frac{Y}{\bar{I}} \simeq 0.61; \quad \frac{Y}{\bar{X}} \simeq 0.73.$$

As might have been expected these multipliers are rather less than the ones in Appendix 1.

Some Comments on
Professor Gibson's Paper

NORMAN CUTHBERT

PROFESSOR GIBSON is to be congratulated on producing a valuable paper on the economic implications of various suggested solutions to the Northern Ireland problem. Not only does it throw much light on the special difficulties of Northern Ireland but it also provides a stimulating and thought-provoking basis for the consideration of certain wider aspects of regional analysis and policy and poses a number of important questions for discussion.

The main features of the Northern Ireland economy may be expressed in a series of superlatives in relation to the other regions of the United Kingdom. It has the lowest average gross domestic product and personal income per head of population, the lowest average hourly earnings and hours worked for adult male manual workers, the lowest proportion of persons of working age to total population, the highest rate of population growth and the highest unemployment rate. For these reasons it has the highest rate of subventions from the central government at Westminster per head of population. Some of these relationships are worth looking at in a little more detail.

(1) Gross domestic product per head of population expressed as a percentage of the United Kingdom figure has increased from about 63 in 1960 to about 72 in 1971. A good deal of this improvement is due to the increase in the value of net output per employee in manufacturing industry. In 1958 the value of net output per employee as disclosed by the Census of Production was about 68 per cent of the average for the United Kingdom; in 1968 it was 84 per cent. During the twenty years ending in 1970 new manufacturing firms coming to the province provided employment for some 60,000 workers yet manufacturing employment was about 10,000 less at the end of the period than

at the beginning. By then about one-third of the total number of jobs in manufacturing which were available in 1950 had disappeared; the new firms had merely replaced or supplanted the old, capital intensity had increased, net output per head in manufacturing had increased relative to the rest of the United Kingdom, and so had G D P. As might be expected the proportion of net output in census trades going to wages and salaries decreased. There was some improvement in the average level of wages and salaries compared with the level in the United Kingdom as a whole but it was a good deal less than the relative improvement in the value of net output per worker.[1] On the other hand unlike the Scottish experience mentioned by Dr McCrone, the Department of Employment's Earnings Inquiries show no strongly marked tendency over the long period for average male earnings in manufacturing to come closer to the British average. For male manual workers they were 86.9 per cent of the United Kingdom average in October 1949 and in April, 1972, 86.6 per cent.[2] The implication is that a good deal of the additional G D P generated, leaks out of Northern Ireland in so far as the new projects are of non-resident ownership. Unfortunately it is not possible to say how much leaks away without more knowledge of the investment income flows into and out of Northern Ireland. Estimates of these were made twenty-five years ago[3] and the annual net inflow of income from this source then appeared to be about £20m, but those twenty-five years have seen vast changes in the industrial pattern, and in the proportion of industrial capital owned locally.

Two conclusions follow from this. The first is that unless one can assume that the shareholdings of individuals, both direct and indirect, tend to be closely bound up with the region in which they live, the G D P of a region or its rate of growth is not necessarily a good indicator of the income accruing to residents of the region from work or the ownership of property. The second is that much of the public investment in infrastructure in a region, or the use of public funds for subsidising industrial development in a region may confer considerable benefits by way of income flows to persons in other regions of the economy. The benefits accruing from central government subventions for these purposes should not be attributed solely to the region to which the subventions are made. This is a complication which should be considered in discussing the financial relations between a central government and a region.

(2) As Professor Gibson states in his paper, probably the most politically sensitive aspect of the Northern Ireland economy is the level of unemployment. In the past twenty years the percentage rate of unemployment has been consistently higher than the United Kingdom average, the difference being generally of the order of 4 to 6 per cent, and the difference is even more unfavourable when comparison is made with the regions of high growth. Basically the problem is lack of balance between the numbers coming on the labour market and the net rate of increase in new jobs, but the position is aggravated by the special circumstances of fairly high emigration, the changing structure of industry and the level of welfare payments compared with expected earnings. It seems likely that areas of high emigration will be left with more than their fair share of unemployables. In addition it should be noted that net outward migration generally involves two-way traffic which is high in relation to the net movement. In 1965–66 the net emigration of 6,900 persons was made up of 22,000 outward and 15,100 inward movements. It is to be expected that a proportion of these immigrants are the unemployed of other regions.

Rapid changes in the industrial structure which involve job changes are also likely to increase unemployment especially where older workers are affected or where the gap between the acquired skill and the required skill is great. The rapid run-down in job opportunities in agriculture, which has been occurring at the rate of 2,000 per year in itself poses a problem which is much larger proportionally in Northern Ireland than in other regions. The same is true of the gap between expected earnings and social security benefits. The lower average earnings coupled with the larger average size of family may adversely affect mobility or provide an incentive to remain unemployed. There is much evidence, even at present, when the recorded unemployment rate is high, that many employers in Northern Ireland are experiencing difficulty in recruiting labour, both skilled and unskilled.

What is a reasonable rate of unemployment to expect in such an area as Northern Ireland? Is regional policy failing if it is persistently above the United Kingdom average? Northern

Ireland's experience during the Second World War may throw some light on this. The lowest level of unemployment ever recorded was in 1944 when the average for the year was 3.8 per cent compared with 0.4 per cent in Great Britain. This was a period when munitions production was at its height, many American and British armed forces were stationed and being trained in the province and the demand for labour in both manufacturing and service industries was extremely high. If we temper our judgement with realism it may be that we should consider full employment in the Northern Ireland context as 4 or 5 per cent rather than 1 or 2 per cent as in Great Britain. The same could probably be said of the Irish Republic.

(3) In assessing the importance of the financial transfers it should be noted that the size of these subventions to Northern Ireland is the outcome of the general tendency to try to smooth out differences in the level of socialised services and personal opportunities in the United Kingdom as a whole. So far as Northern Ireland in its relations with the United Kingdom Government is concerned there has been a gradual evolution of the notion of parity. The Government of Ireland Act of 1920 provided that the amount available for public services would be what was left out of Northern Ireland's share of taxation receipts after the Imperial Contribution, fixed at intervals, had been met. In the first instance this was set at £8m but it was soon clear that such an amount would leave little for the provision of public services. The Colwyn Committee decided in 1923 that the provision of public services must come first and what was left over would form the Imperial Contribution. Parity of services was not clearly defined but the context suggested that what was meant was a kind of proportional parity. Probably the committee had in mind a standard of services in keeping with the level of income in the province. It was a fairly flexible concept and its interpretation left very much to the civil servants who acted as the Joint Exchequer Board.

During the years 1935 to 1938 unemployment pressed heavily on Northern Ireland. In mid-1938 about 30 per cent of the insured were idle. The unemployment reinsurance agreement was drawn up and in these years the subvention under the agreement outweighed for the first time the Imperial Contribution by about £1.4m. But during the war years the Imperial Contribution grew. By 1945 it reached a figure of £36m though this might be reduced if agricultural subsidies and food subsidies were added to the proceeds of the reinsurance agreement. It is clear that by the end of the war the notion of parity was taking on the connotation of equality in the provision of social services. Later agreements covering family allowances, supplementary benefits and the health services all of which emerged from Westminster initiative, reinforced the interpretation of parity as equality. Once the principle of parity in this sense is admitted it can be argued that it should hold for all aspects of social life, for the provision of education or for the provision of employment opportunities. It also subsumes that the capital investment which may be required to make up 'leeway' in the provision of such services is a legitimate provision.

Whether the notion of full parity as it has come to be interpreted is desirable from the point of view of achieving an economic optimum in regional affairs is something you might wish to consider. It certainly has strong emotional and sentimental appeal and some welfare justification. But it should be noted that on the National Income method of formulating government accounts and omitting the transfers under the various special agreements, Northern Ireland, over the years, showed a substantial surplus on revenue account.

Professor Gibson considers three canvassed political solutions, (a) continued membership of United Kingdom, (b) an independent Northern Ireland, (c) a united Ireland. In discussing the first of these he suggests that under the new Constitution Act and the broad objectives outlined in the White Paper, the United Kingdom Government has committed itself to taking fairly drastic action to raise the standard of living in Northern Ireland to something nearer equality with the rest of the United Kingdom. He further suggests that this might be interpreted as achieving over a ten year period income *per capita* of 90 per cent of the United Kingdom average. This is interpreted as 90 per cent of the United Kingdom average per head GDP. On the basis of past population growth and assuming what are probably reasonable capital-output ratios it is estimated that a very substantial increase in gross fixed capital formation would be required on the already high rate at which it is running.

The points which might be considered here are first, should

parity in regional affairs include some sort of parity of income per head and if so what income and which head? In 1971 the relationship between Northern Ireland and the United Kingdom were:

	GDP %	Personal Income %
Per head of total population	71.8	79.5
Per head of population in the working age-groups	75.6	83.7
per head of total working population (including unemployed)	84.9	93.8

Second, is the *aim* of achieving some sort of parity of GDP per head through, for example, the introduction of highly capital intensive manufacturing industries an efficient way of approaching the problem?

Professor Leser[4] pointed out a long time ago that in the conditions which then existed variation in the average value of net output per head in census trades depended more on the variation in industrial structures of regions than on the variation in net output per head in the same trades in different regions. One can envisage a case where, given the situation of a region and the resources available to it, including labour resources, parity of GDP or even a modified parity at some specified level per head may not be possible in a free economy or possible only at prohibitive public cost. The proportion of the population of working age might in itself be an important limiting factor.

Moreover it may be that the more assiduous a development authority is in pumping capital intensive industries into a region the more likely it is that the proportion of GDP which leaks out of the region will increase. Is this the absentee landlord problem in another guise?

Consideration of the second political solution, an 'independent' Northern Ireland, raises the question of the effects of withdrawing the present subventions from Northern Ireland. In the main I think Professor Gibson is right in pointing out that this would lead to an economic mêlée and that the initial contraction in public funds would cause a serious contraction in employment and in both GDP and personal income per head. Could it survive if the subventions were withdrawn? If Northern Ireland became independent against the wishes of its neighbours and with their active opposition involving, for example, trade sanctions, then the situation would be quite impossible. If on the other hand it became independent with the tacit approval of the warring elements of the population and the neighbouring territories I think it could survive economically though with a good deal of tightening of the belt. Many of the services which are at present provided at the same level *per capita* as in the United Kingdom as a whole would be withdrawn or reduced. Personal incomes per head would fall and I suspect that emigration would increase substantially. Initially unemployment would be high. The present programme of capital expansion would have to be cut back and it is difficult to see how and where in present circumstances an alternative source of investment funds could be found. But in the longer run the level of unemployment might not differ substantially from its present level, though the standard of living would be a good deal lower for many years to come.

In looking at the longer term prospects of such a political solution, it might be better to consider the financial relations between Northern Ireland and the United Kingdom Government at the period before rather than after 1968. The 'troubles' have undoubtedly had a considerable effect both on the need for revenue and the willingness of the United Kingdom Government to supply it. Current subventions in that year from the United Kingdom Government were £44m on account of the Social Services Agreement, Selective Employment Premiums and Unemployment Insurance Agreement. We can assume that if these revenues had not been obtained the payments under similar headings would have been substantially below the £135m that they in fact were. The surplus on revenue account would probably not have been much different from what it was, i.e. £74m. It was this £74m which formed the main item in the receipts of the capital account. The total of outside borrowing required to meet capital expenditure was £24.6m. This is a fairly small total of borrowing for a government with a revenue approaching £300m. Moreover it should be noted that this figure covers most local authority borrowing and also borrowing by gas, electricity and transport services and the Northern Ireland Housing Executive.

The final political solution canvassed is that of a 'united' Ireland. The suggestion here is that at some stage the government of the Republic would have to face up to the problem of making good the hole in Northern Ireland revenues created by the eventual withdrawal of the United Kingdom subsidies and subventions.

As Professor Gibson points out GDP *per capita* in the Republic is 62 per cent of United Kingdom compared with 72 per cent in Northern Ireland. This makes it unlikely that Dublin would be prepared to accept London's burden till the gap was closed and indeed if we use GDP as our measure federal equity would dictate that it should not. Even if the rate of growth in GDP in the Republic continues at 4 per cent (as it has over the last 14 years) it would still be a heavy burden to bear in fifteen years' time.

It should be noted that according to the published statistics, GDP in Northern Ireland over the past fourteen years has been increasing at approximately 4.9 per cent and over the past 6 years at 5 per cent per annum in real terms. Thus if we make our comparisons on a basis of recent rates of growth in GDP either in total or per head of population it would appear that the gap may be widening rather than narrowing. If these relative rates of growth continue there seems little chance of the Republic playing the part of fairy godmother. A united Ireland solution would I think be economically disadvantageous to Northern Ireland unless the effect was greatly to increase the relative growth rates in both parts of Ireland or United Kingdom subventions continued.

SECTION FIVE

SECTION FIVE

The Economic Problems of Ireland, Scotland and Wales

DAVID LAW

'All round the ultimate rim of North Western Europe were the fascinating fringes of a twilit Celtic world . . . The early Tudors, especially Henry VIII, had got forward with the job of absorbing Wales and Cornwall into the pattern of English government and life. These still retained their different inflection and remained different, for they were in a less advanced stage of development than progressive English agrarian society already being energised by commerce and industry : they were poor and they were backward. Still ruder, more backward, and more of a problem, were the Scottish borders; and, most of all, Ireland.'

A. L. Rowse,
The Expansion of Elizabethan England

Introduction

I R E L A N D, Scotland and Wales have several characteristics in common which make them, as a group, an interesting subject for discussion. First, they are the major relics of Celtic civilisation,[1] each having developed and to varying degrees retained, a separate language, literature and culture which have much in common with each other but little with English culture. Second, they share a subsystem of the world economy with England, by far the dominant partner, and as might be expected in such relationships, they are the poor relations. Third, and no doubt for both the above reasons, they are distinctive in modern times in being the only areas of the British Isles where a substantial part of the population have expressed a desire for independence. One of the strands of argument taken up later in this paper is that although economic matters may not be the predominant issues of contention in peripheral areas either within the British Isles or elsewhere, there exists a two-way connection between relative poverty in peripheral areas and the strength of nationalist feeling.

What is it that distinguishes the economic problems of Ireland, Scotland and Wales from those experienced elsewhere? In a very general and trivial sense the economic problems of the Irish, Scots and Welsh are no different from those of people anywhere. But the severity of these problems obviously depends on the standard of comparison. They would appear in a very different light if they were compared to those in say, Denmark, than they would if related to those in Greece. Of the many standards of comparison which are possible the most obvious, and the one which this paper is largely concerned with, is the extent to which prosperity and economic opportunity have kept pace with England. It is this context which seems most relevant, since Northern Ireland, Scotland and Wales are constitutionally regions of the United Kingdom, whilst the Republic of Ireland, though a sovereign state, remains closely connected by virtue of historical ties and the ease of movement of capital, goods and people. Also, in economic as in other aspects of life, it is the comparison with England which matters most to the residents of Ireland, Scotland and Wales.[2]

It has been pointed out that regional income-inequalities within the United Kingdom are small in comparison with other countries,[3] and that their removal would reduce only slightly the inequality of income in the country as a whole, to which the population as a whole seems to have become reconciled.[4] Why then, have small regional disparities become, and remained, such an important cause for public concern in the United Kingdom? Whilst this question cannot be answered in a couple of sentences, if at all, part of the answer must surely lie in the fact that regional disparities were very substantial during the inter-war years when the problem first became obvious, and that regional policy has been inspired by a determination that these conditions should not return. It is more than simply a question of income inequality; as a result of public disquiet regional policy has been more concerned to ensure the fundamental 'right to work' than to equalise between regions the income of those already at work. Further, spatial inequalities may be more keenly felt because, of all inequalities, they are the only ones which require the economic and 'psychic' costs and the inconvenience of movement to reduce them.

In this framework the economic problems of Ireland, Scotland and Wales are seen as the extent to which they have fallen short of English standards of prosperity. There is, of course, a range of other viewpoints which might prove equally interesting. To take a wider view, for instance, the economic experience of Ireland, Scotland and Wales has been conditioned by their close involvement in the British economy which has been in decline relative to the industrialised countries of the world for the past century. To what extent are the economic problems of the peripheral countries due to this attachment, and how does their experience compare with that of peripheral areas of faster-growing economies? To what extent will entry into the European Economic Community change this environment of slow growth, and contribute to a solution of the problems faced by Ireland, Scotland and Wales? To take a narrower view, each of the countries discussed in this paper has itself got problems of internal balance, of dominance and congestion in urban centres, of rural depopulation and industrial unemployment. Each country is, in other words, a microcosm of what, at the risk of offending the Irish, might be called the British economy as a whole. The title of this paper, however, is pretentious enough without a consideration of these issues, and only passing mention is made of them.

Relative Poverty in the Celtic Fringe

The first basic point is that the Irish, Scots and Welsh are indeed the poor relations of the English. As shown in Table 1, income per head of the population in 1967, measured by Gross Domestic Product, ranged from £304 in the Republic of Ireland to £564 in Scotland, compared with £652 in England. These differences are substantial compared with regional disparities in other countries. For example, the Republic of Ireland appears to be poorer in relation to England than the Mezzogiorno is in relation to the rest of Italy. Indeed the same is true of the two constituent islands of the British Isles as a whole. The *per capita* G D P in Ireland as a whole, at £343 in 1967, was only 53.8 per cent of that in Great Britain, whereas in the Mezzogiorno it was 54 per cent of the rest of Italy in 1951 and 58 per cent in 1970,[5]

TABLE 1
Indicators of Prosperity

	Republic of Ireland (1)	N Ireland (2)	Scotland (3)	Wales (4)	England (5)
GDP at factor cost, 1967					
£ per head of pop.	304	419	564	532	652
as % of England	46.6	64.3	86.5	81.6	100
Percentage unemployed average for 1966–71 inclusive	7.4	7.2	4.1	4.0	2.3
Net emigration, 1961–71 Annual rate per 1,000 pop.	5.0	5.0	6.3	3.4	0.003
Female activity, rate, 1966	28.2	35.7	41.3	33.4	42.8
Percentage of labour force engaged in agriculture, 1966	30.8	9.9	5.2	5.3	2.8

Sources.
(1) National Income and Expenditure, Dublin 1972; The Trend of Employment and Unemployment in 1971, Dublin 1972; Census of Population of Ireland, 1966 and 1971.
(2) Digest of Statistics for Northern Ireland, Annual Abstract of Statistics, Northern Ireland Census of Population, 1966 and 1971.
(3) Scottish Abstract of Statistics, Annual Abstract of Statistics, Census of Population for Scotland, 1966 and 1971.
(4) Digest of Welsh Statistics, Annual Abstract of Statistics, Census of Population for England and Wales, 1966 and 1971.
(5) Annual Abstract of Statistics; estimates of G D P and net emigration were obtained by subtracting those for N. Ireland, Scotland and Wales from the U K totals.

The other indicators of prosperity shown in Table 1 confirm that the Celtic countries are relatively depressed. The unemployment percentage in Scotland and Wales for the years 1966–71 inclusive was nearly twice the English figure, and in both parts of Ireland it was more than three times that level. Not surprisingly, there was substantial net emigration from the four countries between 1961 and 1971, ranging from 3.4 per cent of the initial population in Wales to 6.3 per cent in Scotland. The activity rate, that is, the economically active proportion of the population aged 15 years and over, is another commonly used indicator of the extent of economic opportunities. For males, however, there is very little regional variation, and in any case this is largely explained by the age-structure of the population.[6] There is, however, substantial variation in the activity rates for females, which ranged in 1966 from 28.2 per cent in the Republic of Ireland to 42.8 per cent in England. It was only in Scotland that the rate (41.3 per cent) approached the English level. In keeping with Bowers's conclusions, these differences are to be explained mainly in terms of the local industrial or occupational structure rather than the intensity of the overall demand for labour in the area.[7] Wales, for example, has a low female activity rate not because men do jobs which would be done by women elsewhere, but because the Welsh industrial structure is oriented towards male-intensive industries. Nevertheless these low activity rates suggest that there is a considerable reserve of labour, which, if mobilised by the introduction of female-employing industry, might substantially raise local incomes. In Great Britain this process was already under way; the activity rate increased by 4.6 percentage points in England, and by 5.4 both in Scotland and Wales between 1961 and 1966. In Northern Ireland the increase, at 0.4 percentage points, was marginal whilst in the Republic the rate actually fell by 0.4 per cent.

The final indicator presented in Table 1 is the percentage of the labour force which was engaged in agriculture in 1966. According to this test the four Celtic countries again appear more backward than England, though it is doubtful whether the relatively small differences between England, Scotland and Wales have any significance. It is in the Republic of Ireland, where agriculture employed more than 30 per cent of the labour force, and to a much lesser extent in Northern Ireland, that this seems to indicate the lack of alternative employment prospects. Agricultural employment has continued to fall in all five countries of the British Isles, but by 1971 the figure for the Republic of Ireland was exceeded only in Greece, Portugal, Spain, Turkey and Yugoslavia out of a total of twenty-four member countries

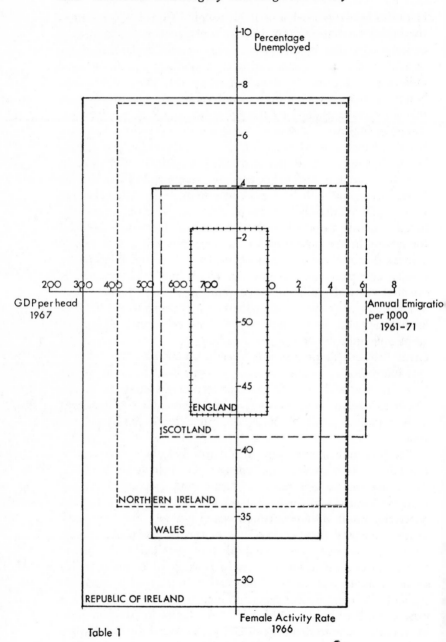

Table 1

of O E C D.[8] In this sense at least, in making a belated effort to industrialise, the Republic seems more comparable to these countries (though its income per head is substantially above that of Greece, its nearest rival) than to the countries of the United Kingdom.

One of the interesting features in this comparison is that each country demonstrates its relative backwardness in a somewhat different fashion. It might have been expected that the ranking of each country would be the same no matter which indicator of prosperity was used. In terms of Chart 1, where each rectangle represents one of the five countries, the rectangles would be concentric, without any intersections. But it is only in the case of England (placed first on all counts) where all four indicators agree. At the other end of the scale, the Republic of Ireland is unambiguously last, except for (or perhaps because of) having less emigration than Scotland and no more than Northern Ireland. If we ignore the very low female activity rate, due, as we have seen, to a preponderance of male-intensive industry, Wales is clearly above Ireland.

Perhaps the most puzzling aspect of Chart 1 is the apparently very high propensity of the Scots, and the relatively low propensity of the Irish, to emigrate. Emigration is arguably the ultimate test of the well-being in an area, since it represents the extent to which people are so dissatisfied with local economic conditions that they leave the area altogether. It is therefore surprising that the Scots, with G D P per head higher, and unemployment only marginally higher than the Welsh, emigrate on a scale even greater than the Irish.[9]

This is a very complex question and, as Mr A. B. Jack says, 'there is clearly still scope for considerable academic research into the problems of migration'.[10] Unfortunately this is not the place to pursue it, but a few points might be made. First, it seems unlikely that high Scots emigration in the 1960s can be explained in terms of the traditional habit of the Scots to emigrate, since this is even more so a characteristic of the Irish: nearly half of those born in the Republic of Ireland in the years 1926–46 found their livelihood abroad.[11] Second, it may be that a particularly mobile section of the Scottish population were prompted to emigrate by the contraction during the 1960s of the shipbuilding, metal manufacture and coal-mining industries. If

TABLE 2

Emigration and Growth of GDP in Ireland and Scotland

	% Growth of G D P, 1950–58	Net emigratiion 1951–61 rate per 1,000	% Growth of G D P, 1958–70	Net emigration 1961–71 rate per 1,000
Republic of Ireland	44.2	14.1	177.8	5.0
Northern Ireland	57.8	6.8	150.8	5.0
Scotland	59.0	5.5	103.9	6.3

Note. G D P at factor cost, current prices; for the Republic of Ireland, G N P at factor cost, current prices.

Sources. Net emigration 1961–71, as for Table 1; figures for 1951–61 were taken from J. Simpson, *Regional Analysis: the Northern Ireland Experience*, Economic and Social Review, Dublin 1971. G D P

(a) Northern Ireland: 1950 and 1958 figures come from Appendix. I, p. 144, of Professor Tom Wilson's report, in *Economic Development in Northern Ireland*, cmnd. 479, H M S O Belfast 1965. The 1970 figure: the Northern Ireland Digest of Statistics.

(b) Scotland: 1950 and 1958 figures are from G. McCrone, *Scotland's Economic Progress*. Dr Crone's estimate for 1951 was scaled down on the assumption that Scottish G D P increased at the same rate as for the U K as a whole between 1950 and 1951. The 1970 figure is taken from the Scottish Abstract of Statistics.

(c) Republic of Ireland: G N P for 1950, 1958 and 1960 comes from K. A. Kennedy, *Productivity and Industrial Growth: the Irish Experience,* Clarendon Press, Oxford, 1971, p. 3. The 1970 figure is taken from *National Income and Expenditure*, Prl 2779, S O, Dublin 1971.

each of the men released from these industries between 1959 and 1971 had emigrated, and taken two dependants with him, this would account for over 85 per cent of the net migration from Scotland between 1961 and 1971. We cannot, of course, presume that all of them did emigrate, or that they had two dependants each: the exercise is intended only to compare the broad orders of magnitude. This hypothesis must be considered as a real possibility, but it rests on the unproven assumption not only that these workers were much more mobile than the Irish, but also that their preponderance in the Scottish economy ensured that Scots workers as a whole were more mobile than the Irish.

Finally, whilst it seems generally accepted that net emigration is associated with the levels of unemployment and income relative to other areas, it may also be related to their rates of change. Thus, taking the 1950s and 1960s together, both parts of Ireland were much more depressed than Scotland throughout, with lower incomes and higher unemployment, and on this account alone emigration would be expected to exceed that from Scotland. But this was not so. As Table 2 shows, net emigration during the 1950s was much higher in Ireland than in Scotland, whilst the reverse was true of the 1960s. However, this is perfectly understandable in the light of the differing growth experience of the three countries. Before 1958 G D P grew more slowly in Northern Ireland, and much more slowly in the Republic, than it did in Scotland; emigration was substantially greater than in Scotland. After 1958 growth was much faster, and emigration somewhat lower, than in Scotland.

The differential growth rates might also help to explain why Irishmen south of the border emigrated during the 1960s only to the same extent as those in the north. Again, throughout both decades the Republic was poorer, with lower incomes and more disguised unemployment than the north, though there was little difference in the percentage registered as unemployed. On this ground emigration should have been higher in the Republic throughout the period. In the 1950s it was, when growth was considerably less than in the north; but during the 1960s, when growth was faster in the Republic than in the north, it was not.

Causes of the Regional Problem

The relatively backward state of the Celtic nations is part of the more general regional problem in the British Isles where some regions, such as the South-East of England, are buoyant and prosperous whilst others, such as the North of England, are backward and depressed. But in the Celtic nations the existence of a sense of national identity adds an extra dimension to the problem—the issue of whether or not a measure of independence would improve the situation. This topic is taken up in the next section.

The regional problem in the British Isles is normally seen as a problem of relative imbalance in the excess demand for labour. Since at any point in time some industries are growing whilst others are in decay there is no reason why the particular industrial mix in each area should produce a demand just equal to the current increase in the potential labour force. The demand for, and supply of, labour are substantially but far from completely independent. Regional demand is conditioned by the local mix of industries, and also by the extent to which any particular industry is growing faster in one region than in another, for reasons such as economies of agglomeration and regional specialisation, and general locational advantage. Changes in the indigenous labour pool, on the other hand, are determined basically by past birth rates which are in turn partly caused by the age-structure of the local population at various stages in the past, and partly by the features peculiar to each region which determine fertility rates.

This is far from saying that the two sets of factors are completely independent. To some extent, for example, the presence of population, which partly determines the supply of labour, also causes demand (e.g. jobs in service industries); up to some unspecified limit the greater the concentration of population the more this is so (economies of agglomeration). This interdependence is particularly important in the dynamics of the regional problem. Thus the present population of working age in a region—the labour pool—is a partial function of the size and age-structure of the population at previous dates, but *both* are partly determined by the historical interplay of demand and supply factors throughout the country as a whole. Regional imbalance thus produces both a long-run and a short-run effect, most obviously in terms of population and the local labour supply, but also in terms of demand, partly for reasons mentioned above.

Much work has been devoted to analysis of the extent to which differences in employment growth are due to the regional structure of industry, and how much to factors peculiar to the region. Its application to Ireland, Scotland and Wales is discussed later on in this paper. Much less work has been devoted to the other part of the problem, namely how far imbalances are due to regional variations in the growth of population and the supply of labour. For purposes of policy it is obviously the demand side which deserves most attention—it would be politically impossible and economically ludicrous to attempt to regular the present number of births to the expected demand for labour in fifteen or more years' time. Yet it still makes sense to argue that unemployment and emigration would have been reduced if birth rates had been lower in the past. The higher the birth rate the more industrial expansion is required to avoid high unemployment, low incomes and emigration.

The Great Famine of the 1840s in Ireland and the Highlands of Scotland is the most dramatic illustration in British history of this Malthusian type of situation, where the growth of population outstrips its means of support. But, as Dr Cullen points out, a rise in emigration and a falling population would have been inevitable in Ireland even if the Great Famine had not occurred.[12] The previous rise in population had been accompanied by a disproportionate increase in population with no secure stake in the land, and the decline of domestic industry removed the prospect of industrial employment. The famine simply dramatised what was inevitable anyway, since Ireland did not share in the industrial expansion in the rest of the British Isles (except for the north-east of the country, where population resumed its growth between 1901 and 1911 under the stimulus of industrial growth). The same is true of areas of Britain such as Mid-Wales and the Highlands of Scotland.

Irish history in the twentieth century presents the same Malthusian-style problem, resulting from a failure to expand economic opportunities to accommodate the continuing large natural increase of the population, which has therefore been syphoned off through emigration. It is only in the last decade that rapid industrial growth in the Republic has been able to reduce the rate of emigration below the rate of natural increase.

The Irish economic problem of the last 150 years could therefore be ascribed either to a failure to industrialise, or a failure to restrain the natural increase of the population to a level that could be supported.

The same is true of Northern Ireland, Scotland and Wales, which have all been areas of net emigration since the last third of the nineteenth century, except for the period 1901–11 when the growth of the Welsh coal industry induced immigration. In

Scotland and Wales, of course, industrial growth was able to absorb much of the natural increase in population, so that their population increased more or less steadily throughout the last two hundred years. In Northern Ireland, however, industrial expansion was unable to reduce emigration below the rate of natural increase until just before the last decade of the nineteenth century, since when population has increased.

Nevertheless it remains true that in all of the countries discussed above the natural increase of the population could not be accommodated by the expansion of economic opportunities, and they were therefore depressed relative to England. It seems likely that a lower rate of natural increase in population would have reduced emigration and alleviated their relatively depressed economic conditions.

Though the strictly limited policy implications of the point must be stressed, it may be that their relatively high natural increase of population has a bearing on the economic conditions of the Irish, and to a lesser extent, of the Scottish. In 1968 the birth rate per thousand was 21.0 in the Republic of Ireland, 22.1 in Northern Ireland, 18.3 in Scotland, 16.3 in Wales and 16.9 in England. The contrasts are even more marked if births are related to the population of women aged 15–44. Thus, the fertility rate was 114.3 per thousand in the Republic, 113.3 in Northern Ireland, 93.5 in Scotland, 86.0 in Wales and 87.1 in England. This means that industrial expansion would have to be much greater in Ireland and to some extent also in Scotland, in order to prevent their economies from being depressed relative to England. It is hard to resist the conclusion that the poverty of the Celts is as much due to a high birth rate as it is to the relative failure of industry.

The Degree of Independence

If we rank the Celtic countries according to their degree of poverty and their degree of independence there is a substantial measure of agreement. The most independent, the Republic of Ireland, has lowest GDP per head; Northern Ireland, with its own local Parliament, has the second lowest; Scotland and Wales with a more or less equal lack of independence are roughly similar in having the highest level of GDP per head next to England. The question is whether this similarity of ranking is significant, and if so whether relative economic backwardness leads towards independence or whether independence leads to backwardness.

These are complex questions which are far from resolved. Obviously more than simply economic factors are involved in nationalist aspirations, and the subject deserves, and needs, much more extended treatment than is possible here. All that can be done is to sketch some of the main outlines.

One of the major disadvantages of regional status is that regional interests may conflict with, and have to give way to the interests of the state as a whole. Thus, at times when the country as a whole suffers from demand-inflation, the policy of deflation required at national level seems to run counter to the needs of the depressed regions, where the problem is one of inadequate rather than excess demand. More generally, it may be argued that it is more in the national economic interest to allow depressed regions to remain depressed, than to interfere in natural processes which are presumed to maximise economic welfare in the state as a whole.

In these circumstances it would hardly be surprising if those in the relatively depressed regions resented the fact that their interests were over-ridden, and begin to wonder whether they could best take care of them themselves. This feeling would obviously be all the stronger if their relative deprivation appeared to result, not from any conflict of regional and national interest, but from a lack of ability or interest, on the part of the national government.

To put a little flesh on these bones, there is some evidence to suggest that the strength of support for nationalism in Scotland and Wales is at least partly associated with the performance of the Scottish and Welsh economies. It was in the inter-war years, for instance, that both Plaid Cymru and the Scottish National party were formed. In Scotland, which 'for the first time since the eighteenth century . . . ceased to be the cutting edge of a world industrial economy, . . . the collapse of industry between the wars . . . turned a derelict country in upon itself.'[13] In post-war Scotland, as Dr McCrone has shown, disillusionment with the progress of the Scottish economy, under Conservative and Labour governments successively, led to increasing support for the nationalist party.[14] The same was also broadly true for Wales, where the run-down of the South Wales coal industry appeared to have been an important factor in electoral success for Plaid Cymru even in areas not noted for nationalist sentiments. It is difficult to fit Northern Ireland into this picture, because economic issues are overlaid with religious divisions, but it does not seem irrelevant to point out that it is in Northern Ireland where nationalist protest is most violent.

It seems likely, however, that achievement of independence would do little to improve the economic prospects of regions such as Northern Ireland, Scotland or Wales. As relatively poor regions of the United Kingdom these areas benefit through paying less taxes for the same level of government services as obtain in more prosperous parts of England, including the finance of their industrial development. One result of this is that they spend more than they earn. In Wales, the only region for which a series of estimates are available, Gross Domestic Expenditure has exceeded GDP every year since 1948.[15] Estimates made for each region of the United Kingdom for 1961 and 1964 suggest that this was also true of Scotland and Northern Ireland, along with the South West of England.[16] It seems from Mr Woodward's estimate that the corresponding net imports into these three areas in 1961 were largely financed by net public sector expenditure, whereas in Wales inflow of private capital was equally important. For Wales this finding stands in sharp contrast to estimates made by Mr Tomkins, which suggest that from 1965 to 1968 Welsh net imports were predominantly financed by net public sector expenditure.

The estimates of course, relate simply to the net public expenditure pumped into the areas. To estimate the extent to which Northern Ireland, Scotland and Wales have been subsidised by England, or the extent to which their independence would require borrowing from 'abroad', some additional charge ought to be made to cover central United Kingdom services such as external relations and defence. If this is done on the basis adopted in the Treasury's 'Scottish Budget', it seems that independence would require substantial net borrowing, either from local residents or from abroad.[17] In 1967–68 an independent Scotland would have had a net borrowing requirement of £476m, or £92 per head of the population; in Northern Ireland the figure would have been £126m, or £85 per head; in Wales, for the calendar year 1967, £241m, or £88 per head. It is fair to say, however, that these estimates are a source of controversy, first as regards their basic accuracy; secondly as to whether government expenditure *in* say, Wales should be calculated rather than government spending *for* Wales; and thirdly, whether central government loans should be regarded as a subsidy. So far only the Scottish National Party has been able to convert a net borrowing requirement into a surplus.

If England were granted independence, the net borrowing requirement would obviously be reduced, by shedding the load of borrowing for the Celtic fringe. On the basis of the calculations above, the English borrowing requirement in 1967–68 would have fallen from £1,292m to £499m, as from £28.5 per head to £11. In comparison with these figures, the net borrowing requirement in the Republic of Ireland was £63m, or £22 per head of population.

There is clearly much scope for disagreement in assessment of the net borrowing requirement of 'independent' regions, not only for reasons mentioned above, but also because with independence the whole structure of government action would be different; for example an independent Wales might choose to spend much less on defence, and proportionately more on industrial development. Thus the main advantage of independence seems to lie in avoiding conflicts of interest between region and the state at large— in 'doing your own thing', whereas the main disadvantage is that this has to be paid for. To put the matter bluntly Northern Ireland, Scotland and Wales have the opportunity to pull themselves up by English bootstraps, whereas the Republic of Ireland has to use her own. In the last analysis this advantage depends on how willing England is to allow her bootstraps to be used for this purpose. In the circumstances obtaining when Ireland was part of the United Kingdom, the advantages of regional status were probably less because public expenditure was in general much lower, and much less devoted to compensatory finance to regions in the form of agricultural subsidies, regional development expenditure, and the automatic fiscal stabiliser. It seems typically ironical that in recent years, when the value of regional status has been great, Ireland was independent; up till 1922, when the value of regional status was small, she was not.

Happily, the Republic, as a new member of the European

I

Economic Community, is reverting towards the status of a region of a larger entity, along with the United Kingdom. It is significant that membership is expected to provide a substantial stimulus, both to industry and to agriculture,[18] which will reduce unemployment and emigration. If the advantages to the Republic of membership of the E E C could be taken as roughly similar to those provided by membership of the United Kingdom, this is some indication of the cost of independence.

The Structure of Industry

In recent years there has been a substantial, and growing, amount of published work devoted to analysis of the extent to which the industrial experiences of different regions can be attributed to their particular mix of industry. Most of this work has been concerned to split differing regional growth of employment into a 'structural' and a 'growth' component.[19] Others have used the structure of industry as an explanatory variable to account for regional variations in female activity rates[20] and, separately, for variations in the level of G D P per worker.[21]

The point I wish to make is that these studies invoke the structure of industry to explain one separate aspect of the regional problem; none, so far as I am aware, use industrial structure to account for the whole cluster of regional variations which constitute the regional problem—variations in the levels of output per worker and of female activity rates, and in the growth of output and employment. How can one factor, the structure of industry, be called upon to account for several things at the same time? The answer to this is surely that 'the structure of industry' is not simply one variable; just as the regional problem exists in several dimensions such as levels and growth rates of income and employment, so too the structure of industry exists in several relevant dimensions such as capital-intensity, male-intensiveness, income demand-elasticity and so on.

In arguing that the structure of industry is an important factor in causing the regional problem as a whole, we are simply saying that one cluster of variables encompassed in the term 'structure of industry' are important determinants of another cluster, collectively known as 'the regional problem'. To the best of my knowledge, no statistical technique is known which will adequately determine the relationships between clusters of variables even if the components of each cluster are mutually independent. In practice the components of the 'regional problem' are interdependent; for example, slow growth of employment in an industry which is a regional speciality may spill over and reduce earnings in the whole regional labour market below what would otherwise be expected on grounds of structure alone. Separate analyses of effects of industrial structure on (a) the growth of regional employment and (b) the level of regional incomes will fail to pick up the combined effect. Similarly the rundown of shipbuilding in Scotland may, because of industrial linkages, cause related industries to contract or grow less fast than their United Kingdom equivalent. A straightforward 'shift-share analysis' of Scottish employment would fail to pick up this effect.[22]

It is less clear whether the several attributes of 'industrial structure', which are called upon to explain different aspects of 'the regional problem', are inter-related. For example, it would presumably be 'capital-intensity' which would be called upon to account for regional variations in output per worker, whilst 'income-elasticity of demand', or 'competitiveness in foreign markets' might be likely causes of employment growth. Are these characteristics of industry functionally related, or do they combine accidentally in explaining the 'regional problem'? This would require a paper on its own, but it is clearly not difficult to see some connections. For example, one would expect a relatively rich and technologically sophisticated country like the United Kingdom to be increasingly pushed by competition from poorer and less advanced countries to specialise more and more on capital-intensive and technologically advanced industries. Hence one might expect capital-intensive industries to be particularly fast-growing. If this is so, one factor which causes a high level of output per worker is also associated with fast growth of output and (perhaps) employment. Regions which depend more than average on these industries would for that reason tend to have a high level of output and income per head, together with fast growth of output and employment. On the other hand there may be no systematic association between different attributes of 'industrial structure'; it may be that those which exist are different as between industries so that no generalisation is possible. In

I*

this event one might expect, for example, that industries of rapid employment growth are not necessarily high-productivity industries, and vice-versa. The specific forms which 'the regional problem' assumes in different regions might then be regarded as an accidental combination of these different attributes. For example, one region might have relatively high wages but slow growth of employment because it just happens to have a combination of industries which are capital-intensive but face a low income-elasticity of demand for their products.

In the present state of knowledge it seems that all that can be done is to take different aspects of the regional problem in turn and attempt to assess how important the regional mixes of industry appear to be as a causative factor. First, it had better be pointed out that the dice are heavily loaded against distinguishing the influence of the industrial structure even in principle. First, the existence of multi-product factories hinders the inclusion in an industry of only those products which have a high mutual cross-elasticity of demand. Second, the existence of large companies serving the national or international market often leads to regional division of functions, e.g. research, marketing and administration near London and production in Wales. Since the former category have been a rising proportion of all manufacturing employment so that 'head-office' areas such as the South-East of England have a more growth-oriented structure of industry than the figures suggest, and conversely for 'workshop' areas such as Northern Ireland, Scotland and Wales. Further, the existence of industrial linkages may imply that a whole regional economy may follow the fortunes of a few leading sectors of industry. More generally inter-regional differences in performance of an industry may be related to dependence on different geographical markets, which obviously need not grow at the same rate. In practice all of these difficulties are compounded by well-known limitations of the data, which are inaccurately classified for the purpose.

In view of the odds against distinguishing the influence of industrial structure on the regional problem the results of published work, on the whole, provide some grounds for confidence in the view that it is the most important factor. As Mr Bowers has shown, regional variations in the level of female activity rates are largely the result of differences in industrial structure.[23]

Further, there is some evidence that the narrowing differentials between regions are associated with changes in the structure of industry.[24]

Regional variations, within Great Britain, in the level of G D P per worker, and in various categories of income also seem explicable largely in terms of industrial structure. According to Mr Woodward's analysis inter-industry variance was greater than inter-regional variance by a factor of 24.7 for G D P per worker, 58.2 for non-employment income per person, 18.9 for average earnings per employee, and 2.6 for male manual earnings per employee.[25]

It is difficult to say how far this applies to Ireland, since no comprehensive analysis has been carried out, but it is certainly possible to identify low-output industries in which Northern Ireland and the Republic both specialise more and have a lower G D P per head than Great Britain. In Northern Ireland the linen industry, characterised by low capital-intensity and high female-intensity, is one obvious example; G D P per worker in 1961 was about 20 per cent less than the textiles industry in the North-West of England and only about one-third of the Welsh textiles industry. Agriculture is another case where G D P per worker in Northern Ireland, and also in Wales, is below the Great Britain average for the industry for structural reasons; farms are small and labour-intensive, specialising in livestock as opposed to the large-scale, capital-intensive farms in parts of England which specialise more in grain production. If we attempted to remove these two intra-industry structural defects by assuming G D P per worker was in each case equal to their Great Britain industry-average, the result would be to raise over-all G D P per worker in Northern Ireland from 78.3 per cent to 85.2 per cent of the level in Great Britain in 1961, thus accounting for almost one-third of the over-all difference.

As between Northern Ireland and the Republic the difference in G D P per worker seems to be accounted for by an enormous difference in agricultural productivity (in 1969 65 per cent higher in the North) and a more modest excess of output per head in the services sector (20 per cent higher in the North).[26] The differential in agriculture is presumably explained by the different structure of output, by more intensive methods, and by agricultural subsidies which are received only in the North.

These three factors are not mutually exclusive, and it would be difficult to distinguish their separate influences. As Dr Fitzgerald has pointed out, output per head is very similar in manufacturing as a whole, at £1,560 in the North and £1,500 in the Republic, despite some substantial differences in particular sectors such as chemicals and 'other textiles', which seem to be due to differences in capital-intensity.

Thus within Great Britain it seems that the industrial structure is predominantly the cause of regional variations in GDP per worker and in various categories of income. More comprehensive work is required to establish how far this is so in Ireland. It seems likely to be important in the North, but the relationship might be expected to be distorted in the Republic by the existence of unsubsidised agriculture and the development of protected industry catering for the domestic market.

It is more difficult to assess the influence of industrial structure on regional employment-growth patterns, partly, no doubt, because the richer variety and quantity of data have prompted a great many studies for different regions and different time-periods, using different systems of classification.[27] Practically all of these studies confirm that on grounds of industrial structure Northern Ireland, Scotland and Wales would be expected to display less buoyant employment trends than the United Kingdom as a whole.[28] They differ substantially, however, in estimates of the 'growth' effect, though this seems to be due partly to the level of aggregation in the data used, and partly to differences in the particular time period considered. In view of the bias against distinguishing the influence of industrial structure, discussed above, Mr Randall's conclusion seems fair: that 'the broad conclusions . . . support the underlying assumption of regional policy that the problems of the Development Area regions of the United Kingdom are largely structural in origin.'[29]

It seems that the relatively slow growth of employment in Northern Ireland during the 1950s was almost entirely due to an unfavourable structure of industry, biased towards agriculture, linen and shipbuilding. This was also true of Wales, where slower than average growth, conditioned by dependence on coal, metal manufacture and agriculture, was slightly better than could have been expected on grounds of structure alone. In Scotland, by contrast, employment growth seemed to be explicable much more in terms of an adverse 'growth' effect than of poor structure.[30] Indeed, as Mr Randall shows, during the period 1959–68 when favourable 'growth' in Wales, and especially in Northern Ireland, overcame poor structure, rather more than half of Scotland's poor performance was attributable to a negative 'growth' effect—and this during a period when regional policy expenditure was growing to record amounts. Mr Randall goes on to establish that this negative growth effect seems to be entirely due to the disastrous experience of West Central Scotland and by an imaginative series of disaggregated tests is able to gain some insight into the problem and show a substantially increased influence of the structural component. For example the decline in employment in the Inner Area (the Glasgow district) combined with growth in the Outer Area would seem to be a phenomenon typical of many cities. But it seems, from independent evidence, that the outlying growth is due more to the introduction of new industry from outside the area than to the more normal overspill development. What then happened to the old jobs in the city? Questions such as this, prompted by Mr Randall's analysis, clearly demand a familiarity with the industries concerned. Another example of the same type follows his finding that, on certain assumptions, the negative growth component for manufacturing would be overestimated by between 15 and 20 per cent because of a failure to take local inter-industry linkages with shipbuilding into account. Did these trades supplying Clydeside shipbuilders with goods and services also supply shipyards in other areas, such as Belfast or the North-East?

Clearly much research work remains to be done, as it seems strange that any depressed region should still register a negative growth component in a period of unprecedentedly active regional policy. It is stranger still that it should be Scotland, for two hundred years 'the cutting edge of a world industrial economy', that fails to keep pace.

Instead of Conclusions

It has been argued, *inter alia*, that the relative poverty of the Celts can be looked at either as a problem of excessive labour supply, due to high birth rates, or as a deficiency of demand stemming basically from a weak industrial structure. In the case of the Republic of Ireland these problems have been aggravated by its independent status.

This leads to a series of fascinating and important questions, for it is clearly not enough to say simply that each country has a weak industrial structure. How is one to account for the particular structure of industry now existing in each of these countries? Why is it that the shipbuilding industry did not develop in South Wales during the nineteenth century, when there were local supplies of coal and iron, whereas it did develop and prosper in Northern Ireland in their absence? Why was industrialisation in Ireland confined largely to its north-eastern corner, in what is now Northern Ireland? In the light of its previous economic performance how does one explain the economic lethargy of Scotland during the last fifty years?

As suggested in the quotation at the beginning of this paper, Celtic backwardness is not a new phenomenon. The present ranking of the countries in order of prosperity is very similar to what it was in the reign of Elizabeth I. Why, in a period of four hundred years, have economic forces been unable to remove this inequality? To what extent has government action helped or hindered in the transformation of the Celtic economies? Which policy measures appear to be most effective? Why have efforts to achieve parity in prosperity with the English remained unsuccessful?

Notes

ECONOMIC SOVEREIGNTY

1. 'It is possible to imagine many different forms of international authority and correspondingly many different limitations on the independence of states . . . It is salutary to consider this range of possibilities because merely to realise that there are many possible forms and degrees of independence, is a step towards answering the claim that because states are sovereign they *"cannot"* be subject to or bound by international law or *"can"* only be bound by some specific form of international law. For the word " sovereign" means here no more than "independent" and, like the latter, is negative in force : a *sovereign* state is one *not* subject to certain types of control, and its sovereignty is that area of conduct in which it is autonomous.' H. L. A. Hart, *The Concept of Law*, Oxford 1961, 217.

2. It is interesting to recall that Austin's sovereign power, for which he claimed so much, was not Parliament but the electorate. But the 'sovereign power' in this sense is impotent over a wide range of decisions unless preferences can be effectively expressed through the market.

3. The expression is, of course, the title of a recent book by Samuel Brittan, *The Price of Economic Freedom*, London 1971.

4. I must confess to being a little puzzled by the fact that some economists who object to variable rates on this ground are also inclined, in other contexts, to deny the importance of cost inflation. The objection that devaluation might be offset by cost inflation was made in an article by Sir Hubert Henderson which is now apparently forgotten. This article, 'The Function of Exchange Rates' appeared in *Oxford Economic Papers* in January 1949. Henderson was prepared to concede that a lower rate might help at a time of deflation, as in the thirties, but not in fully employed economies. He also laid much stress upon the fact that stable rates imposed some discipline upon governments.

5. R. I. McKinnon, 'Optimum Currency Areas', *American Economic Review*, Sept. 1963, 717.
6. R. A. Mundell, 'A Theory of Optimum Currency Areas', *American Economic Review*, Sept. 1961.
7. 'Sovereignty' is a necessary but not a sufficient condition. The states in a federal country are sovereign but have no control over the currency.
8. W. M. Corden, *Monetary Integration*, Essays in International Finance, No. 93, Princeton, April 1972. (Italics added)
9. For an application of the Phillips curve analysis to the problem of international adjustment see J. M. Fleming, 'On Exchange Rate Unification', *Economic Journal*, September 1971.
10. In the contributions to the discussion of this branch of international trade theory, little account is taken of the fact that a low level of migration is a social objective in the view of some of those concerned with regional economics.
11. It is sometimes suggested that the Republic would inevitably be opposed to a separate currency policy for political reasons. This may be so, but political considerations did not prevent the erection of other barriers between South and North.
12. This reduction of barriers was being met in 1973 with some opposition delaying tactics, even with regard to imports from the North.
13. An affirmative answer would be the right one if it were the case that the industrialised North and the agricultural South would constitute an 'economic unit'. Presumably an 'economic unit' is a self-sufficient area; but the island of Ireland is far from being a self-sufficient unit. Great Britain is more important to both North and South than the two parts of the island are to each other, and this is likely to continue. We must therefore dismiss this *simpliste* argument which reflects an almost total neglect of the industrial structure of both areas and of their trade.
14. Corden, *Monetary Integration*. Both quotations are from page 13.
15. Cf. Michael Parkin, 'An Overwhelming Case for European Monetary Union', *The Banker*, September 1972.
16. H. G. Johnson, 'The Monetary Approach to Balance-of-Payments Theory' in Michael B. Connolly and Alexander K. Swoboda (Editors), *International Trade and Money*, Toronto 1973, 213.
17. This neglected point is made and developed in an unpublished paper by my colleague, Dr L. Sirc.

18. The adjustable peg has not had many academic defenders in recent years. There has rather been a tending either to advocate fixed rates or to advocate floating rates. On the other hand public statements by finance ministers, bankers, etc., have tended to favour stability but not rigidity. For one of the few statements in favour of the adjustable peg see Samuel I. Katz, *The Case for the Par-Value System*, Essays in International Finance, No. 92, Princeton, March 1972.

19. On issues such as these see *Social Aspects of European Economic Co-operation*, I L O, Geneva 1956 (Ohlin Report); Carl S. Sharp (Editor) *Fiscal Harmonisation in Common Markets*, Columbia 1967; Bela Balassa, *The Theory of Economic Integration*, Irwin 1961. It should be noted in passing that a switch of emphasis from payroll taxes to V A T could have a similar effect to a devaluation. Such switches would therefore need to be watched by the central authority in a monetary union. When it is recalled that payroll taxes in Italy add more than 50 per cent to the wages bill, it will be appreciated that this may not be a merely trivial point.

20. For example there may be obligation to repurchase one's currency.

21. Such areas are usually termed 'regions'. Mundell, 'A Theory of Optimum Currency Areas', uses the term in a different sense.

22. This paper was written before the report of the Royal Commission on the Constitution was published. Cmnd. 5460 and 5460–1; October 1973. The broad line of reasoning is similar.

23. I have analysed these developments at greater length in a memorandum submitted to the Commission on the Constitution and published as *Written Evidence, No. 6*, H M S O 1972. For earlier discussions see T. Wilson (Editor), *Ulster Under Home Rule*, Oxford 1965; K. S. Isles and Norman Cuthbert, *An Economic Survey of Northern Ireland*, H M S O 1956; R. J. Lawrence, *The Government of Northern Ireland*, Oxford 1965.

24. The official statistics were presented under various accounting headings which did not show the true 'imperial contribution'. Mr John Simpson has estimated that in 1967–68, the year before the political disturbances began, the imperial contribution was negative to the extent of £50m; or rather more than a fifth of current provincial expenditure; or about 7 per cost of gross domestic product. If we add to this a notional figure for what a positive imperial contribution should have been the shortfall was about £120m. J. Simpson, 'Regional

Analysis : the Northern Ireland Experience', *Economic and Social Review*, July 1971.
25. The Report of the Commission on the Constitution now permits us to see this issue in a somewhat clearer perspective. Public expenditure per head in Northern Ireland was not appreciably above the English average before the first Development Plan (1964–70). This plan, which sought to reflect special needs, then lifted the relative index as the following figures from page 178 of the Report show :

Public Expenditure Per Head

	England	Wales	Scotland	Northern Ireland
1963–64	100	116	118	103
1969–70	100	116	131	118

26. Originally Stormont was not allowed to initiate any service which did not exist in Great Britain nor to have any service at a higher level. This ruling which made devolution look a somewhat pointless exercise was later relaxed.
27. Other examples could, of course, be taken such as Western Germany or Australia but my choice of example has been circumscribed by my ignorance of other systems. A review and critical analysis of equalisation arrangements in Britain, Canada, the U S A, Western Germany and Australia has been carried out by Miss Diane Dawson of the University of Glasgow on behalf of the Commission on the Constitution, and this has been published as Research Paper No. 9.
28. On the earlier disparities see Eric J. Hanson, *Fiscal Needs of the Canadian Provinces*, Canadian Tax Foundation 1961.
29. Quebec has stood apart from the tax-sharing arrangements but received equalising benefits on the same principle as other provinces. The earlier arrangement, abandoned in 1967, related only to personal income tax, corporation tax and succession and estate duties—but the proceeds were then brought up to the average for the two provinces with the highest tax-yield *per capita*. The account above is abbreviated to the point of oversimplification. For a more detailed description and statistical analysis, see *The National Finances*, published each year by the Canadian Tax Foundation. See also *In Search of Balance— Canada's Intergovernmental Experience*, the Report of the

Advisory Commission on Intergovernmental Relations, Washington D C, September 1971. This is a useful, if somewhat uncritical, study of Canadian experience.

30. The tax-equalisation arrangements have received more emphasis above than these conditional grants because the former are of interest in principle. The conditional grants, however, are still of much greater quantitative importance.

31. This way of putting the matter implies that the equalisation procedure should be the prior step with adjustments for differing needs as a supplementary refinement. In fact the 'needs' element in the British rate support grants has been about 5–6 times as important as the 'resources'—or equalisation—element, for the latter related to a restricted source of revenue (rates).

32. This danger was clearly foreseen in *The Federalist* and continues to be a relevant consideration—not merely in Northern Ireland.

33. Cf., for example, the reservations expressed by Herr Hans Frederichs, the Economics Minister in Western Germany, at the annual meeting of the German Chambers of Commerce. (Reported in *The Times*, 23 February 1973). If we look further afield, the stresses and strains in the Yugoslav federation come at once to mind.

34. The fact remains that even in Britain, Westminster chooses to exercise control partly by providing rather more than half of the assistance to local authorities in the form of specific grants. This procedure can, of course, be criticised.

35. Even within the context of the British economy, R E P is, in my view, a bad device. It is a prop, a crutch, an invalid chair. What we need are measures for rehabilitation. In so far as R E P helps at all in this respect, it is by raising profits and thus helping in the financing of investment. R E P is thus not a useful substitute for investment subsidies but a costly way of providing such assistance.

I have always been puzzled by the argument that R E P is appropriate because it is analogous to devaluation—as though that were conclusive—or as though the investment subsidies were not, for that matter, also analogous.

It is encouraging that the E E C is laying stress on training. See *Attainment of the Economic and Monetary Union*, Supplement 5/73 to the *Bulletin of the European Communities*.

36. 'Whether a high mobility of capital will mitigate or accentuate the hardship resulting from exchange rate fixity with a group of countries . . . is much more doubtful than in the case

of labour mobility!' J. M. Fleming, *Economic Journal*, September 1971, 472.

FIRST CHOOSE YOUR THEORY

1. John Morris, *The Age of Arthur*, London 1973.
2. This point emerges from F. S. L. Lyons's study, *Ireland Since the Famine*, London 1971 and also from Paul Johnson's *The Offshore Islanders*, London 1972.
3. Adam Smith and a substantial group of the classical economists were Scotsmen. The discovery of Ricardo's papers at Malahide draws attention to the extent to which British economists were concerned with Ireland—Ricardo especially—but Nassau Senior was almost the last great economist to concern himself with these matters. See *Journals, Conversations and Essays Relating to Ireland*, 2 vols, London 1868, and a valuable discussion by Lord Robbins, *Robert Torrens and the Evolution of Classical Economics*, London 1958, and *The Theory of Economic Policy In English Political Economy*, London 1950 and R. D. Collison Black, *Economic Thought and the Irish Question*, London 1960.
4. See Joseph Schumpeter, *History of Economic Analysis*, London 1954.
5. This view was expressed in Lecky's classic work on Irish history and subsequently became an orthodoxy, even in George O'Brien's splendidly balanced *The Economic History of Ireland in the Seventeenth Century*, London and Dublin 1919; *The Economic History of Ireland in the Eighteenth Century*, London and Dublin 1918; *The Economic History of Ireland, From the Union to the Famine*, London 1921. Professor O'Brien modified his views in his masterly *The Four Green Fields*, Dublin and Cork 1936, which surely deserves reprinting, and Professor James Meenan in his *The Irish Economy Since 1922*, Liverpool 1970, has achieved a notable balance.
6. See Patrick Lynch and John Vaizey, *Guinness's Brewery in the Irish Economy, 1759–1876*, Cambridge 1960.
7. Of which the classic instance is E. Strauss, *Irish Nationalism and British Democracy*, London 1951.
8. See a splendid standard text on international trade; Jagdish Bhagwati, *International Trade*, London 1969.
9. See D. Swann, *The Economics of the Common Market* (Second edition), London 1972, and H. W. Richardson, *Elements of Regional Economics*, London 1969.

10. Paul A. Baran, *The Political Economy of Growth*, London 1973, preface by R. B. Sutcliffe.
11. Brinley Thomas, *Migration and Economic Growth* (Second edition), Cambridge 1973.
12. See R. G. L. McCrone, *Scotland's Economic Progress 1951–60*, London 1965 and *Scotland's Future—The Economics of Nationalism*, Oxford 1969; K. S. Isles and Norman Cuthbert, *An Economic Survey of Northern Ireland*, H M S O, Belfast 1957.

THE ECONOMIC CASE FOR CONSTITUTIONAL REFORM

1. When changes in the differential system did have to be made, spillover effects would be minimised by a judicious choice of tax instruments and use of public expenditure for stabilisation purposes : again, this is explained in detail later.
2. 'Public Expenditure to 1976–77', H M S O, Cmnd. 5178.

THE DETERMINANTS OF REGIONAL GROWTH RATES

1. Alfred Weber, *Ueber den Standort der Industrien*, Tuebingen 1909 (translated into English by C. J. Friedrich as *Alfred Weber's Theory of the Location of Industries*, Chicago 1929).
2. Walter Christaller, *Die Zentralen Orte in Sueddeutschland*, Jena 1933 (translated by C. W. Baskin, *Central Places in Southern Germany*, New Jersey 1966; A. Loesch, *Die Raumliche Ordnung der Wirtschaft*, Jena 1940 (translated as *The Economics of Location*, Yale 1954); H. C. Tinbergen, 'The Spatial Dispersion of Production : A Hypothesis'. *Schweizerische Zeitschrift fuer Volkswirtschaft und Statistik,* Vol. 97 No. 4, 1961 and 'Sur un Modele de la dispersion geographique de l'activite economique', *Revue d'Economie Politique*, Numero Special 1964.
3. Francois Perroux, *L'Economie du XXe Siecle*, Paris 1964.
4. See especially written and oral evidence submitted by British Leyland and Chrysler Motors to the *Expenditure Committee (Trade and Industry Sub-Committee) Session 1971–72 and 1972–73*, H M S O, London.
5. J. N. Randall, 'Shift-Share Analysis as a Guide to the Employment Performance of West Central Scotland', *Scottish Journal of Political Economy*, February 1973; also Gavin McCrone, *Regional Policy in Britain*, London 1969, Chapter 7. The point is also established in B. Moore and J. Rhodes, 'Evaluating the

Effects of British Regional Economic Policy', *Economic Journal*, March 1973.

6. 'Inquiry into Average Weekly Earnings of Adult Male Manual Workers in Manufacturing and Certain Other Industries and Services', *Department of Employment Gazette*.

7. Scottish G D P figures show that the Scottish share of United Kingdom G D P has fluctuated between 8.4 and 8.6 per cent of the United Kingdom total during the last decade and stood at 8.6 per cent in 1971. *Scottish Economic Bulletin*, No. 5, Summer 1973, Table 15, 22.

THE ECONOMIC AND EXCHEQUER IMPLICATIONS OF BRITISH REGIONAL POLICY

1. We gratefully acknowledge the invaluable contribution of Mr W. A. H. Godley, Director of the Department of Applied Economics, Cambridge. We have also received valuable comments from Professors N. Kaldor and R. R. Nield, Kevan Allen, John Bowers, Jim Taylor and Peter Townroe. This paper has its origin in a memorandum which we were asked to submit to the Trade and Industry Sub-Committee of the House of Commons Expenditure Committee.

2. There are possibly two origins of this view. One stems from an influential line of reasoning in economics which has its roots in the doctrine that the optimum allocation of a *given* quantity of resources is brought about by the operation of free market forces. The other is based on the contentions of individual firms which claim to have been adversely affected by particular measures of regional policy—for example where firms have been prevented from locating near to their main markets or near to existing plants and have therefore moved to areas where the efficiency of labour per unit of wage costs is lower.

3. Part of this income effect arises from the increase in incomes of previously unemployed persons brought into employment by regional policy.

4. For the rest of this paper the phrase 'regional policy measures' is used to indicate action or effects of a specifically regional kind. We shall use the phrase 'the net effects of regional policy' to describe the overall effects of both regional policy measures and the counterpart demand management measures.

5. The redistribution occurs because, whilst it is mainly manufacturing activity which is diverted to Development Areas, the

resources released may be taken up by a general expansion of demand falling in all sectors.

6. The issue as to how far regional policy reduces or increases the overall level of productivity in the Development Areas is complex. A distinction must be made between incoming and indigenous firms. For the indigenous firms investment incentives are likely to accelerate the rate of investment with consequent improvements in productivity relative to non-Development Areas. On the other hand these firms may have to raise wage rates to hold their labour force in competition with incoming firms or recruit less skilled labour from the unemployment register. Therefore, in the short run these firms may suffer even after allowing for compensating inducements such as R E P, but in the longer run these increasing competitive pressures may themselves generate productivity increases. In the case of incoming firms productivity of Development Area plants is often below that in similar plants in non-Development Areas but this is a transitional factor which emerges in the short run whenever plants are newly established or move from one place to another. More permanent productivity losses may arise from regional policy in firms which are forced to split operations into several factories but this may be offset by increases in productivity in other firms in fully employed areas which can grow more easily as a consequence of regional policy. For the Development Areas as a whole incoming firms almost certainly will raise the overall level of productivity in the medium and long term.

   It should not be overlooked that, in the absence of regional policy, productivity differences between Development Areas and non-Development Areas are likely to increase as new growth would be concentrated in fully employed areas. Regional policy therefore can be seen as having to prevent productivity differences getting larger before any absolute improvements can take place.

7. The consequential loss of productivity in the fully employed areas due to a change in the structure of employment will only be a minor one because the change in the distribution of employment is itself a small one.

8. See Appendix C. This point is discussed in more detail below.

9. Some would argue that by inhibiting migration even to a small extent regional policy involves losses in efficiency in the growth centres of fully employed areas, resulting from unexploited internal and external scale economies. However, there are

equally strong arguments on the other side concerned with the social costs and external diseconomies which cannot be adequately measured and which are associated with growing concentrations of population, i.e. the costs of congestion.

10. The I D C policy is specifically designed to restrain expansion in the fully employed areas and thereby divert manfacturing firms to assisted areas. Evidence to the Trade and Industry Sub-Committee of the House of Commons Public Expenditure Committee confirms that the I D C policy has in fact diverted some large firms to Development Areas. Other evidence to this Committee indicated that firms now in Development Areas would have been in the fully employed areas were it not for financial inducements available in Development Areas. The D T I data on industrial movement in the United Kingdom indicate that movement of firms to Development Areas is substantial and responsive to the strengthening of regional policy. Our more recent work which takes the form of an industrial enquiry and a detailed analysis of firms attracted into Government factories suggests a considerable diversionary effect of regional policy.

11. B. C. Moore and J. Rhodes, 'Evaluating the Effects of British Regional Economic Policy', *Economic Journal*, March 1973.

12. A. J. Brown, *The Framework of Regional Economics in the United Kingdom*, Cambridge, 1972. See also D. J. C. Forsyth and K. Doeherty, *The United States Investment in Scotland*, New York, 1972; P. A. Hart, 'The Distribution of New Industrial Building in the 1960s, *Scottish Journal of Political Economy*, June 1971; Hunt Committee Report on Intermediate Areas, 156; T. W. Buck and J. F. Lowe, 'Regional Policy and the Distribution of Investment', *Scottish Journal of Political Economy*, November 1972.

13. The operation of this policy may have two effects—firstly to divert demand to Development Areas away from fully employed areas and secondly to delay or thwart the expansion plans of firms in fully employed areas. The outcome of both these effects is a reduction in the pressure of demand in fully employed areas.

14. The Green Paper on the Regional Employment Premium asserted that whilst this conclusion might hold for R E P it did 'not hold good for other measures'. (Para. 35.)

15. Whilst this is true for each region as a whole there may be firms or individuals in any one fully employed region who lose income at the expense of others in the same region.

16. See for instance N. Kaldor, 'The Case for Regional Policies', *Scottish Journal of Political Economy*, November 1970, 347.

17. This pre-emption of resources is not always pound for pound. For instance, in the case of family allowances some of the initial Exchequer cost is recovered directly through higher income tax rather than increasing the demand for goods and services.

18. For details of expenditure on these incentives see Table A1.

19. Including the reduction in Exchequer outlays on unemployment benefits.

20. A number of different assumptions on migration and other variables were tried two of which are presented above. It appears that the overall outcome of the analysis is not very sensitive to a wide range of alternative assumptions about income effects, migration and multipliers.

21. N B. This does not imply that the growth rate is 1 per cent higher, merely that G D P is 1 per cent higher after seven years of regional policy than it would otherwise have been.

22. In calculating direct output and employment effects of a subsidy or income change we adopt the following conventions: $S = .15$ (higher than average to take account of progressive taxes), direct taxes $= 0.3$, indirect tax content of consumption $= .15$, marginal propensity to import $= 0.2$, corporation tax at $.4$, dividends $= .4$ of after tax profits, $.3$ of retained profits used for further investment, output/employment relationship $1:1$.

23. A multiplier of 1.4 was used.

24. B. C. Moore and J. Rhodes, 'Evaluating the effects of British regional economic policy'.

25. A. J. Brown, *The Framework of Regional Economics in the United Kingdom*.

26. This higher migration figure is based on research published by the Development Commission for Mid-Wales which indicated that, *at least in sparsely populated rural areas*, for every 10 new jobs created, the net outward migration of employed persons declined by 4 or 5.

27. A. J. Brown, *The Framework of Regional Economics in the United Kingdom*, 276.

28. A study of American firms moving into Scotland in the post-war period suggests that regional policy was a powerful force in attracting some of these firms to the United Kingdom and that their favourable contribution to the Balance of Payments

was substantial. See D. J. C. Forsyth and K. Doeherty, *The United States Investment in Scotland.*

THE IMPLICATIONS OF EUROPEAN MONETARY INTEGRATION FOR THE PERIPHERAL AREAS

1. This paper has been revised from the version presented to the conference, in the light of useful comments made by the participants (particularly Professor D. McKay and Mr J. Martin) and the constructive criticism of Dr M. Corden and Mr J. Marcus Fleming. I hope that the last two, and the other economists whose models are sketched in the paper, will forgive me for continuing to attribute to them what is undoubtedly a simplified version of their full analysis, but which I believe captures the essential features of their contributions. I am also indebted to Mr M. Goldstein for comments on an earlier draft, and to Miss N. Calika for statistical assistance. Views expressed are those of the author and do not necessarily represent those held in the International Monetary Fund.

2. I. F. Pearce, 'Some Aspects of European Monetary Integration', a paper presented at the Bournemouth Conference of the Money Study Group, February 1972.

3. Use of the term 'money illusion' to describe a willingness to accept market-clearing rather than monopolistic prices is an obfuscation that would be better banished from the literature. Indeed, the term seems a serious source of confusion. Thus Ingram was led to argue that currency depreciation can work only in the presence of money illusion, since if the population is determined to force up real wages faster than productivity there is no system that can reconcile internal and external balance. J. C. Ingram, *The Case for European Monetary Integration*, Essays in International Finance, No. 98, Princeton, April 1973, 20. What this overlooks is that the process of cost inflation can perfectly well result from the attempt to do as well as possible, rather than to achieve certain immutable real income goals; or from the attempt to make gains relative to certain reference groups, rather than of a determinate absolute size. In so far as those reference groups are within the monetary area, it is quite feasible for devaluation to 'work', even in the presence of an environment that produces cost inflation. Indeed, it is precisely in an environment where a competitive scramble for real income is keenest that it is most difficult to

envisage a decrease in real income (to make way for a payments improvement) that did not represent an across-the-
board sacrifice, such as is imposed by a devaluation.
4. Neither, incidentally, does it establish that wage differentials
are equilibrating; in fact, the table shows Irish labour to be
more highly paid than British labour in 15 occupations and
less well paid in only 5 occupations.
5. P. M. Oppenheimer, 'The Problem of Monetary Union',
mimeographed. Oppenheimer is not alone in having toyed with
this theory, which the author at one time partially subscribed
to; but his clear statement provides a convenient focus for
discussion.
6. P. M. Oppenheimer, 'The Problem of Monetary Union', 3.
7. Prices and Incomes Commission, *Inflation, Unemployment and
Incomes Policy*, Ottawa 1972, 92; W. Thirsk, *Regional Dimensions of Inflation and Unemployment*, Prices and Incomes
Commission, Ottawa 1973, 18.
8. J. M. Fleming, 'On Exchange Rate Unification', *Economic
Journal*, September 1971.
9. W. M. Corden, *Monetary Integration*, Essays in International
Finance, No. 93, Princeton, April 1972; W. M. Corden, 'The
Adjustment Problem', in L. B. Krause and W. S. Salant
(Editors), *European Monetary Unification and Its Meaning for
the United States*, Washington D C 1973.
10. J. M. Parkin, 'An Overwhelming Case for European Monetary
Union', *The Banker*, September 1972.
11. The literature surveyed by Goldstein suggested that the wage
response to expected price changes appears to be less than
unity for the United States, but close to unity for Canada. M.
Goldstein, 'The Trade-Off Between Inflation and Unemployment', *I M F Staff Papers*, November 1972, 667. On the other
hand, Gordon and Nordhaus found coefficients close to unity
for the United States, and Nordhaus was unable to reject the
hypothesis for 3 of 6 other countries (with Canada being one
of those for which it was rejected). R. J. Gordon, 'Wage-Price
Controls and the Shifting Phillips Curve', *Brookings Papers on
Economic Activity*, 1972; W. D. Nordhaus, 'The Worldwide
Wage Explosion', *Brookings Papers on Economic Activity*,
1972. Duck *et al* found a unitary coefficient for the 'world'
(actually the Group of Ten). N. Duck, M. Parkin, D. Rose, G.
Zis, 'World Inflation: 1956–70', Inflation Workshop, University of Manchester, February 1973. Spitäller found a coefficient
that increases (though still less than unity) above a certain

threshold, for the United States. E. Spitäller, 'Inflationary Expectations and the Trade-Off Between Unemployment and Inflation in the United States', mimeographed, June 1973.

12. J. M. Fleming, 'On Exchange Rate Unification', 469.

13. D. E. Laidler, 'Price and Output Fluctuations in an Open Economy', University of Manchester, December 1972.

14. See L. B. Krause and W. S. Salant, *European Monetary Unification and Its Meaning for the United States*, 198.

15. Sources of these figures are as follows:

Canada: *Canadian Statistical Review*, Ottawa, December 1970, November 1971, January 1973, Table 8.

Iceland: Iceland: *General Economic Review*, Reykjavik 1971, Vol. II, Table 30, and Fund Sources.

Ireland: *Quarterly Economic Commentary*, Economic and Social Research Institute, Dublin, October 1972, Table 6.1.

Northern Ireland: *Digest of Statistics*, Northern Ireland, Ministry of Finance, Stormont, September 1972, Table 10.

Norway: *Arbeidsmarkadstatistikk 1971*, Central Bureau of Statistics of Norway, Oslo, 1971, Tables 8 and 15.

Scotland: *Department of Employment Gazette*, London, October 1972, Table 116.

16. The literature contains two recent articles whose empirical findings seem consistent with this hypothesis. One is the finding of Packer and Park that distortions in relative wages tend to push the Phillips curve upwards. A. H. Packer and S. H. Park, 'Distortions in Relative Wages and Shifts in the Phillips Curve', *Review of Economics and Statistics*, February 1973. The second is Brechling's conclusion that the aggregate long-run Phillips curve varies with shifts of sectoral unemployment between sectors with strong and weak expectational leadership, and that regions with high expectational leadership are those with high relative earnings rather than those with low unemployment. Brechling explained his finding by a theory of migration, but Thirsk has pointed out that this theory is empirically indistinguishable from one based on wage emulation, as sketched in the text. F. Brechling, 'Wage Inflation and the Structure of Regional Unemployment', *Journal of Money, Credit and Banking*, February 1973, Part II; W. Thirsk, *Regional Dimensions of Inflation and Unemployment*, 42.

17. The potential importance of this third effect has been strikingly demonstrated by the capricious distributional consequences of the geographical location of oil deposits and the sharp rise in oil prices in late 1973. However, the relationship

between monetary union and fiscal integration is not clearly established : Corden has argued that the former may not be a necessary condition for the latter, and the existence of the common agricultural policy substantiates this view. Nevertheless, a political-economy viewpoint would suggest that monetary union is likely to promote a commonly-financed regional policy. W. M. Corden, *Monetary Integration*, 38.

18. G. Magnifico and J. Williamson, *European Monetary Integration*, Federal Trust, 1972.
19. Oppenheimer has challenged this on the ground that adoption of a Europa 'would encourage inter-country price and wage comparisons . . . with the pernicious result' [of undermining the ability of individual European countries to remain feasible currency areas]. (A 'feasible currency area' is defined as one within which 'money illusion' is sufficient to make devaluation an effective instrument for reducing real wages.) The encouragement of such comparisons is indeed a probable consequence of full monetary union, but it is far-fetched to suppose that replacement of the Euro-dollar by the Europa, or the use of the Europa for denominating international debts, would exert a perceptible influence on the process. P. M. Oppenheimer, 'The Problem of Monetary Union', 28.

IRELAND IN THE ENLARGED EEC:
ECONOMIC CONSEQUENCES AND
PROSPECTS

1. The author gratefully acknowledges the many helpful criticisms and suggestions received from Dr K. A. Kennedy and Professor R. O'Connor of The Economic and Social Research Institute, Dr W. Black of Queen's University, Belfast, John O'Hagan of Trinity College, Dublin and Paid McMenamin of the Industrial Development Authority. A special debt is owed to John Martin of Nuffield College, Oxford, for his careful and critical reading of the first draft of this paper. Any remaining faults or omissions are the author's sole responsibility. The author wishes to thank The Economic and Social Research Institute for providing office and typing facilities during the period in which the present paper was prepared.
2. T. Garvin and A. Parker, 'Party Loyalty and Irish Voters : The EEC Referendum as a Case Study', *Economic and Social Review*, October 1972.
3. For further details, see *The Accession of Ireland to the Euro-*

pean Communities, Government Stationary Office, January 1972 (Prl 2064).

4. T. Garvin and A. Parker, 'Party Loyalty and Irish Voters: The E E C Referendum as a Case Study'.

5. Only some economic implications are examined, chiefly the comparative static balance of payments effects. The effects of economic monetary union, for instance, are not considered, nor the long-run implications of the E E C's common competition and industrial policy etc.

6. O E C D *Examiners' Report on National Science Policies: Ireland*, Paris 1973 (mimeo) 20–1.

7. See Dermot McAleese, *Effective Tariffs and the Structure of Industrial Protection in Ireland*, The Economic and Social Research Institute, Paper No. 62, June 1971, Dublin. Irish tariffs are also compared with other countries' tariffs in P. G. Elkan, *Industrial Protection in New Zealand 1952 to 1967*, New Zealand Institute of Economic Research, 1972, Table 14, with similar results to the above.

8. For further details of Ireland's export performance, see Dermot McAleese and John Martin, 'Ireland's Manufactured Exports to the E E C and the Common External Tariff, *Economic and Social Review*, July 1972.

9. Committee on Industrial Progress, *General Report*, Prl. 2927, December 1972, 13. This report also contains a highly critical commentary on the quality of management in the older-established enterprises. Further analysis of grant-aided enterprises is contained in Dermot McAleese, 'Capital Inflows and Direct Foreign Investment in Ireland 1952–70', *Journal of the Statistical and Social Inquiry Society of Ireland*, Vol. XXII, Part IV, 1971–72.

10. Since 1966, the percentage of domestic consumption of manufactured goods allocated to competing imports has increased from 16 per cent to 23 per cent. *Review of 1972 and Outlook for 1973*, Prl. 3090, Table (1).

11. See, for example, B. Balassa and M. E. Kreinin, 'Trade Liberalisation under the "Kennedy Round": The Static Effect', *Review of Economics and Statistics*, May 1967.

12. Details are provided in the Appendix.

13. C. E. V. Leser, *A Study of Imports*, The Economic and Social Research Institute, Paper No. 38, April 1967, Dublin; Dermot McAleese, *A Study of Demand Elasticities for Irish Imports*, The Economic and Social Research Institute, Paper No. 53, March 1970, Dublin. The latter study contains price elasticity

estimates for *total* imports of between -0.9 and -1.5. If *manufactured* imports are broken down according to use (producers' capital goods, intermediate goods, consumers' goods) and the elasticities for these commodity groups (as estimated in McAleese's study) are applied, weighted by import shares, elasticity estimates of -0.9 and -1.2 are obtained.

14. M. E. Kreinin, 'The Static Effects of E E C Enlargement on Trade Flows', *Southern Economic Journal*, April 1973. We use the average of his elasticities for E E C and Other E F T A of 1.8 for semi-manufactures and 3.6 for manufactures. This accords closely with Hitiris's estimate of the substitution elasticity for Greece of -2.5. T. Hitiris, 'Price-import Effects of Economic Association', *Bulletin of Economic Research*, November 1971,101.

15. The third and fourth columns of Table 2 are derived from the formula :

$$\triangle M = M \cdot t/(1 + t) \cdot \eta$$

where M = 1971 imports, t = average nominal tariff and η = the price elasticity of demand.

16. This figure is obtained by averaging the G A T T estimates of commodity tariffs on semi-manufactured and manufactured goods. See *European Community*, June 1972, 21.

17. Rising G N P will, of course, ensure that the import base keeps increasing annually. The integration effect becomes as a result larger in absolute terms. Hence the figure for percentage increase in imports in Table 3 are probably more significant than the absolute figures. This point deserves to be brought out explicitly in any study of integration effects, especially when the transitional period is long.

18. Dermot McAleese and John Martin, *Irish Manufactured Imports from the U K in the Sixties: The Effects of A I F T A*, The Economic and Social Research Institute, Paper No. 70, May 1973, Dublin.

19. In this instance, we implicitly assume infinite supply elasticities over the relevant output range, whereas for imports we availed of the small-country assumption of infinite supply elasticities of imports.

20. Improvements in our competitive position *vis-à-vis* the developed Commonwealth countries (Australia, Canada etc.) and disimprovements in our competitive position *vis-à-vis* All Other Area imports due to the alignment of the high United King-

dom tariff to the lower C E T are assumed to be of negligible importance.

21. Dermot McAleese and John Martin, 'Ireland's Manufactured Exports to the E E C and the Common External Tariff'.

22. An arithmetic average of tariff estimates relating manufactured and semi-manufactured goods for each of the six Other E F T A countries (Iceland excluded).

23. The approach here is a non-rigorous one. Ideally, we ought to stick to the 'own' elasticity of about −3 and add the substitution effects directly. This would have entailed a detailed computation of All Other Areas' exports to the United Kingdom in order to apply substitution elasticities. Since all we need is an approximate estimate, it was felt that such an elaborate exercise would not be worthwhile undertaking.

24. See, for example, Kreinin's already cited article on E E C enlargement and references therein.

25. These results may be compared with those of John O'Hagan and Hugh Neary, 'E E C Entry and Ireland's Balance of Payments', *Quarterly Bulletin*, Central Bank of Ireland, Autumn 1972.

26. We follow Williamson here who, in his study of the effects of E E C membership on British trade in manufactured goods, estimates these effects by first projecting trade values to 1978 on a non-entry assumption and then applying the formula to these end-period flows. (See Williamson's contribution in John Pinder (Editor), *The Economics of Europe*, London 1971.) The same procedure could, of course, be applied to imports, but in view of the greater base values the difference between the trade effects as measured from the extrapolated 1978 import base and those measured from the 1971 base would not be as great proportionately as in the case of exports.

27. See, for example, the results referenced and cited in *The Trade Effects of E F T A and the E E C, 1959–1967*, European Free Trade Association, Geneva 1972.

28. The various Associated territories can safely be excluded from consideration in this table for obvious reasons.

29. See Dermot McAleese and John Martin, 'Ireland's Manufactured Exports to the E E C and the Common External Tariff', 625.

30. Many foreign industrialists viewed Ireland's acceptance into the E E C as a seal of approval from the Community, reflecting favourably on the 'soundness' both of the Irish Economy

and of present and prospective future economic policy of the Irish Government.

31. The notion that free trade affects only those industries which are directly competitive with imports is surely mistaken. The managerial 'slack' permitted by high effective tariffs conduces to a careless attitude towards cost control. Faced with intensified competition from abroad, it is only to be expected that the Irish industrialist will demand higher standards from the service sector. Hence the redundancy observed in that sector in recent years cannot be viewed in isolation from the trend towards free trade.

32. To generate *net* exports of £100m would require roughly twice that amount of *gross* exports. While capital investment/sales ratio differ widely from enterprise to enterprise, an increase in investment of up to £400m might be required to generate £200m of gross exports. An E E C effect on foreign investment of this magnitude is clearly implausible.

33. For a useful discussion of these estimates, see J. O'Hagan and H. Neary, 'Irish Agriculture and the E E C: An Examination of Some of the Macro-Economic Issues', *Irish Journal of Agricultural Economics and Rural Sociology*, Vol. 4, No. 1, 1972–73.

34. The White Papers of 1970 and 1972 give estimates of 58 and 50 per cent respectively. The latter estimate is also used to estimate the balance of payments effects of entry in *The Irish Farmer in the European Community*, Occasional Paper 111, published by the Irish Council of the European Movement.

35. International comparisons are provided in Tables 3.1 and 3.2 of D. G. Johnson, *World Agriculture in Disarray*, London 1973.

36. This is because the E E C Guide price is a weighted average of many different types of beef price—cows, steers of different quality etc.

37. A comparison between E E C and Irish reference prices for beef, computed in April 1973, shows a gap of 26 per cent between the two price levels. These prices were as near to being exactly comparable as one can get. I am grateful to Mr R. Dunne of the Irish Livestock and Meat Board for his assistance on this matter.

38. The live equivalent of cattle and beef exports was as follows:

	1968	1969	1970	1971	1972
Number (000)	1211.8	1150.7	1195.3	1290.2	1108.8

(Source: *Irish Statistical Bulletin*, March 1973).

39. T. Josling and D. Lucey, 'The Market for Agricultural Goods in an Enlarged European Community', paper read to the Irish Agricultural Economics Society, Dublin, 22 October 1971. R. O'Connor, 'Projections of Irish Cattle and Milk Output under E E C Conditions', *Economic and Social Review*, April 1972.

40. For example, see *Agricultural Projections for 1975 and 1985*, O E C D, Paris 1968.

41. This conclusion would be further strengthened if account were taken of the high import content of domestic manufacturing in a small country like Ireland. The net balance of payments effect of import substitution, in other words, is significantly less than the gross effect. The import content of increased agricultural output is, by contrast, quite small.

42. 'Sensitive' products consist of paper products, aluminium, ferro-alloys, magnesium, silicon carbide, zinc and certain synthetic fibres. See *E F T A Bulletin* November 1972.

43. Raymond Crotty, *Ireland and the Common Market*, Dublin 1972. Crotty incidentally, was the only Irish economist to commit to print a substantial set of arguments *opposing* E E C entry.

44. Baker, O'Connor and Dunne, *A Study of the Irish Cattle and Beef Industries*, The Economic and Social Research Institute, Paper No. 72, July 1973, Dublin, 122.

45. Dermot McAleese, *Effective Tariffs and the Structure of Industrial Protection in Ireland*, Table 3 and A2 respectively. The 12 per cent average was obtained by weighting each of the three commodity group tariffs (producers' capital goods, intermediate goods and consumption goods) in Table A2 by their share in 1971 total merchandise imports.

THE INDUSTRIAL DEVELOPMENT PROCESS IN THE REPUBLIC OF IRELAND 1953–72

1. I would like to acknowledge the invaluable contributions to this paper by my colleagues Mr F. L. Benson and Mr D. Flinter. The opinions expressed in the paper are mine and do not necessarily reflect the views of the Industrial Development Authority.

SOME ECONOMIC IMPLICATIONS
OF THE VARIOUS 'SOLUTIONS' TO
THE NORTHERN IRELAND PROBLEM

1. An earlier draft of this paper was delivered at the Royal Economic Society and British-Irish Association conference on 'The Relation of Small Economies to a Dominant Neighbour' on 12 September 1973. I am indebted to the participants at the conference and to the chief discussant of the paper, Norman Cuthbert, for most helpful comments.

2. If 1950 is compared with 1970 instead of 1972 the numbers employed in manufacturing industry would have fallen by some 6,000. This is probably a fairer comparison.

3. The estimated borrowing requirement for 1973–74 is £83.3m. The borrowing requirement is generally financed from a number of sources including borrowing from the United Kingdom government.

4. The cost of army operations in Northern Ireland for 1972–73 has been estimated at £29m. See *Hansard*, 16 February 1973.

5. The payments also include, for example, unemployment and related benefits paid to those who were formerly employed in Britain but during periods of slack demand return to Northern Ireland. Should these payments be deducted in whole or in part from the 'net' payments figure mentioned in the text on the grounds that if they could not be made in Northern Ireland they would, at least to some degree, have been made in Britain to those who might have remained there?

   Clearly some very difficult theoretical and measurement questions arise when an attempt is made to determine a 'net' figure for transfers. For instance, on the theoretical level it would seem to raise the whole issue of externalities and their measurement and possible questions relating to the costing and pricing of joint-products.

6. For some information about public sector expenditure in Northern Ireland see, 'Public Expenditure to 1976–77', especially pages 84–5, Cmnd. 5178.

7. Cmnd. 5259 and the Northern Ireland Constitution Act 1973 (c. 36).

8. The Finance Corporation acts both as merchant bank in putting up equity or loan capital for new and established companies and as lender of last resort to companies in financial difficulties. Enterprise Ulster is a direct labour organisation concerned with providing continuous labour-intensive employ-

ment mostly on social improvement schemes. The Local Enterprise Development Unit promotes employment through aiding small firms, which employ less than 50 persons by means of grants and loans, management and financial advice etc. The counter redundancy scheme provides for the payment, during periods of temporary slack demand, of what is in effect a wage subsidy to firms which are prepared to keep workers on for re-training. The industrial regeneration programme is designed primarily to stimulate expansion of existing industry by examining with the help of representatives from individual industries the factors inhibiting growth.

9. Many other assumptions are, of course, involved. Suppose we postulate a Cobb-Douglas production function so that

$$Q = AK^\alpha L^\beta \qquad \text{then}$$

$$\frac{dQ}{Q} = \alpha \frac{dK}{K} + \beta \frac{dL}{L}$$

This implies immediately that changes in output depend on both capital and labour, including given technology, constant intensity of use of capital and fixed quality of labour. Moreover, to relate output to capital as is done in the text is to imply for the Cobb-Douglas production function that the rate of change of labour is a constant multiple of the rate of change of capital.

$$\text{Suppose} \quad \frac{dL}{L} = \gamma \frac{dK}{K}$$

$$\text{then} \quad \frac{dQ}{Q} = (\alpha + \beta\gamma) \frac{dK}{K}$$

Assumptions such as these are all reasons for treating the argument in the text with reserve.

10. Capital-grants to the private sector were £47.7m for 1970–71 and £46.2m for 1971–72 at out-turn prices. Northern Ireland Economic Report on 1972, Table 4.

11. See the Appendix.

11a. By income here is meant income from economic activity in

Northern Ireland. But in addition to this there would be the loss in transfers from Britain.

12. Northern Ireland would also be involved in additional expenditure on defence, diplomacy etc. which is now carried by Britain, thus the £250m to £300m is probably an *under* estimate of the costs of 'independence' to Northern Ireland.

13. There is some tentative evidence that the output elasticity of labour for manufacturing industry is about .58. See W. A. McCullough, 'Embodied and Disembodied Technical Change in Northern Ireland Manufacturing 1950–68', unpublished MSc. dissertation, New University of Ulster, 1973.

14. The model would need further development to try and take account of 'balance of payments' complications which would certainly arise if there was a cut-off of funds from Britain and an attempt to implement offsetting measures. The likelihood of a devaluation of what presumably would by then be the Northern Ireland pound would be very high. The anticipation of this possibility would probably precipitate a massive flight of funds from Northern Ireland.

15. See below for some discussion of offsetting during transition to a federal Ireland.

16. To expect Britain to support a 'foreign' federation on a large financial scale may seem politically unrealistic. However, it would almost certainly be economically less expensive than Northern Ireland's continued membership of the United Kingdom.

17. In so far as £300m refers to 1973–74 and includes special payments connected with the troubles it may be on the high side. However, to reduce it to say £250m would still constitute a major task in relation to the likely gross domestic product and tax revenue of the Republic. The task would, of course, be less onerous if the economy of the Republic were to grow at 5 per cent or 6 per cent per year.

18. I have not dealt with what might happen at the end of the period following a cessation of payments from Britain to Northern Ireland. However, if a 'full' federation was to come about with harmonisation of taxes etc. then the Republic could scarcely be expected to continue indefinitely to make payments to Northern Ireland. In effect, uniform progressive taxation would ultimately imply that the 'richer' area would make payments to the 'poorer' one.

19. It is in principle possible to use the formulae in the appendices to answer this question within the framework of the particular

models employed there. However, the usefulness of such a procedure may be doubted because of the short-run, static and incomplete nature of the models, including the absence of monetary, production and employment sectors. Some crude figuring suggests that a unit reduction in net payments to Northern Ireland might, as far as income is concerned, be offset by a 0.4 per cent to 0.5 per cent reduction in tax rates. Thus a £30m to £40m cut in net payments might require some 12 per cent to 20 per cent cut in the rates. However, this is not a complete answer as it, amongst other things, begs the question of how government expenditure is financed following a reduction in tax rates.

20. It is possible that radical measures, including if need be devaluation, to achieve full employment might allow rather more of the net British payments to be offset though perhaps at some cost to the future in terms of accumulation of foreign debt.

21. As living standards in Northern Ireland increased the transfer payments component of the total payments involved would be likely to decrease, but this would probably be more than offset by other payments for a growing public sector expenditure.

22. It is perhaps conceivable that the E E C might be willing to contribute financially towards the establishment of an Irish 'federation'. This would clearly help but it may be doubted if it would be on a scale that would require a major modification of the conclusions which follow in the text.

23. If the White Paper commitments are not fulfilled along the lines indicated this conclusion might need substantial alteration.

24. My chief debt is to A. J. Brown, *The Framework of Regional Economics in the United Kingdom*, Cambridge 1972, see especially 180–88. It will also be noticed that the model above employs some of the same symbols as used by Brown. In addition, I have drawn on the work of others such as T. Wilson, 'The Regional Multiplier—A Critique', *Oxford Economic Papers*, November 1968.

25 and 26. These are the values used by A. J. Brown, *The Framework of Regional Economics in the United Kingdom*.

27. See A. J. Brown, *The Framework of Regional Economics in the United Kingdom*, 184.

SOME COMMENTS ON
PROFESSOR GIBSON'S PAPER

1. This is not a very useful average since working proprietors are included in the total of employment but not in the total of salaries.
2. There has been a considerable variation in this figure over the years; 88.2 per cent in April 1948, 81.2 per cent in April 1963, 87.6 in October 1967, 85.9 in October 1969. Average earnings in Northern Ireland were not published in the fifties.
3. K. S. Isles and Norman Cuthbert, *An Economic Survey of Northern Ireland*, H M S O, 1957.
4. C. V. Leser, 'Output per head in Different Parts of the United Kingdom', *Journal of the Royal Statistical Society, Part II*, 1950.

THE ECONOMIC PROBLEMS OF
IRELAND, SCOTLAND AND WALES

1. The others being Brittany, Cornwall and the Isle of Man.
2. In various sports, it is the match with England which arouses most enthusiasm.
3. J. G. Williamson 'Regional Income Inequality and the Process of National Development: a Description of the Patterns', *Economic Development and Cultural Change*, 1965.
4. A. J. Brown, *The Framework of Regional Economics in the United Kingdom*, Cambridge 1972, 81–4.
5. The Italian data comes from *O E C D Economic Surveys: Italy*, O E C D Paris, November 1972.
6. John Bowers, *The Anatomy of Regional Activity Rates*, N I E S R Regional Papers I, Cambridge 1970, 17.
7. John Bowers, *The Anatomy of Regional Activity Rates*, 40.
8. *O E C D Economic Surveys: Ireland*, O E C D Paris, March 1973, Basic Statistics: International Comparisons.
9. Dr R. C. Geary and Mr J. G. Hughes suggest that net migration of insured persons from the Republic between 1961 and 1966 is consistent with a highly significant relationship they have discovered, between unemployment and net migration of insured workers, for seven British regions (including Scotland and Wales) in the period 1962–66: *Certain Aspects of Non-Agricultural Employment in Ireland*, The Economic and Social Research Institute, Paper No. 52, Dublin, February 1970. This result must, however, remain open to doubt because of the

recent discovery that Ministry of Labour estimates of inter-regional migration are unreliable.

10. A. B. Jack, *The Scottish Council Study of Migration within the U K*, Regional Studies, September 1968.

11. R. C. Geary and J. G. Hughes, *Certain Aspects of Non-Agricultural Employment in Ireland*, 12.

12. L. M. Cullen, *An Economic History of Ireland since 1660*, London 1972, 134.

13. E. J. Hobsbawm, *Industry and Empire*, London 1968, 308–9.

14. G. McCrone, *Scotland's Future*, Oxford 1969, chapter 1.

15. E. T. Nevin, A. R. Roe and J. I. Round, *The Structure of the Welsh Economy*, Welsh Economic Studies No. 4, Cardiff 1966; C. R. Tomkins, *Income and Expenditure Accounts for Wales 1965–1968*, report commissioned by the Welsh Office, 1971; and the Welsh *Digest of Statistics*.

16. J. Bowers and V. H. Woodward, *Regional Social Accounts for the U K*, N I E S S R series, Cambridge 1970, 79.

17. *Estimates of Central Government Revenue and Expenditure attributable to Scotland for the financial year 1967–68, a Scottish Budget*, H M Treasury, 1969. Similar estimates for Wales, for calendar years 1965 to 1968, are contained in C. R. Tomkins, *Income and Expenditure Accounts for Wales 1965–1968;* for Northern Ireland, J. Simpson, 'Regional Analysis : The Northern Ireland Experience', *Economic and Social Review*, Dublin 1971.

18. *The Accession of Ireland to the European Communities*, Prl. 2064, S O, Dublin January 1972.

19. See, for example, the bibliography in J. N. Randall, 'Shift-Share Analysis as a Guide to the Employment Performance of West Central Scotland', *Scottish Journal of Political Economy*, February 1973.

20. Cf. J. Bowers, *The Anatomy of Regional Activity Rates*.

21. Cf. J. Bowers and V. H. Woodward, *Regional Social Accounts for the U.K.*

22. Cf. J. N. Randall, 'Shift-Share Analysis as a Guide to the Employment Performance of West Central Scotland'.

23. J. Bowers, *The Anatomy of Regional Activity Rates*. See p. 248 above. In both parts of Ireland female activity rates may have been influenced both in total and industrial distribution by high fertility rates and the exclusion of married women from many public services.

24. J. Bowers, *The Anatomy of Regional Activity Rates*, 42–52.

25. Calculated from Table 12, J. Bowers and V. H. Woodward,

Regional Social Accounts for the U.K., 89. Regional variations in G D P per worker were less than in G D P per head of the population, because of different demographic and labour market conditions. This is also true of the countries discussed in this paper. Thus in 1967 G D P per worker in the Republic of Ireland was 59.7 per cent of the English level; in Northern Ireland 80.5 per cent, in Scotland 94.3 per cent and in Wales 98.3 per cent.

26. G. Fitzgerald, *Towards a New Ireland*, Dublin 1973, 83.
27. See, for example, A. J. Brown, *The Framework of Regional Economics in the United Kingdom*, chapter 6; G. McCrone, *Regional Policy in Britain*, London 1969, chapter 7; J. N. Randall, 'Shift-Share Analysis as a Guide to the Employment Performance of West Central Scotland'.
28. I have discovered only three analyses which include Northern Ireland : those of A. J. Brown, *The Framework of Regional Economics in the United Kingdom*, chapter 6 and J. N. Randall, 'Shift-Share Analysis as a Guide to the Employment Performance of West Central Scotland', also M. F. W. Hemming, 'The Regional Problem', *National Institute Economic Review*, August 1963. None have included the Republic of Ireland.
29. J. N. Randall, 'Shift-Share Analysis as a Guide to the Employment Performance of West Central Scotland', 4.
30. M. F. W. Hemming, 'The Regional Problem'.